BARRON'S

CDL

DISCARDED

COMMERCIAL DRIVER'S LICENSE
TRUCK DRIVER'S TEST

Fourth Edition
by Mike Byrnes and Associates, Inc.

© Copyright 2016, 2010, 2004, 1991 by Barron's Educational Series, Inc.

All inquiries should be addressed to:
Barron's Educational Series, Inc.
250 Wireless Boulevard
Hauppauge, NY 11788
www.barronseduc.com

ISBN: 978-1-4380-0750-2

Library of Congress Control Number: 2016931317

Printed in the United States of America

9 8 7 6 5 4 3 2 1

Table of Contents

Dedication

This book is dedicated to the late Mike Byrnes, who left a legacy of enthusiasm and dedication to excellence in truck driver education.

We continue on in that tradition, guided by his principles and concern for you, the student.

Mike Byrnes & Associates, Inc.
Devorah Fox, President

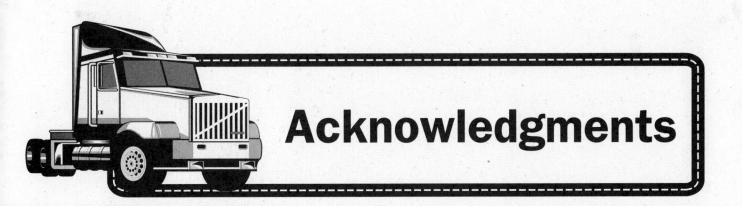

Acknowledgments

Special recognition is due John M. Rojas, Director, Del Mar College Transportation Training Services, Corpus Christi, Texas, and Joyce Walters. You are deeply appreciated.

Direction of travel

Traffic cone or marker

At least 40 ft.

At least 40 ft.

Figure 3-3. The CDL Skills Tests are scored to specific standards.

scraping the curb and without turning wider than five feet away from the curb."

You will also be told if you must meet all the conditions, or only most of them. Sometimes, it only takes one error to fail a test. This is the case on some of the CDL Skills Tests. Breaking a traffic law or causing an accident during the Skills Test results in automatic failure.

TEST-TAKING TIPS

The best test-taking tip we could give would be "prepare well." There's nothing like having a good grasp of the material that will be tested. Along with that, these tips will help you not to make careless errors.

Understand the Instructions

Before you begin any test, make sure you understand the instructions. On a written test, read any information that comes before the questions. It's there you will find instructions to choose "the right answer" or "the best answer."

If no instructions have been given, ask the examiner. Ask if you should use a pencil or pen to take the test. Find out if you may use scrap paper. Will there be a time limit? Don't make a pest of yourself. Do ask enough questions so you feel you understand the test conditions.

Don't Rush

If there is no time limit, relax and take all the time you need. Rushing will cause you to make careless errors. Take each question or skill test item one at a time. Clear your mind of the other parts of the test.

Read Carefully

Read knowledge test questions carefully. Before you answer, be certain you understand clearly what's being asked. Read any suggested answers just as carefully. When two or more answers seem alike, describe to yourself the difference between them.

Answer the Easy Ones First

Unless you are told to do otherwise, scan through written tests quickly. Answer all the questions you can answer off the top of your·head. Then work on the trickier ones. Finally, before you hand in the test, review the easy ones just to make sure you didn't misread them, or write down "A" when you meant to write "B."

Avoid Careless Errors

When filling out answer forms that are separate from the question forms, avoid careless errors. Make sure the number of the question on the question form and the number of the answer blank match. It's not uncommon for test-takers to put the right answer in the wrong answer space. That throws off the entire answer form and makes all the answers that follow wrong. On provided forms, use your scrap paper, a spare pencil, or your finger to line up the question with the right answer blank.

Write Neatly

Write neatly on printed forms. Mark your answer choices with firm, bold, marks. This is especially important when the answer form will be "read" by a machine. The machine can't read marks that are too light, or that fall outside the fill-in area. Stray marks will be scored as wrong answers.

Don't Change Your Answer

It's recommended that you don't change an answer choice once you have made it. Usually, your first decision about the answer is the best one. More often than not, when test-takers change their answer, they change it to the wrong one!

If you do decide to change your answer, erase the old answer completely. Make sure it's clear that your new answer choice is the one you mean.

Again, with machine-scored tests, this is vital. If you do not erase completely, the machine may see two answer choices marked. This will be scored as a wrong answer, even if one of the answers happens to be the right choice.

Don't Leave Blanks

Don't leave any blanks on written tests. If you don't know the answer, plan to come back to the question later. Often, other questions on the test will refresh your memory of the subject. Even if that doesn't happen, you can make a smart guess. We'll cover that next. Before you leave the question, though, make a circle, X, arrow, or some other mark beside the question or answer blank. That makes it easier to find when you want to tackle it again. It also helps you to see that you have left something blank so you don't hand in the test with questions left unanswered.

It's really not to your advantage to leave any blanks. If there are four answer choices, even if you make a wild guess, you have a one-in-four chance of hitting the right one. You can improve your chances with smart guessing.

Smart Guessing

To make a smart guess, eliminate any answer choices you know are wrong. Does one of the remaining answer choices have words like "all," "every," "always," or "never"? Consider that answer carefully. It's rare that something is always so or never the case. You may be able to eliminate this answer choice after all.

That narrows down your choices. You may be left with only two choices, instead of four. A wild guess will then give you a 50-50 chance of getting the right answer. By now, one of the remaining two answers may look pretty good to you. You may feel quite certain it's the right one after all.

Penalties for Guessing

The only time you want to leave questions unanswered is if there is a penalty for guessing. Some tests are scored as the percentage of right answers compared with the number of total questions answered. This is different from tests where the right answers are compared with the total number of questions asked. On such a test, it's better to leave a question blank if you don't know the answer.

There will usually be some information on the test that tells you when there is a penalty for guessing. Your CDL Knowledge Tests will not likely have such penalties. Unless you are told otherwise, make smart guesses on the questions that have you stumped.

TIPS FOR DIFFERENT TEST QUESTION TYPES

Matching

On a matching test, look for any instructions first. You may be told that the first list is a list of terms and you are to match terms to their definition. Or, each list may have a heading that describes the items in the list. Look for clues about what relationship the two lists have to each other.

If there are an equal number of items in each list, you probably have to make a one-to-one match. If there are more items offered on the answer list than there are on the question list, this isn't the case. You will clearly have some left over. Or, you may have fewer answers than there are questions. In that case, some answers are used more than once. You guessed it—these variations make the test more challenging.

Scan the lists quickly. Make any matches that jump out at you right away. If you may have scrap paper, you may want to use pieces of it to cover up any answer choices you have eliminated in this first pass. Or, draw a line through them (unless you're told not to write on the form). Since you have already "used" them, you don't need to consider them as answers for any of the other questions. If you remove them from "view," you reduce the chance of mistakenly choosing them a second time.

Next, work on any remaining unmatched "question" items. Taking each one in turn, try to answer it without looking at the answer choices. If the question item is a term, define it. If it's a regulation, what does it regulate? If it's an item of equipment, what does it do?

Look over the list of matching choices. Do you see your definition there? If so, match the two. Draw a line through or cover up the answer you have chosen.

Continue to make all the matches you can. Skip over any you can't answer at all. Come back to those when you have done all the "easy" ones. By then you will have eliminated some more answer choices. You'll have a short list of answers to choose from, instead of the entire range.

Consider each of the answer choices with the remaining questions. Examine the questions and answers closely. You may notice some things right away that help you to make the correct matches.

Take these three sample matching question and answer choices.

Term	Definition
duals	riding on the surface of the water
hydroplaning	two tires on one axle
check valve	a part of the braking system

The first item, "duals" seems to be asking about a group of things. Only one of your remaining answers refers to a group. That is "two tires on one axle." That's the correct match for "duals."

Notice also that "hydroplaning" seems to be asking about an action, rather than a thing. "Riding on the surface of the water" is the only answer choice left that is also an action rather than a thing. That's the correct match for "hydroplaning."

Now you're left with one question item, "check valve," and one answer item, "a part of the braking system." Match those two up and you are done.

Use this logic if you are simply flat out stuck on some test questions. Stop racking your brain for definitions you don't know. Take a mental step back and simply look at the words. Try to find any way in which they relate to each other or seem alike. That may lead you to the match the test is asking you to make.

True/False

Usually true/false questions are worded as statements. You decide if it is a true statement or not. Sometimes, true/false questions are worded as questions. An example would be, "Are on-duty drivers who take narcotics prescribed to them by a doctor breaking the law?" If you would answer the question "yes," your answer choice should be "true." If you would answer the question "no," your answer choice should be "false." (In this case, the answer is "yes." The "question" is "true.")

Remember that all parts of the statement or question must be true for you to say it's a true statement. If any part is false, then "false" is your answer choice. Take this true/false question, for example:

It is safe for an on-duty driver to take over-the-counter cold remedies without a prescription.
A. True
B. False

The answer to this question is "B. False." Yes, it's true that over-the-counter cold remedies can be taken without a prescription. But it's not true that on-duty drivers can take them safely. Many of these medications cause drowsiness. It would not be safe for a driver to take them while driving. If the driver in the question were "off-duty," the answer to the question would be "A. True."

Be on the lookout for words like "always," "ever," "never," "all," and "complete." These words should make you read the statement very carefully. Be certain that your answer, true or false, covers every possible case, since a question like this does not allow for any exceptions.

True/false questions look easy. That's why it's especially important to read them closely.

Multiple Choice

Multiple-choice questions are a little easier to answer if you follow a system. We'll assume we're dealing with the "only one answer is correct" type of question.

First, read the question "stem" to yourself. Then read the stem with the first answer choice. Does the combination make a true statement? If so, this answer choice is correct. If not, go on to the next answer choice.

Read the question stem with each answer choice in turn. Note which combinations make a true statement. Most times, only one answer choice will make a true statement of the question stem. If more than one answer seems to be correct, use the elimination and smart guessing techniques already described to narrow down the choices.

Read "best answer" test questions and their answer choices, very carefully. Describe to yourself the difference between the answer choices. Does one include more details than the others? If all the details are true, this may be the "best" answer. It's often true that an answer choice that is a lot shorter, or a lot longer, than all the rest is the correct answer.

All the Answers Are Correct

Be careful when one of the answer choices is "all the above." Just because "all of the above" is an answer choice doesn't mean it's the correct one. Select it only if you have convinced yourself that all the answer choices are correct. It may be that one or more of the answer choices is indeed wrong.

Try each answer choice with the stem. Make certain that each one completes the question stem and makes it a true statement or answers the question correctly. If all the answer choices meet this test, then the answer choice to select is "all of the above."

PASS PRACTICE TESTS

Throughout the rest of this book, you will find many sample tests to practice with. You'll have a chance to work with true/false, matching, fill-in-the-blank, and multiple-choice questions. Try all the techniques described in this chapter.

After you have scored your own tests, examine the questions you missed. Did you make careless errors, or were you simply not prepared enough? Keep track of your results. See if practice doesn't help you make fewer careless errors.

You'll also find some practice performance tests. They will include specific conditions your performance must meet to be considered "passing." Keep these conditions in mind when you self-score your performance.

This concludes Part One. You've covered test preparation and test-taking in general. In Part Two, you'll get into preparation specifically for taking the CDL tests. Before leaving Chapter 3, though, there's one last item to cover.

In the following chapters, you may read about facts or procedures that differ from what you already know or do. The terms used for equipment or maneuvers may not be the ones you are familiar with or use. That doesn't mean you are wrong. Your way may be just fine. You may even be better informed. But to get a CDL, you'll have to do things "by the book." You must "speak the language" used by the CDL tests and the examiners.

When you find a way of doing something or describing something that's different from what you are used to, make a special note of it. Review it and get it firmly in your mind. You don't want to be surprised by it on the test. If you're looking only for answers phrased "your way," you won't recognize the right answers when you see them.

PART TWO

Chapter 4

Commercial Driver Licensing

In this chapter, you will learn about:

- what the Commercial Driver's License is
- who must have a Commercial Driver's License
- how to get a Commercial Driver's License
- penalties for not having a Commercial Driver's License
- areas of knowledge and skill covered by the Commercial Driver's License
- Commercial Driver's License Tests
- other Safety Act rules regarding commercial driver licensing

To complete this chapter, you will need:

- a dictionary
- a pencil or pen
- blank paper, a notebook, or an electronic notepad
- colored pencils, pens, markers, or highlighters
- a CDL preparation manual from your state Department of Motor Vehicles, if one is offered
- a driver license manual from your state Department of Motor Vehicles
- the Federal Motor Carrier Safety Regulations pocketbook (or access to U.S. Department of Transportation regulations, Parts 383, 387, and 390-399 of Subchapter B, Chapter 3, Title 49, Code of Federal Regulations)

PASS PRE-TRIP

Instructions: Read the three statements. Decide whether each statement is true or false. If it is true, circle the letter A. If it is false, circle the letter B.

1. If you do not have a Hazardous Materials Endorsement on your Commercial Driver's License, you can never haul hazardous materials.
   A. True
   B. False

2. It is legal to have a Commercial Driver's License from more than one state if you lived in that state when you got that license.
   A. True
   B. False

3. There is a national Commercial Driver's License required by federal law, but your home state may decide not to adopt the CDL.
   A. True
   B. False

How did you do with these first **PASS** Pre-trip questions? Did you feel confident about your answers? If you felt that you don't know the first thing about commercial driver licensing, don't worry. When you finish this chapter, you will know the answers to the **PASS** Pre-trip questions and more.

CDL BACKGROUND

The Commercial Driver's License is a special type of driving license. Before we explore this special license, it would be helpful for you to have a clear understanding of just what a driver's license is—any type of driver's license.

Driver Licensing

When you receive a driver's license, you have been granted permission to drive by a body of government. That makes driving a regulated activity.

To get your license to drive any vehicle, you go to the Motor Vehicles Department of your home state. This is because it is your state that grants you the license to drive. It's not the city, county, or federal government.

Commercial Driver Licensing

A Commercial Driver's License (CDL) grants permission to people who have passed one or more tests. By passing, they have shown that they have the knowledge and skill to drive certain types of vehicles in certain conditions. The CDL law is quite specific about the types of vehicles, conditions, and drivers concerned. You'll learn about these later in this chapter.

It takes special skill and knowledge to do many important jobs in today's society. Airline pilots, police officers, and other professionals prepare for and take tests to earn special licenses. They take pride in that special testing and licensing. The licensed commercial driver can also take pride in being a member of a recognized skilled profession.

FMCSR PART 383: COMMERCIAL DRIVER'S LICENSE STANDARDS

The CDL is part of a larger body of regulations. These are the regulations set by the U.S. Department of Transportation in Subchapter B, Chapter 3, Title 49 of the Code of Federal Regulations (CFR).

You should, at least once, read these regulations in their "official" language. If you would like your own copy of the Federal Motor Carrier Safety Regulations (FMCSR), you can order one from any number of companies that supply materials to the trucking industry.

*An "appendix" in a book is extra material. Like our **PASS** Billboards, it's material that you may find helpful or may not need at all. That's why you will usually find appendices (that's the plural form of "appendix") at the back of a book, after the main material. This book has several appendices.*

The FMCSR is a compact book and usually not very expensive. If you can't afford or get your own personal copy of the FMCSR, check with the reference librarian at your local public library. The library will either have an FMCSR or a copy of Title 49 CFR, if not both. You can't take either out of the library, however. You can only look at them there.

You can even find the FMCSR on the Internet at:

> *http://www.fmcsa.dot.gov*

CMVSA 1986

In 1986, the Congress of the United States of America passed the Commercial Motor Vehicle Safety Act (CMVSA). The goal of this act was to improve driver quality and remove unsafe and

---

PASS BILLBOARD
Abbreviations and Acronyms

You will see many abbreviations and acronyms in this book. An abbreviation is a shortened form of a word. For example, "Dept." is an abbreviation. It is a shortened form of the word "Department." You can tell it's an abbreviation because it ends with a period. This is true whether it appears at the beginning, in the middle, or at the end of a sentence.

An acronym is a word formed from the first letters of several words in a group. Taking the first letters of the words in the group "Department of Transportation" forms the acronym "DOT." You can tell it's an acronym,

and not a word by itself, because it appears in all capital letters.

In this book, you will always be properly introduced to the abbreviation or acronym. First you will see the whole word, name, or group of words spelled out. That will be followed by the abbreviation or acronym enclosed in curved brackets called parentheses. After the abbreviation or acronym has been introduced in this way, it will be used throughout the book with no further explanation.

However, if you ever forget what an acronym stands for, you can find it in the glossary.

unqualified commercial motor vehicle (CMV) drivers from the highway.

The Federal Highway Administration (FHWA) of the U.S. Department of Transportation (DOT) responded to this Act by changing some regulations and adding Part 383 to the FMCSR. These changes fall into two main areas of interest to commercial drivers:

- the single license law
- commercial driver testing and licensing

These changes occurred at the federal level of government. It's still state governments that issue licenses to CMV drivers. Each state's licensing standards must comply with the federal regulations, however. Within certain limits, states may develop their own tests and licenses for commercial drivers. These tests and licenses must, however, at least meet the federal requirements. State standards can be higher or more demanding than the federal standards, but they can't be lower or less demanding.

The bottom line is, although state governments issue driving licenses, there is a national Commercial Driver's License required by federal law. Effective April 1, 1992, your home state must have a CDL program that meets the federal requirements.

These requirements are set out in Part 383 of the FMCSR. If you have a copy of the FMCSR, follow along as we discuss each section of that Part.

Purpose and Scope

The purpose and scope of the CDL program is described in FMCSR Part 383, Subpart A (General), Section 383.1. As you know by now, the purpose has two targets. They are:

- to help reduce or prevent truck and bus accidents, deaths, and injuries by requiring drivers to have a single commercial motor vehicle driver's license
- to disqualify drivers who operate commercial motor vehicles in an unsafe manner

How does the CDL program achieve this? We'll answer that question briefly, then address each point in greater detail later in the chapter.

First, a CMV driver may have only one CMV driver's license. This is known as the single license requirement.

Next, drivers must notify their current employers and their home state of certain convictions.

Drivers must provide previous employment information when they apply for jobs as CMV drivers.

Employers must not hire anyone with a suspended license to operate a commercial motor vehicle.

Persons convicted of certain criminal acts or traffic violations are subject to fines, suspensions, loss of license, and other penalties.

Commercial motor vehicle drivers must pass tests and receive a special license.

States must give knowledge and skills tests to all qualified applicants for commercial driver's licenses.

There are different classes or types of licenses. To each class or license type, there are additional items that can be added that allow the person to operate specific categories of vehicles or haul certain types of cargo within a particular license class. These categories are called **endorsements**.

Drivers must meet specific knowledge and skills requirements to be licensed to drive certain vehicles and haul certain cargo.

Commercial driver licensing tests must meet specific standards. Commercial driver license applicants must achieve a stated minimum score on these tests.

States must keep records on licensed commercial drivers.

With the exception of some military drivers, and a few other types of CMV drivers under specific conditions, Section 383.3 states that the rules in FMCSR Part 383 apply to all who operate commercial motor vehicles in interstate, foreign, or intrastate commerce. These rules also apply to the employers of these drivers.

Definitions

Section 383.5 defines many of the terms used to describe the CDL program. For the most part, these are terms that won't be found in a dictionary, or terms that have special meanings. For instance, what exactly is a commercial vehicle? A commercial vehicle is one that is used in commerce. The CDL law defines this as trade, traffic, or transportation in the United States (or any area controlled by the United States). The trade can be between a

PASS BILLBOARD

There are three words in the English language that have common, everyday meanings. These are "may," "should," and "must." In common speech, you may hear these words used as if they all had the same meaning, or nearly the same. They don't. It usually doesn't matter much.

When laws are written, however, the meaning of words must be very clear. "May," "should," and "must" have unique and specific meanings when used in a legal sense. They refer to three different levels of "permission."

"May" refers to a relaxed level of permission. When a law says you "may" do something, it means you are allowed. If there is more than one action possible, the choice is yours to make. This is usually used when some conditions have been set. If the situation meets the condition, then you "may" choose to act or not to act.

Take, for instance, a law that says you "may" make a right turn at a red light. This means there is nothing that would stop you, legally, from making that turn. Of course, there may be reasons besides whether it is legal or not for why you wouldn't want to make that right turn. Perhaps you're concerned that oncoming traffic turning left will turn into your lane. So you stop at the red light and wait for a green light before you turn. As far as the law is concerned, though, a right turn at a red light is permitted.

Sometimes, you might see the word "can" used instead of "may." "Can" refers to ability rather than permission. That is, you might have permission to do something, but not the ability. You might have permission to make a right-hand turn, but if your steering system breaks down, you might not have the ability to make it. This is splitting hairs, though. It's all right to assume that if a law says you "can" do something, it means the same as you "may" do something.

"Should" gives you a little less permission than "may." It carries recommendations with it. It's usually used with some conditions. The

Figure 4-1. Some laws state you "may" make a right turn at a red light.

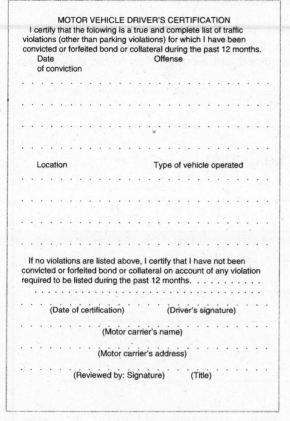

Figure 5-2. Motor Vehicle Driver's Certification

Examinations and Tests

FMCSR Part 391 describes the road test that CMV drivers must take. This road test is different from the CDL skills test. This road test is given to you by your motor carrier employer. The CDL skills test is given to you by the state that gives you your CDL license. You must take both.

The road test required by FMCSR Part 391 must include at least the following:

- a pre-trip inspection (described in FMCSR 392.7)
- coupling and uncoupling any combination units
- putting the vehicle in operation
- use of the vehicle's controls and emergency equipment
- operating the vehicle in traffic and while passing other vehicles
- turning the vehicle
- braking, and slowing the vehicle without using the brakes
- backing and parking the vehicle

Your motor carrier employer will give you the road test. It can also be given by someone the employer appoints to do this. (If you yourself are the motor carrier, you cannot give yourself the road test. You must assign someone else to give you the test.) Your performance will be rated on a form. The person who gave you the test will sign the form.

When you complete the road test, you will get a copy of the Certification of Road Test. It will look like the one in Figure 5-3.

If you recently had a road test elsewhere and have a valid CMV license, the motor carrier may waive (excuse you from taking) another road test. The motor carrier may also waive the road test if you have a valid certificate of driver's road test that is no more than three years old. The only exception to the road test waiver is if you were going to work for a motor carrier driving tankers or double/triple trailers.

On the other hand, even if you have such a certificate, the motor carrier may still have you take a new road test.

Physical Qualifications and Examinations

CMV drivers must meet certain physical qualifications. These are described in FMCSR Part 391. We won't list them here. A doctor will check for these qualifications by giving you a physical. This isn't an ordinary physical. You've probably heard it called a "DOT physical." What makes this CMV driver physical special is described in this section of the FMCSR.

Among other things, your hearing, sight, and reflexes will be tested. You'll be asked about your use of drugs and alcohol. You may be tested for drug and alcohol use. It's here that the doctor will advise you about any medicines you may be taking. The doctor must assure you that such drugs are safe to use while driving. If they are not, taking them can get you disqualified as we mentioned before. This is true even if the doctor prescribed them.

This physical must be completed by a medical examiner listed on the National Registry of Certified Medical Examiners. Vision tests (visual acuity, field of vision, and the ability to recognize colors) may be performed by a licensed optometrist.

CERTIFICATE OF DRIVER'S ROAD TEST

Instructions: If the road test is successfully completed, the person who gave it shall complete a certificate of the driver's road test. The original or copy of the certificate shall be retained in the employing motor carrier's driver qualification file of the person examined and a copy given to the person who was examined. (49 CFR 391.31(e)(f)(g))

CERTIFICATION OF ROAD TEST

Driver's Name _____

Social Security Number _____

Operator's or Chauffeur's License Number _____

State _____

Type of Power Unit _____

Type of Trailer(s) _____

If passenger carrier, type of bus _____

This is to certify that the above-named driver was given a road test under my supervision on _____, 20____, consisting of approximately _____ miles of driving.

It is my considered opinion that this driver possesses sufficient driving skill to operate safely the type of commercial motor vehicle listed above.

_____
(Signature of Examiner)

_____
(Title)

_____
(Organization and Address of Examiner)

Figure 5-3. Certification of Road Test. You'll sign the original, and the motor carrier will keep it on file.

The physical must follow the guidelines in FMCSR Part 391. The doctor will sign and date the examination form and a medical examiner's certificate. The doctor will keep the exam form on file. Both you and your motor carrier will be given a copy of the medical examiner's certificate. It will look like Figure 5-4 on page 64.

You must have the physical if you have never had a so-called "DOT physical" before. If your last DOT physical was more than two years ago, you must be examined again and whenever a physician specifies. Exempt intracity zone drivers must get a DOT physical if their last one was more than one year ago. You must also get an exam if your ability to drive has been reduced by injury or illness.

FMCSR Part 391 tells you what to do if you disagree with the doctor's findings. Also, certain physical problems that might disqualify you may be waived. The process of getting a waiver is also described in this part.

Some states require that a DOT physical be submitted to the Department of Motor Vehicles before it will administer the CDL Knowledge Test.

Files and Records

FMCSR Part 391 describes the files and records motor carriers must keep on each of their drivers. They're of concern mainly to motor carriers. Read them enough to be familiar with them. Unless you yourself are a motor carrier, though, you don't need to be concerned about complying with them.

Limited Exemptions

FMCSR 391.61, 391.62, 391.63, 391.65, 391.67, and 391.69 are also of interest mainly to the motor carrier. These regulations list the few drivers who are exempt from FMCSR 391. There are few indeed. Some drivers who only work now and then are exempt from some of the regulations. So are drivers who usually work for one motor carrier but are doing a job for another motor carrier. Drivers of farm vehicles are exempt from some of the regulations. So are some drivers in Hawaii and some intrastate drivers hauling combustible liquids.

When you read these sections, you will see that most drivers are covered by FMCSR 391.

FMCSR PART 392

The next part of the FMCSR that all drivers must know is Part 392, Driving of Motor Vehicles. This part covers:

- illness, fatigue, drugs, intoxicating beverages, driver schedules, equipment, safe loading, and other general topics
- driving of vehicles
- stopped vehicles
- safety while fueling
- unauthorized passengers
- coasting and other prohibited practices
- texting and cell phone use

This part introduces the concept of "higher standard of care." The FMCSR says that drivers must obey local laws first. If the federal law is more strict, though, the federal law must be obeyed instead. This results in a "higher standard of care." Simply put, the stricter rule applies.

You've read about higher standard of care before, although not in so many words. It's what allows states to have a more strict definition of DUI than the federal law. Federal law considers a driver with 0.04 percent AC as DUI. A state could make that 0.03 percent, or less. That would result in a higher standard of care. If a state set the AC at 0.05 percent, the federal law would apply, since that would result in the higher standard of care.

The following are highlights of the other sections of FMCSR 392.

Ill or Fatigued Operator

Illness or fatigue is not to be taken lightly. A sick or tired driver is not a safe driver. It's not merely being lazy to get rest when you need it. You're not being a hero by continuing to drive. You are in fact breaking the law. FMCSR Part 392 says a driver must not drive if too tired or ill to be fully alert and in control. Only in an emergency should you continue to drive. Then, you should go on only as long as needed to handle the emergency.

Once in a while, you may become so ill that you cannot operate a motor vehicle safely. If this happens to you, you must not drive. However, in case of an emergency, you may drive to the nearest place where you can safely stop.

MEDICAL EXAMINER'S CERTIFICATE

I certify that I have examined _____ in accordance with the Federal Motor Carrier Safety Regulations (49 CFR 391.41-391.49) and with knowledge of the driving duties, I find this person is qualified, and, if applicable, only when:

☐ wearing corrective lenses
☐ wearing hearing aid
☐ accompanied by a _____ waiver/exemption

☐ driving within an exempt intracity zone (49 CFR 391.62)
☐ accompanied by a Skill Performance Evaluation Certificate (SPE)
☐ qualified by operation of 49 CFR 391.64

The information I have provided regarding this physical examination is true and complete. A complete examination form with any attachment embodies my findings completely and correctly, and is on file in my office.

SIGNATURE OF MEDICAL EXAMINER	TELEPHONE	DATE

MEDICAL EXAMINER'S NAME (PRINT)	☐ MD ☐ DO ☐ Physician Assistant	☐ Chiropractor ☐ Advanced Practice Nurse ☐ Other Practitioner

MEDICAL EXAMINER'S LICENSE OR CERTIFICATE NO./ISSUING STATE	NATIONAL REGISTRY NO.	

SIGNATURE OF DRIVER	INTRASTATE ONLY	CDL	DRIVER'S LICENSE NO.	STATE
	☐ YES ☐ NO	☐ YES ☐ NO		

ADDRESS OF DRIVER

MEDICAL CERTIFICATION EXPIRATION DATE

Figure 5-4. Medical Examiner's Certificate.

PASS BILLBOARD
Fatigue

Driving a vehicle for long hours is tiring. Even the best of drivers will become less alert. To stay alert and safe, get enough sleep. Leaving on a long trip when you're already tired is dangerous. If you have a long trip scheduled, make sure that you get a good sleep before you go. Most people require seven to eight hours of sleep every 24 hours.

Schedule trips safely. Your body gets used to sleeping during certain hours. If you are driving during those hours, you will be less alert. If possible, try to schedule trips for the hours that you are normally awake. Many heavy motor vehicle accidents occur between midnight and 6 A.M. You can easily fall asleep at these times, especially if you don't regularly drive at those hours. Trying to push on and finish a long trip at these times can be very dangerous. See Figure 5-5.

Avoid medication. Many medicines can make you sleepy. Those that do have a label warning against operating vehicles or machinery. The most common medicine of this type is an ordinary cold pill. If you have to drive with a cold, you are better off suffering from the cold than from the effects of the medicine. Keep cool. A hot, poorly ventilated cab can make you sleepy. Keep the window or vent cracked or use the air conditioner, if you have one.

Take breaks. Short breaks can keep you alert. However, the time to take them is before you feel really drowsy or tired. Stop often. Walk around and inspect your vehicle. It may help to do some physical exercises.

When you are sleepy, trying to push on is far more dangerous than you think. It is a major cause of fatal accidents. When your body needs sleep, sleep is the only thing that will work. If you have to make a stop anyway, make it whenever you feel the first signs of sleepiness, even if it is earlier than you planned. By getting up a little earlier the next day, you can keep on schedule and not have to drive while you're not alert.

Take a nap. If you can't stop for the night, at least pull off the road and take a nap. A nap as short as a half-hour will do more to overcome fatigue than a half-hour coffee stop.

Avoid drugs. There are no drugs that can overcome being tired. While they may keep you awake for a while, they won't make you alert. Eventually, you'll be even more tired than if you hadn't taken them at all. Sleep is the only thing that can overcome fatigue.

Figure 5-5. Most heavy motor vehicle accidents happen between midnight and 6 A.M.

Drugs and Other Substances

The misuse of drugs and alcohol while on-duty is forbidden by several regulations. Some are found in FMCSR Part 40 and FMCSR Part 382. FMCSR 392.4 states that no driver shall be on-duty and possess, be under the influence of, or use:

- a Schedule I substance
- amphetamines ("pep pills" or "bennies")
- narcotics or their derivatives
- any substance that keeps a driver from being able to drive safely

This part reminds you that it is OK to use drugs a doctor has prescribed for you. This is only if the doctor has assured you the drug will not affect your driving ability.

This part also clears up the definition of "possession." It is legal to "possess" and transport these drugs as cargo. They must be listed on the manifest, however.

Alcohol

All drivers are affected by drinking alcohol. Alcohol affects judgment, vision, coordination, and reaction time. It causes serious driving errors, such as:

- increased reaction time to hazards
- driving too fast or too slow
- driving in the wrong lane
- running over the curb
- weaving
- straddling lanes
- quick, jerky starts
- failure to signal or use lights
- failure to stop at stop signs and red lights
- improper passing

All these can mean increased chances of a crash and chances of losing your driver's license. Accident statistics show that the chance of a crash is much greater for drivers who have been drinking than for drivers who have not.

FMCSR Part 392 states that no driver shall drink an intoxicating beverage within four hours before going on-duty, driving, or otherwise being in control of a motor vehicle. This means any and all intoxicating beverages. It doesn't matter how much alcohol is in them. A little or a lot, they are

prohibited. Remember, alcohol is alcohol. Beer and wine are no safer than liquor.

You must not even be under the influence of such a beverage within four hours of going on-duty. This may mean that if you are drinking, you must stop much sooner than four hours before going to work. It's possible to be "under the influence" of drinking for more than four hours. Here's why.

You have seen that drunkenness is measured as a percentage of alcohol in the blood. Three factors affect this percentage. These factors are time, the amount of alcohol, and your weight.

Alcohol, like any food or drink, is used by the body over time. After a certain amount of time, your body has used up the alcohol. There is no more in your system. It no longer affects you.

12 ounces of beer   5 ounces of wine   1½ ounces of liquor

Figure 5-6. It takes most people about one hour to burn off one 12-ounce bottle of beer, one 5-ounce glass of wine, or one 1 1/2-ounce shot of liquor.

How much time must pass before you are free of the effects of alcohol? It depends on how much you drank and your weight. It takes most people about one hour to burn off one 12-ounce bottle of beer, one 1 1/2-ounce shot of liquor, or one 5-ounce glass of wine. Smaller people feel the effects of alcohol more than larger people.

Put together the facts that you have just learned so far about the effects of alcohol and the requirements of the law. The law requires you to be free of the effects of alcohol for four hours before you go on-duty. Say you have one beer at noon. You are due to go on-duty at 4 P.M. Is it safe? No, it's not. You had the beer at noon. At 1 P.M., you were still affected by it. By 4 P.M., only three hours have passed. You still have an hour to go. Only then have you been free for four hours of the effects of that one beer you drank at noon.

Right away, you can see why you must stop drinking far in advance of when you plan to drive.

What if you had more than one drink? What if you are lighter or heavier than the average person? The charts in Figure 5-7 help answer that question.

Read down the left side to find the row with the figure closest to the number of drinks that concern you. Read along the top to find the column with the body weight closest to yours. The number where the column and row come together is your blood alcohol content at that weight at that number of drinks.

Take, for example, a 200-pound man who has four drinks. The chart shows his AC would be 0.08 percent. He is clearly under the influence. As far as the law is concerned, he will be for some time.

One drink would take one hour to burn off. Four drinks would take far longer to burn off. For each hour that passes since that last drink was consumed, subtract 0.15 percent. That's a little less than the alcohol in one drink. Our 200-pound drinker will need at least four hours after he finally has that last drink to get his AC below 0.04 percent. (He will need eight hours to completely burn off all four drinks.) Then he needs the additional four hours required by FMCSR 392.5. This man cannot legally drive for eight hours after he has his last drink! If you have many drinks spread throughout an afternoon or evening, you can easily still be affected by them the next day. You may feel fine and think you are sober. Your judgment and reflexes simply won't be up to par.

Don't think you can hurry the process of getting sober. Coffee and cold showers will make you feel more alert. You will still be under the influence. Only the passing of enough time will return you to a normal state.

Certainly, you must not consume an intoxicating beverage while on-duty, much less before.

You may transport intoxicating beverages, of course. As with controlled substances, such cargo must be on your manifest and transported as part of a shipment to be legal.

A driver who violates these regulations is immediately put out-of-service for 24 hours. You would have to report this to your employer within 24 hours. You would also have to report this to the state that gave you your license. You must make this report within 30 days, unless you request a review.

If you want a review of the out-of-service order, you must request it within 10 days. You must write to the Division Administrator or State Director for

Provided to TABC by the National Highway Safety Traffic Administration

Figure 5-7. Blood alcohol content and weight. The numbers in the chart are AC percentages. Remember the legal limit? It's 0.04.

PASS BILLBOARD

There are many beliefs about how alcohol works in the body. So many of them are not based on fact. A common one is "I can handle it better than other people." It's simply not true.

The first thing that alcohol does is affect your judgment. It also gives you a false sense of competence. All it takes is one drink. After that, you simply can't trust yourself to decide if you are drunk or not. You must assume you are, even if you feel fine. Of course you'll feel great—you've been drinking! You won't be great, though. You'll be impaired. Most people are legally under the influence after having one drink.

Perhaps you wait until your reaction time slows before you decide you've had enough. That's too late. By the time you notice your reactions have slowed, you are at about 0.05 percent AC. This is already over the legal limit. Maybe you decide to stop when you begin to stagger and your speech slurs. At this point you are at 0.2 percent AC. This is five times the 0.04 percent AC that the law considers the limit. You could go on drinking until you pass out. For most people this will happen by the time they reach 0.3 percent AC. If you drink enough to reach 0.4 percent AC, you will definitely not be driving. At 0.4 AC, you will fall into a coma, and likely die.

It's hard not to conclude that drinking and driving don't mix.

---

the geographical area in which the out-of-service order was issued. The addresses of the Motor Carrier Safety offices are listed in Appendix D of this book. The Regional Director may overturn the order or let it stand.

Schedules and Speed Limits

You must drive within the speed limit. It's no excuse to claim you can't complete your run without driving at an illegal speed. FMCSR Part 392 states your carrier must not schedule runs that force you to exceed the speed limit.

Equipment Inspection and Use

Your vehicle cannot be operated safely without certain parts. Before you take a vehicle out, you must make sure these parts are in place and working. Also, you must know how to use them, and use them when needed. These parts are listed in FMCSR Part 392. They are:

- service brakes, including trailer brake connections
- parking (hand) brake
- steering mechanism

- lighting devices and reflectors
- tires
- horn
- windshield wiper or wipers
- rear-view mirror or mirrors
- coupling devices

Before you take a vehicle out, you must make sure your emergency equipment is in place and working. Also, you must know how to use:

- a fire extinguisher
- spare fuses
- warning devices for stopped vehicles (like flares or reflectors)

and use them when needed.

Safe Loading

You must not drive a vehicle unless you are certain the cargo is loaded properly and secure. Tarps, tie-downs, and other items such as tailgates, tailboards, doors, and spare tires must be in good condition and in place. The cargo may look tied down and secure, but the weight could be unbalanced. This could cause the rig to overturn in curves and sharp turns. So you must know both proper cargo distribution and securement. FMCSR Part 392 also states the cargo must not block your view or your ability to move around. It must not block emergency equipment or the vehicle's controls.

All must be in good order before you start your trip. It must remain that way through the trip. You must inspect the cargo and how it's secured within the first 50 miles after you start your trip. Then you must check it again

- when you, the driver, change your duty status
- after the vehicle has been driven for three hours
- after the vehicle has been driven for 150 miles

whichever of these three comes first.

Slowing and Stopping

CMV drivers hauling certain cargo must take special action when crossing railroad tracks at grade. These regulations also apply to drivers hauling hazmat that requires placards. These steps must be taken at railroad crossings without signal lights, or a flagman, or some other way of telling you that it's safe to proceed.

FMCSR 392.10 states you must stop no farther than 50 feet and no closer than 15 feet of the track. Look both ways and listen for oncoming trains. When it's safe, you must proceed at a speed that will let you get all the way across without changing gears. You must not change gears while crossing the track.

You do not have to stop at a streetcar crossing or a track used only for industrial switching purposes within a business district. You also don't have to stop at a railroad grade crossing if a police officer or flagman directs you to proceed. You may cross tracks without stopping if they are controlled by a light that signals green for "go." A sign indicating that the rail line has been abandoned or is "exempt" gives you permission to cross without stopping.

If you are driving a vehicle other than the types just described, you must at least slow down when you approach a railroad crossing. Proceed at a speed slow enough that you could stop before reaching the nearest rail. You must not cross the track until you are sure it is safe to do so.

Hazardous Conditions

FMCSR Part 392 states you should slow down when hazardous conditions exist. This could be snow, ice, fog, mist, dust, smoke, rain, or slick roads—anything that reduces your ability to guide or control the vehicle. If conditions are bad enough, you are to stop altogether.

Seat Belts

You must not operate the CMV unless you have secured yourself with the seat belt.

Stopped Vehicles

Drivers must also take special action when their vehicles are stopped. They must use emergency signals—hazard flashers. Such signals and their use are described in FMCSR Part 392. You must use these signals when you stop on the traveled portion of the highway (other than traffic stops) or shoulder. Briefly, the rule is to turn on your four-way flashers when you first stop. Keep your flashers on until you put out your warning devices. These are the flares or reflective devices described in FMCSR Part 393. You'll learn about these devices later in this chapter.

You must put these warning devices out within 10 minutes of stopping. You must put one at the traffic side of your stopped vehicle. This placement is for traffic going both ways on an undivided highway. It must be within 10 feet of the vehicle in the direction of approaching traffic.

You must put another warning device 100 feet from your vehicle, in the center of the traffic lane in the direction of approaching traffic. Put a third device 100 feet from your vehicle in the opposite direction of the other two, away from approaching traffic.

This is almost easier to show than to describe. See Figure 5-8 on page 70.

You place your warning devices slightly differently when you are stopped on a hill, in a curve, or on a divided or one-way road. Figures 5-9 and 5-10 show the correct placement of warning devices under these conditions.

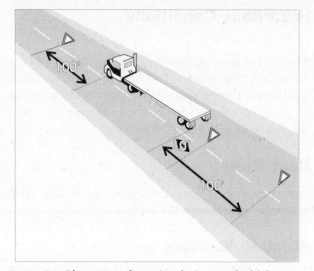

Figure 5-8. Placement of warning devices on the highway.

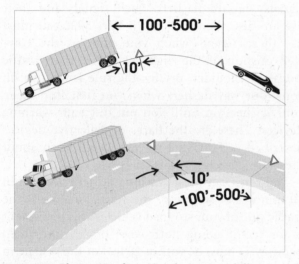

Figure 5-9. Placement of warning devices on a hill.

Figure 5-10. Placement of warning devices on a one-way road.

For older vehicles, flares and liquid-burning flares (called fusees or pot-torches) may be used instead of reflective triangles. However, when flammable liquids are leaking onto the road, the fusees may be used only at a distance where they won't create a fire or explosion. They also may not be used to protect vehicles hauling explosives. You must not use flame-producing flares to protect a vehicle used to haul flammable cargo, even if it's empty. Last, you may not use fusees to protect a vehicle fueled by compressed gas. Use reflective triangles, red lanterns, or red reflectors instead.

Fueling Procedures

The fuel your vehicle runs on can be dangerous if mishandled. The rules in FMCSR Part 392 describe how to handle fuel safely. Unless you need to run the engine to fuel your vehicle, you must not fuel your vehicle with the motor running. Do not smoke or have any open flame in the fueling area. Fueling lets off vapors you can't see. A cigarette or match could ignite these vapors.

Keep the nozzle of the fuel hose in contact with the fuel tank's intake pipe at all times. Do not allow anyone else to smoke or do anything else in the fueling area which would cause an explosion.

Prohibited Practices

The last part of FMCSR 392 describes actions that are forbidden. One is "no passengers." You must not transport anyone else in your motor vehicle. There are some exceptions to this rule. One is that you may transport other people who have been assigned to the vehicle, such as co-drivers. Another is an attendant charged with caring for livestock. You may take a passenger when your motor carrier has authorized it, in writing. This authorization must name the person, the beginning and end points of the transport, and the date on which the authorization expires.

The only time you may carry unauthorized people is to help them in an emergency. Then you may take passengers only as far as needed to get them to safety.

The last few rules in this section have to do with personal safety while inside the vehicle. First, motor vehicles must have an exit. The exit must be one that can easily be operated by the person inside.

Chapter 6

Safety Control Systems

In this chapter, you will learn about:

- CMV safety control systems:
  —lights
  —horns
  —side and rear-view mirrors and their proper adjustment
  —fire extinguishers
  —instruments and gauges
- troubleshooting

To complete this chapter you will need:

- a dictionary
- a pencil or pen
- blank paper, a notebook, or an electronic notepad
- colored pencils, pens, markers, or highlighters
- a CDL preparation manual from your state Department of Motor Vehicles, if one is offered
- the Federal Motor Carrier Safety Regulations pocketbook (or access to U.S. Department of Transportation regulations, Parts 383 and 393 of Subchapter B, Chapter 3, Title 49, Code of Federal Regulations)
- the owner's manual for your vehicle, if available

PASS PRE-TRIP

Instructions: Read the statements. Decide whether each statement is true or false. If it is true, circle the letter A. If it is false, circle the letter B.

1. The proper way to use a fire extinguisher is to douse the flames with the dry chemical.
   A. True
   B. False

2. A vehicle will have warning lights or warning buzzers, but not both.
   A. True
   B. False

3. Vehicles with diesel engines don't have vacuum brakes because diesel engines don't create a vacuum on the intake stroke.
   A. True
   B. False

You just finished a long "tour" of FMCSR Parts 391, 392, 393, 396, and 397. It was quite an effort, but very important. Thorough knowledge of the FMCSR is vital to your success on the CDL tests.

Return now to Part 383. You'll recall this part contains the CDL laws themselves. If your copy of the FMCSR contains Subpart G, Required Knowledge and Skills, turn to it now. You'll see that item (a) states you must have knowledge of the safe operations regulations. Now that you've covered that requirement, let's tackle item (b), CMV safety control systems.

SAFETY CONTROL SYSTEMS

Know what equipment makes up your vehicle's safety control systems. Know where they are and how and when to use them.

Lights

Lights help you to communicate with other drivers. Lights help others to see you and help you to see others. You use lights to signal your plans to change lanes, slow, or stop. Many states require that you must have your lights on one-half hour after sunset until one-half hour before sunrise. Also turn on your lights any time you need more light to see clearly.

As you recall, FMCSR Part 393 describes the types of lights and reflectors CMVs must have. This part also describes the lights and reflectors needed in towaway operations. You studied tables and figures in Chapter 5 that illustrated these required devices. How much do you recall? Stop now and select the figure that fits the vehicle you plan to test in. Use the scanning recall technique to identify the lights and reflectors. Compare your recall with the completed figures that follow.

To check your drawings, refer to the illustrations on pages 72–81.

To review, you need the following:

Headlights. Two white headlights, one at the left and one at the right, on the front of the tractor. These are required on buses, trucks, and truck tractors. They must offer a high and low beam setting.

You may have fog lamps and other lights for bad weather or dark roads. These are in addition to, not instead of, headlights.

Front side-marker lamps. Two amber lights, one on each side, at the front of the side of buses and trucks, tractors, semitrailers, and full trailers.

Side-marker lamps. Two amber lights, one on each side, at or near the center between front and rear side-marker lamps of buses and trucks, semitrailers, full trailers, and pole trailers.

Front side reflex reflectors. Two amber reflectors, one on each side, toward the front of buses and trucks, tractors, semitrailers, full trailers, and pole trailers.

Side reflex reflectors. Two amber reflectors, one on each side, at or near midpoint between front and rear side reflectors of buses and trucks, large semitrailers, large full trailers, and pole trailers.

Front turn signals. Two amber signals, one at the left and one at the right side, on the front of the tractor, above or below the headlights. These are required on buses, trucks, and truck tractors.

Front identification lamps. Three amber lights, at the center of the vehicle or cab. These are required on large buses and trucks and truck tractors.

Front clearance lamps. Two amber lamps, one on each side of the front of larger buses and trucks, truck tractors, large semitrailers and full trailers, pole trailers, and projecting loads.

Rear side-marker lamps. One each at the lower left and lower right rear of the side of buses and trucks, semitrailers and full trailers, and pole trailers. These lights are red.

Rear side reflex reflectors. Found just below the rear side-marker lamps. These reflectors are red. These are required on buses and trucks, semitrailers, full trailers, and pole trailers.

Rear identification lamps. Three red lights centered at the top rear of large buses and trucks,

large semitrailers and full trailers, pole trailers, and projecting loads. They're not required on smaller trucks and buses.

Rear clearance lamps. Two red lights, one at the top right and one at the top left of the rear of large trucks and buses, tractors, large semitrailers and full trailers, and projecting loads. These describe the overall width. They're not required on smaller trucks and buses.

Rear reflex reflectors. Two red reflectors, one at the lower right and one at the lower left of the rear of small and large buses and trucks, semitrailers, full trailers, and pole trailers.

Stop lamps. Two red lights, one at the lower right and one at the lower left of the rear. All vehicles must have these. Stop lamps are not required on projecting loads.

License plate lamp. One white light at the center rear, low, on trucks, tractors, semitrailers and full trailers, and pole trailers.

Backup lamp. One white light at the rear of buses and trucks and truck tractors.

Rear turn signal lamps. Two amber or red lights, one at the lower right and one at the lower left of the rear of buses and trucks, tractors, semitrailers, full trailers, pole trailers, and converter dollies.

Rear taillamps. Two red lights, one at the lower right and one at the lower left of all vehicles, even on projecting loads and converter dollies.

Parking lamps. Two amber or white lights, just below the headlights on small buses and trucks.

Four-way flashers. Two amber lights at the front and two amber or red lights at the rear of the vehicle. These are usually the front and rear turn signal lamps. They're equipped to do double-duty as warning lights. You can set them to flash simultaneously. They're required on buses and trucks, truck tractors, semitrailers and full trailers, pole trailers, and converter dollies.

Trailers and semitrailers with a width of 80 inches or more and a GVWR of 10,001 pounds or more must also have retroreflective sheeting and reflectors. Newer vehicles come equipped with these features. Older vehicles have been retrofitted to include them. They're usually red and white. Sheeting should run horizontally along the sides and across the full width of the lower rear area. On the upper rear area, it should run horizontally and vertically on the right and left corners. Reflectors

Figure 6-1. Select the drawing that looks most like your vehicle. Draw in the required lights and reflectors.

Front

Rear

Each Side

Figure 6-2. Select the drawing that looks most like your vehicle. Draw in the required lights and reflectors.

Over 80 Inches

Figure 6-3. Select the drawing that looks most like your vehicle. Draw in the required lights and reflectors.

Under 80 Inches

Figure 6-4. Select the drawing that looks most like your vehicle. Draw in the required lights and reflectors.

Under 80 Inches

Figure 6-5. Select the drawing that looks most like your vehicle. Draw in the required lights and reflectors.

Pole Trailers - All Vehicle Widths

Front

Rear

Each Side

Figure 6-6. Select the drawing that looks most like your vehicle. Draw in the required lights and reflectors.

Container Chassis

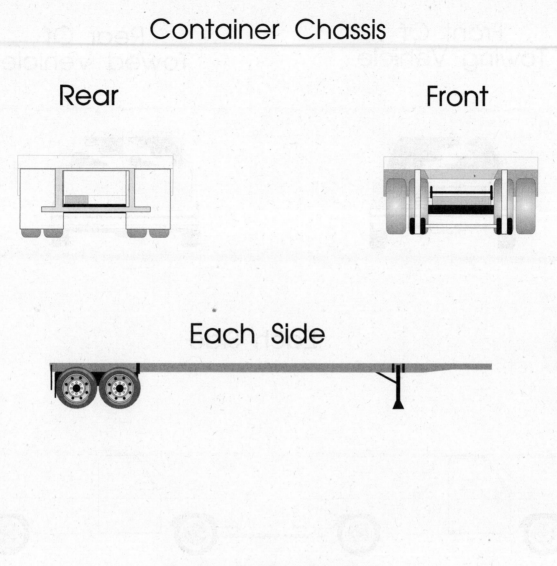

Rear

Front

Each Side

Converter Dolly

Rear

Figure 6-7. Select the drawing that looks most like your vehicle. Draw in the required lights and reflectors.

Front Of
Towing Vehicle

Rear Of
Towed Vehicle

Each Side

Figure 6-8. Select the drawing that looks most like your vehicle. Draw in the required lights and reflectors.

Also, when you inspect your vehicle, check for leaks. If your fuel system is leaking, of course you'll lose precious fuel. But leaking fuel can also be a hazard. If it drips on a hot surface, it could ignite.

Coupling Devices and Towing Methods

Vehicles that tow other vehicles must do it in a way that meets the requirements of FMCSR Part 393. There are two main ways you will see vehicles towed. One is trailers being pulled by tractors. The other is tractors or other towing vehicles being towed as cargo. This is a driveaway-towaway operation. In this section we'll look at the parts used to pull trailers. Then we'll look at saddle mounts and drawbars.

Fifth Wheel

The fifth wheel allows the trailer to articulate (pivot). FMCSR Part 393 states that the towed vehicle must not trail more than three inches to either side of the tractor.

The fifth wheel also allows the trailer to oscillate (rise or drop) along with the tractor.

Of course, the fifth wheel allows you to separate the trailer from the tractor. The power unit isn't "married" to the cargo unit, as it is with a straight truck.

The fifth wheel is mounted on the rear of the tractor frame. The proper brackets and fasteners must be used to do this. The lower half of the fifth wheel (the mounting assembly) must not shift around on the frame. There must not be any bent parts or loose bolts in the fifth wheel lower half.

The placement of the fifth wheel is important. It controls how much weight is on each axle between the front and rear of the tractor. Poor weight distribution can reduce steering control. It also causes uneven wear on tires, brakes, and wheels.

You'll find fifth wheels on converter dollies as well as on tractor frames. A converter dolly converts a semitrailer to a full trailer.

Locking Device

The fifth wheel must have a locking device. This device keeps the towed and towing vehicles together until you release them on purpose. You might hear this locking device referred to as the "jaws." The jaws lock around the shaft of the trailer kingpin. This makes a secure connection. Any forward or backward movement of the tractor will be transmitted to the trailer. You have to get out of the cab and manually pull a lever to open the jaws.

Tow Bars

Full trailers must have tow bars. There must be a locking device on the towing vehicle. This keeps the two trailers coupled with a converter dolly from separating accidentally. You must use a pair of safety chains or cable with the tow bar connection to the towing vehicle.

Saddle Mounts

A saddle mount (see Figure 6-26) is a steel assembly used to couple a towed vehicle to the towing vehicle. The saddle mount has a kingpin that fits into the locking jaws and fifth wheel of the towing vehicle. Then it has a set of U-bolts or clamps that clamp securely to the front axle of the towed vehicle.

The kingpin of the saddle mount provides an articulation point the way the kingpin of a semitrailer does.

You may need to prop up the fifth wheel so it's level. You may use hardwood blocks to do this. You may also have to raise the towed vehicle so it doesn't bump against the frame of the towing vehicle. You may use hardwood blocks for this as well.

Tires

Tires provide proper traction and reduce vibration. They absorb road shock. They transfer braking and driving force to the road. There are many different tire designs, but all tires are made about the same way.

Tires are made up of:

- plies
- bead coils and beads
- sidewalls
- tread

and the inner liner.

Plies consist of separate layers of rubber-cushioned cord. They make up the body of the tire. The plies are tied into bundles of wire called the bead coils.

Saddle mount

Wood blocking

Figure 6-26. A saddle mount.

Plies can be bias, belted bias, or radial. Bias plies are placed at a crisscross angle. This makes the sidewall and tread rigid. In a belted bias ply tire, the plies cross at an angle. There's an added layered belt of fabric between the plies and the tread. The belts make the tread of this tire more rigid than the bias ply tire. The tread will last longer because the belts reduce tread motion when the tire is running.

In radial tires, the plies on this tire do not cross at an angle. The ply is laid from bead to bead, across the tire. Like the belted bias ply tire, the radial also has a number of belts. Radial construction supports the tread better than either the bias ply or the belted bias ply. The radial design means the sidewalls flex with less friction. That requires less horsepower and saves fuel. Radial tires also hold the road better, resist skidding better, and give a smoother ride than the bias types.

Bead coils form the bead. This is the part of the tire that fits into the rim. It secures the tire to the rim. Bead coils provide the hoop strength for the bead sections. This is so that the tire will hold its shape when it's being mounted on a wheel.

The sidewalls are layers of rubber covering. They connect the bead to the tread. Sidewalls protect the plies in the sidewall area.

The tread is the part of the tire that contacts the road. Treads are designed for specific driving jobs. Some jobs require that the tread provide extra traction. Others call for a tread designed for high-speed use. Tires on steering axles must roll well and provide good traction for cornering. Drive tires must provide good traction for both braking and acceleration. Trailer tires mostly need to roll well. Tire treads are also designed to face specific road conditions. For example, drive wheel position tires need maximum traction in rain, snow, sleet, and ice. The inner liner is the sealing material that keeps the air in the tire.

That's the basics of tire construction.

Tire size is shown by either a number or a series design designation. You find this information on the sidewall of your tires. An example of the number designation is a 10.00 × 22 tire. The first number is the tire's width. This means the inflated tire measured 10 inches from the farthest outside point on one sidewall to the farthest outside point

Figure 6-27. Cross sections of the three tire types.

on the other sidewall. The second number is the rim size. Our example tire will fit a 22-inch diameter rim.

The series designation system was developed because of the low profile tire. This tire is wide in relation to its height. Once again, let's take an example to look at this. Say a tire sidewall reads 295/75 R 22.5. This means the section width is 295 millimeters. (Low profile tires are measured in millimeters rather than inches.) The aspect ratio (the height compared with the width) is 75. The type is radial. The rim is 22.5 inches in diameter.

The government requires tire manufacturers to label all tires with several items of information. For example, tire labels must show the tire brand and manufacturer. Tire labels must also show the load rating and maximum load pressure.

Load rating refers to tire strength. This is rated from A to Z. "Z" is the strongest. The maximum load the tire can carry in terms of weight is shown in pounds. FMCSR Part 393 states you must not use a tire that is too weak to support the load. The load rating helps you select the right tire for the load.

The maximum pressure is shown in psi. It is given for cold tires that have been driven for less than one mile. This is why you check tire pressure before you drive. Don't try to check tire pressure by hitting your tires with a stick or a billy or kicking them. These methods will tell you a tire is not completely flat. They will not give you an accurate tire pressure reading. Instead, use a calibrated tire gauge. It wouldn't hurt to have one, and know how to use it, when you inspect your vehicle for the CDL test.

All this pertains mainly to new tires. Used tires can sometimes be made like new. These are regrooved tires and recaps or retreads.

A regrooved tire is one in which the grooves in the tread have been cut deeper into the surface of a tire that is nearly worn down to the legal minimum. A retreaded, or recapped, tire has had the old tread surface removed. Then new tread is bonded to the outside layers of the belts or body plies.

The legal minimum for tire tread depth is set in FMCSR Part 393. A motor vehicle must not use tires that:

- have any fabric exposed through the tread or sidewalls.
- have less than 4/32 of an inch of tread measured at any point in a major tread groove on the front axle.
- have less than 2/32 of an inch of tread measured at any point in a major tread groove on all other axles.
- have front tires that have been regrooved, if the tires have a load-carrying capacity equal to or greater than 4,920 pounds.

Most states do not allow any of the front tires to be regrooved. You must make yourself aware of any such local regulations.

You should measure tread depth when you inspect your vehicle. When you make groove measurements, you must not make them at a tie bar, hump, or fillet. A hump is a pattern of tire wear that looks a little like a cupped hand. The hump is the edge or higher part of the cup. Tie bars and fillets are not patterns of tire wear. They are design factors. So is a sipe. Sipes are cut across the tread to improve traction on wet road surfaces.

You must take the tread depth measurement on a major tread groove. Find a spot where the way is clear all the way to the body of the tire. See Figure 6-28.

You can use a special tread depth gauge for this. Or, you could use a common Lincoln-head penny. Insert the penny in the groove, with Lincoln's head upside down. The edge of the penny touches the body of the tire. The tread should come up to the top of Lincoln's head. That's about 2/32 of an inch. For 4/32 of an inch, the tread should come up to Lincoln's eyebrow.

Figure 6-28. Measure tread depth in a major tread groove, not on a hump or in a fillet or sipe.

Regrooved tires, recaps, and retreads, then, can be used on drive wheels and trailer wheels. They cannot be used on steering, or front, wheels on buses and most trucks.

Wheels

Wheels provide a mounting for the tires. The wheel supports and connects the tire to the truck axle. There are spoke wheels and disc wheels.

Spoke wheels use separate rims. They are clamped onto the wheels with wheel clamps. If the wheel clamps are not installed just right, the wheel may be out of round and wobble.

The rim and center portion of the disc wheel are one piece. The rim is part of the wheel and the wheel is bolted to the hub and brake drum assembly. No clamp is used. There is less chance of the wheel being out-of-round. A wheel that is out-of-round or wobbling is said to be not true running.

The rim's job is to support the tire bead and the lower sidewall.

Neither the wheel nor the rim should be cracked or broken. The stud or bolt holes on the wheels should be perfectly round. When you inspect your vehicle, look for holes that are egg-shaped (out-of-round). These are signs of defects. All the nuts and bolts should be in place, tightened down.

Cracked or broken wheels or rims could cause an accident. A damaged rim can cause the tire to lose pressure or come off. Missing clamps, spacers, studs, and lugs could cause problems. Mismatched, bent, or cracked lock rings are dangerous. If you see signs that the wheels or rims have been repaired by welding repairs, note that as a defect.

Rust around wheel nuts may mean the nuts are loose. Use a wrench to check tightness. You can't judge tightness well enough with just your hands. (If you have just had a tire changed, stop after you have driven on the new tire a while. Double-check to see that the nuts have not loosened.)

Make sure there is a good supply of oil in the hub. Check the oil level mark on the hub cap window. Check that there are no leaks.

Suspension System

The suspension supports the vehicle's weight. It keeps the frame from resting directly on the axles. It provides a smoother ride for the driver and the cargo. The suspension absorbs road shocks. Your vehicle may have one of the following suspension types:

- leaf spring
- coil spring
- torsion bar
- air bag

In a leaf spring suspension, layers of flexible metal are bolted together. The axle rests on the middle of the spring. The front and rear of the spring are attached to the frame.

Figure 6-29. A multi-leaf front suspension.

A coil spring suspension puts a spiral of heavy-duty metal at each wheel. The top of the coil is attached to the frame, while the bottom is indirectly connected to the wheel.

Torsion bars absorb shock by twisting. They're made of special metal that returns to its original shape even after it's been twisted.

In these suspension types, the metal contracts and extends, or twists, in response to bumps or low spots in the road. This allows the wheel to move up and down with the road surface, while the frame remains level.

Your vehicle may have an air bag suspension instead of leaf springs or coils. The air bags are made of rubber fabric and are supplied with compressed air. The air supply allows the bag to expand or shrink, just as springs contract or extend.

Shock absorbers are attached to the springs. These are cylinders partly filled with hydraulic fluid. A piston moves up and down in the cylinder in response to the action of the spring. This helps to lessen the amount of springing motion that's transmitted to the driver.

Springs must always be in good condition. Suspension system defects can reduce your ability to control the vehicle.

Air bags are subject to leaks and valve problems. With air bag suspensions, the braking system should get charged with air before the air bag does. The air pressure valve on the air bag should not let air into the suspension until the braking system has at least 55 psi. The air bags should fill evenly all around. Otherwise, the vehicle will not be level. When the vehicle's air pressure gauge reads "normal," there should be no air leakage greater than 3 psi over five minutes.

Steering

The steering system enables the tractor to change direction and get around corners. A good steering system provides precise rolling, without slipping, when you turn a corner or take a curve.

The wheel in your hands is the steering wheel. It controls the steering wheels on the road that are connected to the steering axle. Between the steering wheel and the steering axle are the parts that make steering possible. Figure 6-30 shows you the basic steering components. You can see how the steering action flows through the system.

The steering wheel is connected to the steering column by a nut. The steering wheel transfers the driver's movements to the steering system.

As you turn the steering wheel, the column turns in the same direction. This turning motion continues through the U-joint to the steering gear shaft. From there the motion continues through another U-joint to the steering gear box. The steering gear box is also called the steering sector. It changes the rotating motion of the steering column to the reciprocating (back and forth) motion, of the Pitman arm. The Pitman arm is a lever attached to the steering gear box. The drag link joins the Pitman arm and the steering lever.

The steering lever or steering arm is the first part of the steering axle. The steering, or front axle, does two jobs. First, it carries a load just like

Figure 6-30. These components make up all types of steering systems, whether manual or power.

other axles. Second, it steers the vehicle. The steering lever or arm turns the front wheels left and right when the Pitman arm pulls it back and forth. The steering lever is connected to the steering knuckle. This is a moveable connection between the axle and the wheels. It allows the wheels to turn left or right.

There is a steering knuckle at the end of each axle. The steering knuckles contain the seals, bushings, and bearings that support the vehicle's weight. The steering knuckles transfer motion to the cross-steering lever, or tie rod arm, and the tie rod, or cross-steering tube.

The spindles are the parts of the steering axle knuckles that are inserted through the wheels.

The cross-steering tube, or tie rod, holds both wheels in the same position. As the left wheel turns, the right wheel moves in the same direction. A kingpin in the steering knuckle allows each wheel to have its own pivot point. The wheel rotates on a spindle. The spindle is also called the stub axle. It's attached to the kingpin.

Your vehicle may have manual or power steering. Power steering systems use hydraulic pressure or air pressure to assist the mechanical linkage in making the turn. This requires less of your strength to turn the steering wheel.

When hydraulic pressure is used to assist steering, a hydraulic unit replaces the steering gear box. A hydraulic pump is added to the engine to supply the pressure used to help turn the wheels. When you turn the steering wheel to the right, the hydraulic valve senses it. A valve opens. Fluid pressure helps turn the wheels to the right.

That's it—a quick tour through the major systems in most commercial motor vehicles. Now you know how wiring and electrical, braking, and fuel systems, coupling devices, tires, emergency equipment, body components, suspension, and steering systems support your vehicle.

All these systems and equipment are "necessary for safe operation" according to the FMCSR. The CDL examiner may, and probably will, ask you questions about some or all of these. You must be able to identify the parts on your vehicle. You must be able to give a basic description of how they work. You must be able to recognize defects and state how they affect safe operations.

EMERGENCIES

It's not enough to know how to operate your vehicle under normal conditions. FMCSR Part 393 states you must know how to use these systems and controls in emergencies. Two examples are mentioned. They are skids and loss of brakes. Of course there are others. The next chapter, on basic vehicle control, will include emergency maneuvers.

PASS POST-TRIP

Instructions: For each true/false test item, read the statement. Decide whether the statement is true or false. If it is true, circle the letter A. If it is false, circle the letter B. For each multiple-choice test item, choose the answer choice—A, B, C, or D—that correctly completes the statement or answers the question. There is only one correct answer. Use the answer sheet provided on page 141.

1. When you first start your engine, you should get a normal reading on the dashboard's _____ within a few seconds.
    A. oil pressure gauge
    B. fuel pressure gauge
    C. tire pressure temperature gauge
    D. all of the above

2. The proper way to use a fire extinguisher is to douse the flames with the dry chemical.
    A. True
    B. False

3. A high pyrometer reading could mean _____.
    A. a leak or a clog in the air intake
    B. problems with the fuel ignition
    C. you're in the wrong gear ratio for the grade
    D. any of the above

4. A vehicle will have warning lights or warning buzzers, but not both.
    A. True
    B. False

get caught between dual tires and cause severe damage.

Some obstacles that appear to be harmless can be very dangerous. For example, cardboard boxes may be empty. They could also contain some solid or heavy material that could cause damage. The same is true of paper and cloth sacks.

Be alert for objects of all sorts. If you see them early enough, you can avoid them without making sudden, unsafe moves.

Off-ramps and On-ramps

Freeway and turnpike exits can be particularly dangerous for commercial vehicles. Off-ramps and on-ramps often have speed limit signs posted. Remember, these speeds may be safe for automobiles, but may not be safe for larger vehicles or heavily loaded vehicles. The safest speed is not the posted one. It's the one that gives you the most control over your vehicle.

Figure 7-19. The speed posted for the off-ramps may be too high for your CMV.

Exits that go downhill and turn at the same time can be especially dangerous. The downgrade makes it hard to reduce speed. Braking and turning at the same time can be a dangerous practice. Make sure you are going slowly enough before you get on the curved part of an off-ramp or on-ramp.

As you learned earlier, off-ramps can be dangerous for other reasons. Drivers ahead of you may slow in order to exit. They may decide suddenly to move for the exit. Or, they may start to exit and change their minds.

On-ramps mean drivers entering the highway. They may not always be very skilled at doing this. They'll probably assume you can slow to make room for them. If you can't, a crash can result. If you're in the merge lane, manage your space and speed very carefully.

Dangerous Drivers

Other drivers can present still more hazards. Learn how to read the clues.

Confused drivers often change direction suddenly or stop without warning. Confusion is common near freeway or turnpike interchanges and major intersections. Stopping in the middle of a block, changing lanes for no apparent reason, backup lights suddenly going on are all clues to confusion. Hesitation is another clue. So is driving very slowly, using brakes often, or stopping in the middle of an intersection. You may also see drivers who are looking at street signs, maps, and house numbers. These drivers may not be paying attention to you.

Tourists unfamiliar with the area can be very hazardous. Clues to tourists include car-top luggage and out-of-state license plates.

Slow drivers are hazards. Seeing slow-moving vehicles early can prevent a crash. Some vehicles (mopeds, farm machinery, construction machinery, tractors, etc.) by their nature are slow. Some of these will have the "slow moving vehicle" symbol to warn you. This is a red triangle with an orange center. Watch for it. Proceed with caution around slow moving vehicles.

Drivers signaling a turn may be a hazard. They may slow more than expected or stop. If they are making a tight turn into an alley or driveway, they may go very slowly. If they are blocked by pedestrians or other vehicles, they may have to stop on the roadway. Vehicles turning left may have to stop for oncoming vehicles.

Drivers in a hurry may feel your CMV is keeping them from getting where they want to go on time. Such drivers may pass you without a safe gap in the oncoming traffic, cutting too close in front of you. Drivers entering the road may pull in front of you in order to avoid being stuck behind you. Be careful around drivers who are going faster than the flow of traffic and making many lane changes.

Drivers who are sleepy, have had too much to drink, are on drugs, or who are ill are hazards. Be suspicious of drivers who are:

- weaving across the road or drifting from side-to-side
- leaving the road (dropping right wheels onto the shoulder, or bumping across a curb in a turn)
- stopping at the wrong time (stopping at a green light or waiting for too long at a stop)
- driving with the window open in cold weather
- speeding or slowing suddenly, driving too fast or too slow

As you learned earlier, you should be especially alert for drunk and sleepy drivers late at night.

Learn to read the body movements of other drivers. Drivers look in the direction they are going to turn. You may sometimes get a clue from a driver's head and body movements that this driver may be going to make a turn even though the turn signals aren't on. Drivers making over-the-shoulder checks may be going to change lanes. These clues are most easily seen in motorcyclists and bicyclists. Watch other road users and try to tell whether they might do something hazardous.

Be alert for drivers whose vision is blocked. Vans, loaded station wagons, and cars with the rear window blocked are examples. Rental trucks should be watched carefully. The driver's vision to the sides and rear of the truck is limited. A rental truck's driver is likely unfamiliar with the vehicle. In winter, vehicles with frosted, ice-covered, or snow-covered windows are hazards.

Vehicles may be partly hidden by blind intersections or alleys. If you only can see the rear or front end of a vehicle but not the driver, then he or she can't see you. Be alert because the driver may back out or enter into your lane. Always be prepared to stop.

Delivery trucks can present a hazard. The driver's vision is often blocked by packages or vehicle doors. Drivers of step vans, postal vehicles, and local delivery vehicles often are in a hurry. They may suddenly step out of their vehicle or drive their vehicle into the traffic lane.

Parked vehicles can be hazards when the people start to get out. Or, they may suddenly start up and drive into your way. Watch for movement inside the vehicle or movement of the vehicle itself that shows people are inside. Brake or backup lights and exhaust are clues that a driver is about to move.

Be careful of a stopped bus. Passengers may cross in front of or behind the bus. Often, they can't see you.

Some situations are just accidents waiting to happen. Anywhere vehicles meet there is a chance of danger. Be cautious where lanes of traffic merge. This could be at an on-ramp, as you've seen. Another example is the end of a lane, which forces vehicles to move to another lane of traffic. Other situations include slow moving or stalled traffic in a traffic lane and accident scenes.

Dangerous Non-Drivers

There can be others on the road besides drivers, and they can be hazards. Pedestrians, joggers, and bicyclists may be on the road with their back to the traffic, so they can't see you. Sometimes, they wear portable stereos with head sets, so they can't hear you either. On rainy days, pedestrians may not see you because of hats or umbrellas. They may be hurrying to get out of the rain and may not pay attention to the traffic.

People who are distracted are hazards. Watch for where they are looking. If they are looking elsewhere, they can't see you. Be alert to what's distracting them.

Be alert to others even when they are looking right at you. They may believe that they have the right-of-way.

Children tend to act quickly without checking traffic. Children playing with one another may not look for traffic and are a serious hazard. Look for clues that children are in the area. For example, someone selling ice cream is a hazard clue. Children may be nearby and may not see you.

Drivers changing a tire or fixing an engine often do not pay attention to the danger that roadway traffic is to them. They are often careless. Jacked-up wheels or raised hoods are hazard clues.

Accidents are particularly hazardous. People involved in the accident may not look for traffic. Passing drivers tend to look at the accident. People often run across the road without looking. Vehicles may slow or stop suddenly.

People in and around shopping areas are often not watching traffic because they are looking for stores or looking into store windows.

You should always be looking for hazards. They may turn into emergencies. Look for the hazards in order to have time to plan a way out of any emergency. When you see a hazard, think about the emergencies that could develop. Figure out what you would do. Always be prepared to take action based on your plans. That makes you a prepared, defensive driver. You will improve not only your own safety but the safety of all road users.

EMERGENCY MANEUVERS

In spite of your best efforts, you may be faced with an emergency. Traffic emergencies occur when two vehicles are about to collide. Vehicle emergencies occur when tires, brakes, or other critical parts fail. Your chances of avoiding a crash depend upon how well you take action.

Figure 7-20. How many hazards can you spot in this picture?

Stopping May Not Be Safe

Stopping is not always the safest thing to do in an emergency. When you don't have enough room to stop, you may have to steer away from what's ahead. You can almost always turn to miss an obstacle more quickly than you can stop. Keep in mind, though, that top-heavy vehicles may flip over.

Turn Quickly and Safely

To turn quickly, you must have a firm grip on the steering wheel with both hands. The best way to have both hands on the wheel if there is an emergency is to keep them there all the time. Use the grip described at the beginning of this chapter.

A quick turn can be made safely, if it's done the right way. Don't apply the brake while you are turning. It's very easy to lock your wheels while turning. If that happens, you may skid out of control. If you have been managing your speed, you should be going slowly enough to control the vehicle without braking.

Don't turn any more than needed to clear whatever is in your way. The more sharply that you turn, the greater the chances of a skid or rollover.

Countersteer

Be prepared to "countersteer." Countersteering is turning the wheel back in the other direction once you've passed whatever was in your path. Unless you are prepared to countersteer, you won't be able to do it quickly enough. Think of emergency steering and countersteering as two parts of one driving action.

Steer to the Right

In most cases, steer to the right. If an oncoming driver has drifted into your lane, a move to your right is best. If that driver realizes what has happened, the natural response will be to return to his or her own lane.

If something is blocking your path, the best direction to steer will depend on the situation. If the shoulder is clear, going right may be best. No one is likely to be driving on the shoulder, but someone may be passing you on the left. You will know if you have been using your mirrors.

If you are blocked on both sides, a move to the right may be best. At least you won't force anyone into an opposing traffic lane and a possible head-on collision.

If you have been using your mirrors, you'll know which lane is empty and can be safely used.

Leaving the Road

In some emergencies, you may have to drive off the road. It may be better than colliding with another vehicle. Most shoulders are strong enough to support the weight of a large vehicle.

If you do leave the road, avoid using the brakes until your speed has dropped to about 20 mph. Then brake very gently to prevent skidding on a loose surface. Keep one set of wheels on the pavement if possible. This helps to maintain control.

Stay on the shoulder. If the shoulder is clear, stay on it until your vehicle has come to a stop. Signal and check your mirrors before pulling back onto the road.

If you are forced to return to the road before you can stop, use the following procedure. Hold the wheel tightly and turn sharply enough to get right back on the road safely. Don't try to edge gradually back on the road. If you do, your tires might grab unexpectedly. You could lose control.

When both front tires are on the paved surface, countersteer immediately. The two turns should be made as a single "steer-countersteer" move.

Stop Quickly and Safely

If somebody suddenly pulls out in front of you, your natural response is to hit the brakes. This is a good response if there's enough distance to stop and you use the brakes correctly. You should brake in a way that will keep your vehicle in a straight line and allow you to turn if it becomes necessary. You can use the "controlled braking" method or the "stab braking" method.

In controlled braking, you apply the brakes as hard as you can without locking the wheels. Keep steering wheel movements very small while doing this. If you need to make a larger steering adjustment or if the wheels lock, release the brakes. Reapply the brakes as soon as you can.

In stab braking, you apply your brakes all the way. Release the brakes when the wheels lock up. As soon as the wheels start rolling, apply the brakes fully again. It can take up to one second for the wheels to start rolling after you release the brakes. If you reapply the brakes before the wheels start rolling, the vehicle won't straighten out.

Don't jam on the brakes! Emergency braking does not mean pushing down on the brake pedal as hard as you can. That will only cause the wheels to lock up and skid. If the wheels are skidding, you cannot control the vehicle.

Brake Failure

You've learned about the loss of braking power on downgrades. There, a runaway ramp is your escape route. What if your brakes fail and there is no escape ramp?

First, remember that brakes kept in good condition rarely fail. That's why brake inspection and maintenance is so important.

Most hydraulic brake failures occur for one of two reasons:

- loss of hydraulic pressure
- brake fade on long hills

When the system won't build up pressure, the brake pedal will feel spongy or go to the floor. If this happens, downshift. Putting the vehicle into a lower gear will help to slow the vehicle. You can also pump the brakes. Sometimes pumping the brake pedal will create enough hydraulic pressure to stop the vehicle.

The parking or emergency brake is separate from the hydraulic brake system. Therefore, it can be used to slow the vehicle. However, be sure to press the release button or pull the release lever at the same time you use the emergency brake. That way you can adjust the brake pressure and keep the wheels from locking up.

Find an escape route. While slowing the vehicle, look for an escape route. This could be an open field or side street as well as a designated escape ramp. Turning uphill is a good way to slow and stop the vehicle. Make sure the vehicle does not start rolling backward after you stop. Put it in low gear and apply the parking brake. You may have to roll back into some obstacle that will stop the vehicle.

When your brakes fail on a downgrade, use the tactics described in the "Mountain Driving" section of this chapter.

Tire Failure

There are four important things that safe drivers do to handle a tire failure safely:

- Be aware that a tire has failed.
- Hold the steering wheel firmly.
- Stay off the brake.
- After stopping, check all the tires.

The sooner you realize you have a tire failure, the more time you will have to react. Having just a few seconds to remember what it is you're supposed to do can help you. Recognize the major signs of tire failure.

Sound is your first clue. The loud "bang" of a blowout is an easily recognized sign. Because it can take a few seconds for your vehicle to react to the tire failure, you might think the sound is coming from some other vehicle. To be safe, any time you hear a tire blow, assume it's yours.

If the vehicle thumps or vibrates heavily, it may be a sign that one of the tires has gone flat. With a rear tire, that may be the only sign you get.

If the steering feels "heavy," it is probably a sign that one of the front tires has failed. Sometimes, failure of a rear tire will cause the vehicle to slide back and forth or "fishtail." However, dual rear tires usually prevent this. Any of these signs is a warning of possible tire failure. To maintain control of the vehicle, hold the steering wheel firmly. If a front tire fails and you're holding the wheel loosely, the force can twist the steering wheel out of your hand. You must have a firm grip on the steering wheel with both hands at all times.

Stay off the brake. It's natural to want to brake in an emergency. However, braking when a tire has failed could cause you to lose control of the vehicle. Unless you're about to run into something, stay off the brake until the vehicle has slowed down. Then brake very gently, pull off the road, and stop. After you've come to a stop, get out and check all the tires. Do this even if the vehicle seems to be handling all right. If one of your dual tires goes, the only way you may know it is by getting out and looking at it.

SKID CONTROL AND RECOVERY

Recovering from a skid can really challenge your emergency maneuvering skills.

A skid happens whenever the tires lose their grip on the road. A skid can result from over-braking. That is braking too hard and locking up the wheels. Skids also can occur if you use the engine retarder when the road is slippery.

Over-steering can lead to skidding. Don't turn the wheels more sharply than the vehicle can turn.

Supplying too much power to the drive wheels can cause them to spin. That can lead to a skid.

Driving too fast is a common cause of skidding. Most serious skids result from driving too fast for road conditions. If you manage your speed, you don't have to accelerate suddenly, brake hard, or over-steer to avoid a collision.

Drive-Wheel Skids

By far the most common skid is one in which the rear wheels lose traction. This can result from over-braking or over-acceleration.

Skids caused by acceleration usually happen on ice or snow. They can be easily stopped by taking your foot off the accelerator. If it is very slippery, push the clutch in. Otherwise the engine can keep the wheels from rolling freely and regaining traction.

Rear-wheel braking skids occur when the rear-drive wheels lock. Because locked wheels have less traction than rolling wheels, the rear wheels usually slide sideways in an attempt to "catch up" with the front wheels. In a bus or straight truck, the vehicle will slide sideways in a "spin out." When you're towing a trailer, a drive-wheel skid can let the trailer push the towing vehicle sideways, causing a sudden jackknife.

To correct a drive-wheel braking skid, first let off the brake. This will let the rear wheels roll again and keep the rear wheels from sliding any further. If you are on ice, push in the clutch to let the wheels turn freely.

Turn quickly. When a vehicle begins to slide sideways, quickly steer in the direction you want the vehicle to go—down the road. You must turn the wheel quickly.

As a vehicle turns back on course, it has a tendency to keep right on turning. Unless you turn the steering wheel quickly the other way, you may find yourself skidding in the opposite direction. Your quick turn must be followed by countersteering.

Learning to stay off the brake, turn the steering wheel quickly, push in the clutch, and countersteer in a skid takes a lot of practice. You don't often get to "practice" skid recovery. Usually, when you're trying to get out of a skid, it's the real thing. About the only place to get this practice is on a large driving range or "skid pad."

Front-Wheel Skids

Most front-wheel skids are caused by driving too fast for conditions. They can also result from worn front tires. If your cargo is loaded so that not enough weight is on the front axle, you could skid.

In a front-wheel skid, the front end tends to go in a straight line no matter how much you turn the steering wheel. On a very slippery surface, you may not be able to steer around a curve or turn.

When a front-wheel skid occurs, the only way to stop the skid is to let the vehicle slow. Stop turning or braking so hard. Reduce your speed as quickly as possible without skidding.

COUPLING AND UNCOUPLING

We're almost at the end of the skills CDL drivers are required to have. As you learned in Chapter 4, you must have some knowledge about hazardous materials. Even if you don't plan to haul them, you must be able to recognize a hazardous materials shipment when you see one. The basic information about hazardous materials was included in the FMCSR summary in Chapter 5 and is presented in FMCSR Part 397. Make sure you have all the information under your belt.

CDL drivers must also show they know how to inspect their vehicle and why it's important to do so. Vehicle inspections are covered in detail in Chapter 9.

So there's one last area of information to cover before we leave this chapter. That's the coupling and uncoupling of tractors and trailers. If you plan to drive a straight truck and never to pull a trailer, you may not need these skills. You will have to take your CDL Skills Test in a Group B or

C truck, without a trailer. If you plan to drive a Group A truck, or pull a trailer, you will be tested on your knowledge of coupling and uncoupling a tractor and semitrailer. You'll have to know how to inspect this vehicle combination.

Coupling and uncoupling, and inspecting vehicle combinations, is covered in Chapter 11. Don't skip that chapter if you are going for a Group A CDL.

You've covered a lot of ground in this chapter. The "list" of vital skills is long and detailed. You may already have many of these skills. Or, you may have found quite a few new ones to master. To be a safe, skilled, licensed commercial driver, you must be in command of them all.

You may need several sessions with this chapter and quite a bit of practice with the tactics and techniques described here. Keep at it until safe vehicle control comes naturally to you.

PASS POST-TRIP

Instructions: For each true/false test item, read the statement. Decide whether the statement is true or false. If it is true, circle the letter A. If it is false, circle the letter B. For each multiple-choice test item, choose the answer choice—A, B, C, or D—that correctly completes the statement or answers the question. There is only one correct answer. Use the answer sheet provided on page 175.

1. Rough acceleration is not only likely to damage the vehicle, it can cause you to lose control.
   A. True
   B. False

2. How far ahead of the vehicle should a driver look while driving?
   A. nine to 12 seconds
   B. 18 to 21 seconds
   C. 12 to 15 seconds
   D. 12 to 15 feet

3. When driving 55 mph on dry pavement, allow _____ to bring the vehicle to a stop.
   A. the length of a football field
   B. twice the length of the vehicle
   C. half the length of a football field
   D. the length of the vehicle

4. Hydroplaning _____.
   A. only occurs when there is a lot of water
   B. only occurs at speeds above 55 mph
   C. is more likely if tire pressure is low
   D. is more likely if the road is banked

5. You're driving a 40-foot vehicle and keeping with the flow of traffic at 50 mph. You should keep _____ seconds of distance between you and the vehicle ahead.
   A. four
   B. five
   C. six
   D. seven

6. When there are two turning lanes, you should start a left-hand turn from the right or outer lane.
   A. True
   B. False

7. When you are dead tired, the best way to refresh yourself and get ready to drive again is to _____ .
   A. have a drink
   B. go for a brisk walk
   C. drink some coffee
   D. get some sleep

8. Roads are most slippery and dangerous during _____ a rainstorm.
   A. the first 15 minutes of
   B. the last 15 minutes of
   C. the heaviest part of
   D. a pause in

9. "Fanning the brakes" is a recommended downhill braking tactic.
   A. True
   B. False

10. You may hear a drive tire blow out before you feel it.
    A. True
    B. False

similar damage—are permitted, as long as they don't connect with other cracks. A whole spider web of cracks is not allowed.

Figure 9-2. Your viewing area must be clean and free of "illegal" stickers.

Fuel System

Check the fuel tank or tanks. See that they are securely mounted, not damaged or leaking. Make sure the fuel crossover line is secure. It should not be hanging so low that it would be exposed to high grade crossings or objects bouncing up from the road. The filler caps must be on firmly. Of course, see that the tanks contain enough fuel. Tanks should not be more than 95 percent full. Fuel expands as it warms up. Filling your tanks slightly less than full leaves some room for this expansion.

Coupling Devices

If you are following along in your FMCSR, you'll see the next item of required equipment covered is coupling devices. This includes the saddle mounts, tow bars, pintle hooks, and safety chains used in towaway operations. Check all the parts that join vehicles together. They should not be bent or warped. The safety chains should not have any broken or twisted links. Make certain the connections are all secure. Check that the lights, reflectors, steering, and brakes work as required on the towed vehicles as well as the towing vehicle. (Review Chapters 5 and 8 if you don't recall the requirements.)

Figure 9-3. Check for bent or warped coupling devices.

If you are inspecting a vehicle combination as part of your CDL test, then you are going for a Group A CDL or the doubles/triples endorsement. You will find combination vehicle inspection covered in Chapter 11.

Tires

It is simply dangerous to drive with bad tires. Look for problems such as body ply or belt material showing through the tread or sidewall. Neither the tread nor the sidewall should be separating from the tire body. Look for cuts that are so deep that the ply or belt shows through. Look for cut or cracked valve stems or missing valve stem caps. Naturally, a very low or flat tire would have to be repaired. Don't drive on tires with any of these problems.

Listen for air leaks that could result in a flat. Look for bulges in the rubber that could lead to blowouts. Check the inflation pressure. Some drivers become expert enough to do this accurately by just thumping the tire with a tire billy. You'll never go wrong using a tire gauge, though. It would not be a bad idea to use a tire gauge during the CDL test inspection. Simply kicking the tires is definitely not good enough.

Check the tires for wear. You need at least 4/32-inch tread depth in every major groove on front wheels. You need 2/32-inch tread depth on other wheels.

Other problems are dual tires that come in contact with each other or parts of the vehicle. You should not have two tires of different sizes on the same axle. Radial and bias-ply tires should not be used together on the same axle, either.

Figure 9-4. Don't mix tire sizes on the same axle.

Last, remember that you may not have regrooved tires with load-carrying capacity equal to or greater than 4,920 pounds on the front wheel of a tractor.

Sleeper Berths and Heaters

Sleeper berths and heaters are listed among miscellaneous parts and accessories. However, most of their specifications are of concern to manufacturers. There's little for the driver to inspect, and they're not included in the inspection report form. For your own safety, note if anything blocks easy access to the sleeper berth entrance or exit. Be alert to leaks that could allow exhaust or fuel fumes to enter the sleeper berth. Be aware, too, of safety threats presented by the heater, such as leaks, loose mounting, frayed wires, worn hoses, and so forth.

Wipers and Defrosters

Your vehicle must have two windshield wiper blades, one on each side of the centerline of the windshield. They must operate automatically, not by manual control. They must clean the windshield of rain, snow, and other moisture so you have clear vision. (A single blade is acceptable if it performs to the specifications in FMCSR Part 393.78.)

As part of your inspection, make sure the wipers work. Make sure the rubber blades do a good job of cleaning. Blades that are stiff, crumbly, or loose can't clear your windshield well.

If your vehicle has a windshield, it must also have a windshield defroster. Turn the defroster on and off as part of your inspection. Put your hand over the vents to confirm that the defroster is putting out warm air.

Test windshield washers to make sure they work. If they don't, you could simply be lacking fluid in the washer reservoir. Or, the fluid lines could be kinked, broken, or leaking.

Rear-view Mirrors

Your vehicle must have a rear-view mirror at each side of the cab. (Some vehicles may have one outside mirror on the driver's side. Another mirror inside the vehicle gives a view to the rear.) Make sure the mirrors are clean and undamaged. Adjust them so that when you are in the driver's seat, you have a view of the highway to the rear along both sides of the vehicle.

Horn

All vehicles must have a horn. As you inspect the vehicle, make sure your horn is working.

Exhaust System

A broken exhaust system can let poisonous gases into the cab or sleeper berth. You should check for loose, broken, or missing exhaust pipes, mufflers, tail pipes, or stacks. Loose, broken, or missing mounting brackets, clamps, bolts, or nuts can lead to problems. Look for exhaust system parts that rub against fuel system parts, tires, or other moving parts of the vehicle. Look for hoses, lines, and wires that are so close to exhaust system parts that they could be damaged by the heat.

Check for exhaust system parts that are leaking. Hold your hand close to the exhaust manifold. You'll be able to feel any leaks. (Don't put your hand too close, though. It's hot, and you could burn yourself.)

Defects in the exhaust system may not be repaired with wraps or patches. If you see such repair work, note it as a defect.

Floor

The floor of your vehicle should be free of holes and openings. Remember, such holes could allow fumes and exhaust gases into your vehicle, which could make you ill. Also make sure that the floor is clean, free of oil or grease. Slippery floors could lead to accidents.

Rear Bumper

Vehicles that are higher than 30 inches off the ground (when empty) must have rear bumpers. If your vehicle requires or has such a bumper, check to see that it is securely attached.

Flags on Projecting Loads

Any part of the vehicle or load that extends more than four inches from the side or four feet from the rear must be marked with a red flag. If you have an oversized load or vehicle, make sure it's marked with a red flag, 12 inches square.

Seat Belts

Most trucks and buses must have a seat belt for the driver. When you inspect your vehicle, make sure the seat belt is firmly attached and in good condition.

Don't forget to put the seat belt on when you take the driving portion of the CDL tests. Nearly all states require the driver (and often the passenger) to wear seat belts.

Emergency Equipment

You must carry a fire extinguisher in all but lightweight vehicles. Most vehicles are required to have one with a 5 B:C rating, or two with a 4 B:C rating. (Fire extinguishers on vehicles hauling hazmat must have a 10 B:C-rated fire extinguisher.) Include the fire extinguisher in your inspection. Check the gauge that tells you the fire extinguisher is fully charged. Check the nozzle to make sure it's clear. Check the ring pin to make sure the tip is intact. Check the pressure gauge. The needle should be in the green area. The extinguisher must be securely mounted to the vehicle, not rolling around loose. It must be stored where you can get to it easily.

Know how to use the fire extinguisher. Do you recall the proper method? If not, review Chapter 6.

If your truck was made on or after January 1, 1974, you must carry three emergency triangles that reflect from both sides. There are other devices you may carry to supplement the triangles, but you must carry the triangles. (If you're driving a truck that was built in 1974 or earlier, there are other warning devices you may use instead of the triangles. If your vehicle is this old, check Section 393.95 of the FMCSR for a full description of those devices.)

Figure 9-5. Make sure you have the required warning devices and emergency equipment.

Unless your vehicle uses circuit breakers, make sure you have spare fuses. You should know how to install them.

Cargo Securement

Cargo must be safely and securely loaded. We covered cargo loading in more detail in Chapter 8. Briefly, though, inspect the following:

- tailgate
- doors
- tarps
- spare tire
- binders
- chains
- winches
- braces and supports

All must be in good working order. Nothing should be flapping or hanging loose.

Tarps must be tied down so they don't flap or billow. If they are too slack, they could fill with air and balloon out. This could block your view in your rear-view mirrors.

Cargo must be loaded so it won't shift or fall off the vehicle.

If your vehicle doesn't have a cab guard, your load may call for a header board or similar device. Make sure it's strong, free of damage, and securely in place.

Cargo that could shift sideways must be held in place by sideboards or stakes. Again, make sure these are in good condition and securely in place. The cargo must not block the view you have while driving. Cargo must not block you in so that you can't move your arms or legs freely. You must be able to get around the cargo easily so you can reach emergency equipment or exit the vehicle in an emergency.

Curbside doors should be securely closed, latched, and locked. Otherwise they could swing open and hit someone on the sidewalk.

If you're hauling a sealed load, you should have security seals in place on the doors.

If you are hauling hazardous materials, you must have the correct papers and placards to go with them. You might also need a Hazardous Materials Endorsement. Review Chapter 5 if you don't exactly recall the rules about hauling hazmat.

Frame

As you inspect your vehicle, check the condition of the frame. Look for loose, cracked, sagging, bent, or broken parts. The frame should not be missing any bolts. Make sure all bolts are in good condition and tightened down. Anything attached to the frame must be bolted or riveted. Check these fastenings to make sure they are tight.

Cab

Check the condition of the doors. They should open easily and close securely. Doors may not be wired shut or held closed in a way that makes them hard to open again. Look for any loose, cracked, sagging, bent, or broken parts. The hood must be securely fastened. The seats must not be loose and wobbly. Your vehicle must have a front bumper. It must be firmly attached to the vehicle. It must not stick out so far that it becomes a hazard.

The cab should be clean and neat. Papers, cups, and other loose items could become hazards. If you stop short or turn sharply, they could fly around and hit you or get in your way.

Wheel and Rim Problems

Look for cracked or broken wheels or rims. Missing clamps, spacers, studs, and lugs could cause problems. Mismatched, bent, or cracked lock rings are dangerous. Wheels or rims should not have been repaired by welding.

Rust around wheel nuts may mean the nuts are loose. Use a wrench to check tightness. Examine the stud or bolt holes on the rims. If they are egg-shaped (out-of-round), that signals a problem. Check the supply of oil in the hub. See that there are no leaks.

Suspension System

Broken suspension parts can be extremely dangerous. Look for cracked or broken spring hangers. Note as defects torque rod or arm, U-bolts, spring hangers, or other axle positioning parts that are cracked, damaged, or missing. Loose or bent spring hangers will allow the axle to move out of its proper position. That could result in problems with the steering or driveline. The axle must be in the proper alignment and secure. Power axles should not be leaking lube or gear oil.

Figure 9-6. Check your suspension for broken parts.

If your vehicle has sliding tandems, make a close inspection of the locking pins. They must not be missing or out of place. The tandems should be securely locked in position.

Another problem to look for is missing or broken leaves in a leaf spring. In many states, if one fourth or more are missing, it will put the vehicle out of service. However, cracks, breaks, or missing leaves are prohibited. Leaves that have shifted might hit and damage a tire or other vehicle part. If your vehicle has coil springs, check the coils for cracks or breaks.

Look for leaking shock absorbers. Air suspension systems that are damaged or leaking are considered defects. Make sure the air pressure regulator valve works properly. First check to see that the vehicle's air pressure gauge shows normal operating pressure. Then check to see that the air suspension doesn't leak any more than three psi in five minutes, if at all.

Steering System

You'll include the steering system in your vehicle inspection. The steering wheel must not be loose. It must not have any missing or cracked spokes.

Remember what steering wheel lash is? That's the number of turns the steering wheel must make before the wheels begin to move. Another term for this is "steering wheel free play." FMCSR Part 393 sets limits on steering wheel lash. It should not exceed the limits set in the regulations for steering wheels of various sizes, manual or power. Anything more than that can make it hard to steer. The steering wheel should move easily both to the right and left.

Look at Figure 9-7. Note the steering wheel lash limit for the steering wheel in your vehicle.

Steering wheel diameter	Manual steering system	Power steering system
16" or less	2" +	4 1/4 " +
18"	2 1/4 " +	4 3/4 " +
20"	2 1/2 " +	5 1/4 " +
22"	2 3/4 " +	5 3/4 " +

Figure 9-7. Steering wheel lash limits.

The steering column should be securely fastened.

Check both the ball-and-socket and U-joints for signs of wear, flaws, or welding. (Damaged U-joints may not be repaired by welding.) There should be no cracks in the steering gear box. All its bolts and brackets should be secure. The Pitman arm must not be loose.

If your vehicle has power steering, all the parts must be in good working order. Look for loose or broken parts. Frayed, cracked, or slipping belts will have to be replaced or adjusted. Look for leaks in the power steering fluid tank and lines. Make sure there is enough power steering fluid. Check for missing nuts, bolts, cotter keys, or other parts. A bent, loose, or broken steering column, steering gear box, or tie rod is a defect.

STATE AND LOCAL REQUIREMENTS

There may be state and local vehicle laws on top of the federal ones we just covered. These may require vehicles to have still more equipment. Remember, you should inform yourself about the requirements of your home state and every state through which you will pass. You could be put out of service in one state for a vehicle condition that was acceptable in another state.

Here are some common state requirements you should know about. You may have to check for these items during your vehicle inspection as well as all those we already covered.

Mud Flaps

Federal law does not require you to have mud flaps on your vehicle. However, some states do. They may have mounting guidelines with which you must comply. It's your responsibility to find out what those guidelines are.

If there are no regulations on mounting mud flaps, use the following as a guide. These suggestions come from the Society of Automotive Engineers.

Measure from the ground to the bottom edge of your vehicle's mud flap. This measurement should be no more than six inches (measured when the vehicle is loaded). This will allow the mud flap to clear snow, curbs, or road hazards.

Your mud flaps should be at least as wide as the tires they cover.

Mud flaps should be mounted as far as possible to the rear from the wheel. They work best at that position.

Remember, check state regulations to see if mud flaps are required, and how they should be mounted.

One-third the horizontal distance from the bottom edge to the centerline of the axle, but no closer to the road then six inches when the vehicle is loaded

As far to the rear from the wheel as practical

At least the width of the tire

Figure 9-8. Some states may require mud flaps.

Tire Chains

Many states require tire chains during snowy weather. This is especially true in the West. Often, you'll see highway signs telling you to put chains on your tires.

Again, check the regulations of your home state and every state on your route. Include tire chains in your stock of equipment. Practice mounting and removing them. That way you'll be prepared if you're asked to put them on during your CDL tests.

Other Equipment

It is often recommended that you carry the following items as emergency equipment, in addition to flares and reflectors:

- tire changing kit
- accident notification kit
- list of emergency phone numbers

Read the CDL manual your state offers carefully. It may mention these items and others besides. You may see them referred to as "suggested" or "recommended." Take that as a very strong recommendation. Have those items on your vehicle when you take your CDL tests. Know what they are for and how to use them.

INSPECTION ROUTINES

Now you know what equipment you must have on your vehicle. You know what condition is considered safe. You know what defects to include in your inspection. You know why they threaten your safety and the safety of others on the road.

All you need is a system for checking these items. Follow the routine outlined on the next pages. This routine is more or less the same whether you inspect a straight truck or vehicle combination. Pair the checklist with the illustration that matches your vehicle. Stop and perform each check described in the routine at the location marked on the diagram that follows.

Usually, you may have the checklist with you when you take your test. Check with your state to see if for some reason this is not permitted. Otherwise, feel free to use the checklist. You'll be less likely to overlook something if you check off items as you go.

As you inspect your vehicle, tell the examiner what you are inspecting and why. Describe what you find. You're not likely to take a defective vehicle to the test. However, the examiner will want to know that you would recognize a defect if you saw one. So as you inspect your vehicle, mention the defects typically found at the different sites. Explain how those defects impair safety.

There are seven main steps in this inspection routine. They are:

- approach the vehicle
- raise the hood or tilt the cab and check the engine compartment
- start the engine and inspect inside the cab
- check the lights
- walk all around the vehicle, inspecting as you go
- check the signal lights
- check the brakes

Step One: Vehicle Overview

As you walk toward the vehicle, notice its general condition. Look for damage. Note if the vehicle is leaning to one side. This could mean a flat tire. Cargo may be overloaded or may have shifted. Or, it could be a suspension problem. Look under the vehicle for fresh oil, coolant, grease, or fuel leaks. Check the area around the vehicle for people, other vehicles, objects, low hanging wires, or limbs. These could become hazards once the vehicle begins to move.

Look over the most recent vehicle inspection report. Drivers typically have to make a vehicle inspection report in writing each day. The vehicle owner then should see that any items in the report that affect safety are repaired. If the mechanic repaired the defects, or determined no repairs were needed, there will be a certification for that on the form.

You should look at the last report to find out what was the matter, if anything. Inspect the vehicle to find out whether problems were fixed, or whether repairs were not needed.

Step Two: Engine Compartment Check

Check that the parking brakes are on and/or wheels chocked. You may have to raise the hood or open the engine compartment door. If you have a tilt cab, secure loose items in the cab before you tilt it. Then they won't fall and break something.

At this site, check the engine oil level. The oil should be above the "Low" or "Add" mark on the dipstick. See that the level of coolant is above the "Low" level line on the reservoir. Check the condition of coolant-carrying hoses.

Check the radiator shutters and winterfront, if your vehicle has one. Remove ice from the radiator shutters. Make sure the winterfront is not closed too tightly. If the shutters freeze shut or the winterfront is closed too much, the engine may overheat and stop. Inspect the fan. Make sure the blades are sound and not likely to catch on hanging wires or hoses.

If your vehicle has power steering, check the fluid level and the condition of the hoses. Check the dipstick on the oil tank. The fluid level should be above the "Low" or "Add" mark.

Check the fluid level for the windshield washers.

If your battery is located in the engine compartment, perform the battery check described earlier here.

If you have an automatic transmission, check the fluid level. You may have to do this with the engine running. The owner's manual will tell you if that is the case.

Check drive belts for tightness and excessive wear. Press down on the center of the belt. The owner's manual will tell you how much slack there should be. Also, if you can easily slide a belt over a pulley, it is definitely too loose or too worn. Look for leaks in the engine compartment. These could be fuel, coolant, oil, power steering fluid, hydraulic fluid, or battery fluid.

Look for cracked or worn insulation on electrical wiring.

Motor Carrier retain for 3 months
One copy must be carried on power unit

DRIVER'S DAILY VEHICLE INSPECTION REPORT

DRIVER'S NAME: _____ **DATE:** _____

Check items which are defective (X) and supply details about the defect in the "Remarks" section below. Use (✓) if inspection was satisfactory.

TRUCK/TRACTOR NO.	DRIVER	MECHANIC	TRUCK/TRACTOR NO.	DRIVER	MECHANIC
Air Lines			Brakes		
Brakes (Emergency)			Brake Connections		
Brakes (Parking)			Bumper		
Body			Coupling Device		
Clutch			Doors		
Cooling System			Hitch		
Coupling Chains			Kingpin		
Coupling Devices			Landing Gear		
Defroster			Lights		
Drive Line			Reflectors		
Engine			Securement Systems		
Exhaust System			Suspension System		
Frame			Tires		
Fuel Tanks			Wheels and Rims		
Heaters			Other		
Horn			**SAFETY/EMERGENCY EQUIPMENT**		
Leaks			Fire Extinguisher		
Lights			Flags		
Oil Pressure			Fuses and Flares		
Rear Vision Mirrors			Reflective Tape		
Reflectors			Reflective Triangles		
Speedometer			Seatbelts		
Steering System			Other		
Suspension System			**REMARKS**		
Tires					
Wheels and Rims					
Windows					
Windshield Wipers/Washers					
Other					

❑ Condition of above vehicle is satisfactory

_____
DRIVER'S SIGNATURE

❑ Above Defects Corrected

❑ Above Defects Need Not Be Corrected for Safe
Operation of Vehicle

_____
MECHANIC'S SIGNATURE

I certify that I am satisfied that this vehicle is in safe operating condition and I have reviewed the last Vehicle Inspection report and verified that required repairs have been completed.

Figure 9-9. A typical Driver's Inspection Report.

Lower and secure the hood, cab, or engine compartment door.

Next, check any handholds, steps, or deck plates. Remove all water, ice, and snow, or grease from handholds, steps, and deck plates that you must use to enter the cab or to move about the vehicle. This will reduce the danger of slipping.

Step Three: Inside the Cab

Get in the cab. Inspect inside the cab. Make sure the parking brake is on. Shift into neutral, "Park" if your transmission is automatic. Start the engine and listen for unusual noises.

Check the gauge readings. The oil pressure should come up to normal within seconds after the engine is started. The ammeter and/or voltmeter should give normal readings. Coolant temperature should start at "Cold" (the low end of the temperature range). It should rise gradually until it reaches normal operating range. The temperature of the engine oil should also rise slowly to normal operating range.

Oil, coolant, and charging circuit warning lights will come on at first. That tells you the lights are working. They should go out right away unless there's a problem.

Make sure your controls work. Check all of the following for looseness, sticking, damage, or improper setting:

- steering wheel
- accelerator ("gas pedal")
- foot brake
- trailer brake (if your vehicle has one)
- parking brake
- retarder controls (if your vehicle has them)
- transmission controls
- interaxle differential lock (if your vehicle has one)
- horn(s)
- windshield wiper and washers
- headlights
- dimmer switch
- turn signal
- four-way flashers
- clearance, identification, and marker light switch(es).

If your vehicle has a clutch, test it now. Depress the clutch until you feel a slight resistance. One to two inches of travel before you feel resistance is normal. More or less than that signals a problem.

Check your mirrors and windshield for the defects described earlier.

Check that you have the required emergency equipment and that it is in good operating condition.

Check for optional items, such as a tire changing kit, and items required by state and local laws, such as mud flaps.

Step Four: Check Lights

Next, check to see that the lights are working. Make sure the parking brake is set, turn off the engine, and take the key with you. Turn on the headlights (on low beams) and the four-way flashers, and get out. Go to the front of the vehicle. Check that the low beams are on and both of the four-way flashers are working. Push the dimmer switch and check that the high beams work. Turn off the headlights and four-way hazard warning flashers. Turn on the parking, clearance, side-marker, and identification lights. Turn on the right-turn signal, and start the "walk-around" part of the inspection.

Step Five: Walk-around Inspection

Walk all around the vehicle, inspecting as you go. Start at the cab on the driver's side. Cover the front of the vehicle. Work down the passenger side to the rear. Cover the rear of the vehicle. Work up the driver's side back to the starting position. Do it this way every time.

Clean all the lights, reflectors, and glass as you go along.

Left Front Side

The driver's door glass should be clean. Door latches or locks should work properly.

Perform a tire, wheel, and rim check at the left front wheel. Perform a suspension system and braking system check. Check the steering parts.

Front

Check the condition of the front axle. Perform a check of the steering system parts. You should actually take hold of steering system parts and shake them to say for sure that they are not loose.

Check the windshield. Pull on the windshield wiper arms to check for proper spring tension. Check the wiper blades for the defects described earlier.

Check the lights and reflectors (parking, clearance, and identification and turn signal lights) at this site. Make sure you have all the required ones as described earlier. They should be clean and working.

Right Front Side

The right front has parts similar to the left front. Perform the same checks. The passenger door glass should be clean. Door latches or locks should work properly. Perform the tire, wheel, and rim check at the right front wheel. Perform a suspension system and braking system check. Check the steering parts.

For cabover (COE) trucks, check the primary and safety cab locks here.

Right Side

The fuel tank is located here. Check to see it is mounted securely, not damaged or leaking. The fuel crossover line must be secure, and not hanging so low that it would be exposed to road hazards. The filler caps must be on firmly. Check the fuel supply. Perform these checks for each fuel tank your vehicle has.

Figure 9-10. Check the fuel tank.

Check all parts you can see at this site. See that the rear of the engine is not leaking. Check for leaks from the transmission. Check the exhaust system parts for defects as described earlier.

Inspect the frame and cross members for bends and cracks.

Electrical wiring should be secured against snagging, rubbing, and wearing.

If your vehicle has a spare tire carrier or rack, check it for damage. It should be securely mounted in the rack. Make sure you have the correct size spare tire and wheel. The spare tire must be in good condition and properly inflated.

Cargo Securement

Check the cargo securement at the right front of the vehicle. Cargo must be properly blocked, braced, tied, chained, and so forth. If you need a header board, make sure it is strong enough and secure. If you have sideboards, check them. The stakes must be strong enough for the load, free of damage, and properly set in place.

Make sure you haven't created handling problems for yourself by overloading the front axles.

Any canvas or tarp must be properly secured to prevent tearing and billowing.

If you are hauling an oversized load, have the necessary signs safely and properly mounted. Make sure you have the permits you need to haul this load.

Check that the curbside cargo compartment doors are securely closed, latched, and locked. See that the required security seals are in place.

Right Rear

At this location, check the wheels, rims, tires, brake system, and suspension parts for the defects described in the first part of this chapter. Check that all parts are sound, properly mounted and secure, and not leaking. Check the axle. Powered axles should not leak.

Check the lights and reflectors required at this location. They should be clean and working.

Rear

Make sure you have a license plate. It should be clean and securely mounted.

If mud flaps are required, check them now. They should be free of damage and fastened according to whatever regulations apply. If there are no legal guidelines, make sure they are at least well-fastened, not dragging on the ground or rubbing the tires.

Check the lights and reflectors required at this location. They should be clean and working.

Bent, cracked, or worn metal parts must be repaired or replaced. If you can't do it yourself, get someone who can to give your brake system some attention. You should not drive off with any part of your brake system in less than top condition. It's simply not safe.

AIR BRAKE SYSTEM INSPECTION

If your vehicle has air brakes, you must add some steps to your normal vehicle inspection routine. You'll learn what they are in detail first. Then you'll find an entire seven-step pre-trip inspection, including the air brake checks. This seven-step routine was first described in Chapter 9, but did not include inspecting the air brakes. We repeat it here, with the air brake inspection included, for your convenience.

Air Brake System Inspection

When you are at the engine compartment, you should check the compressor. Check the oil supply and belt as described in the Maintenance section earlier.

During the "walk-around" part of the inspection, check the hoses for leaks and breaks. At each wheel, check the brake assembly. Look for parts that need replacement or repair. You might find a cracked drum or a loose or worn brake lining. Check the slack adjuster. Have it adjusted if necessary.

Drain all air tanks that must be drained manually. You could find air tanks at the right front, left front, or center of the vehicle. It depends on the manufacturer. Don't forget any air tanks on the trailer.

When you're in the cab, your brake system check should include the following tests. Some of them are performed with the parking brakes off. Make sure the vehicle wheels are chocked so the vehicle doesn't roll while you perform these tests with the parking brakes off.

Test One: Air Pressure Build-Up

This procedure tests pressure build-up time, the low pressure warning indicator, and the air governor.

Open the petcock. Drain the wet tank first, then drain the dry air tanks until the gauges read zero, and close the petcock. Start the engine and run it at a fast idle (600 to 900 rpm). The compressor will start to fill the tanks.

Watch the low air pressure warning mechanism. It should come on and stay on until the pressure builds to more than 60 psi. If the compressor cuts out between 70 and 90 psi, it needs to be adjusted.

In a vehicle with a single air system, the pressure should go from 50 psi to 90 psi within three minutes. In dual air systems, pressure should build from 85 to 100 psi within 45 seconds. If the build-up takes longer, the compressor needs attention.

Some vehicles with larger air tanks can take longer. The owner's manual gives the best advice on this.

Keep filling the tanks until the governor stops the compressor. If it stops below 100 psi or above 125 psi, the governor needs to be adjusted.

The owner's manual may give slightly different upper and lower limits. Run the engine at a fast idle. The air governor should cut out the air compressor at the psi stated in the manual. The air pressure should stop rising.

With the engine still idling, release the spring brakes and step on and off the brake, reducing the air pressure.

 TIP *Chock your wheels before you begin this test.*

The compressor should cut in at the psi stated in the manual. The air pressure should begin to rise. If the governor cuts in or out too early or too late, it requires adjustment.

If the warning light doesn't go out once you have reached 60 psi, there could be a problem with the light. More seriously, it could be that one part of the dual braking system isn't working.

Test Two: Air Leakage Rate

With these simple steps, you can test the brake system's ability to hold air pressure. With the pressure fully built up (about 125 psi), turn off the engine. Release the parking brakes. Press the service brake pedal firmly. Watch the reading on the pressure gauge and start timing. The pressure should not drop more than 2 psi in one minute for single vehicles. If the pressure drop is greater, something is wrong. Find out what is wrong and see that it's fixed before you drive.

Test Three: Air Leakage Rate

Here's another way to test the combination system's ability to hold air pressure. With the engine turned off, press on the brake pedal. Bring the pressure to 90 psi on the application gauge. Watch the air pressure gauge. The pressure drop should not be more than 3 psi per minute.

Test Four: Warning Device and Emergency Brake

These two steps test your warning device and your spring brake emergency application. With air pressure at about 90 pounds and the engine off, push and release the foot brake, reducing the air pressure, until the low air pressure warning comes on. If the warning indicator fails to come on when the pressure reaches 60 psi or below, get it adjusted before you drive. The warning device should come on before the spring brakes are automatically applied.

 Remember the air pressure at which the spring brakes will automatically come on? It's usually in a range between 20 and 40 psi.

Continue pushing and releasing the foot brake until the emergency brakes apply. The spring brakes apply automatically. If they apply above 45 psi or below 20 psi, something is wrong.

Test Five: Parking Brake

Begin the test from a dead standstill. You'll be moving the vehicle, so remove any wheel chocks you may have put in place. Get in the vehicle. Put the parking brake on. Put the vehicle in a low gear and try to move forward. The parking brake should hold you back. If it doesn't, it needs attention.

Test Six: Service Brake

Again, you'll be moving the vehicle. If you have wheel chocks in place, move them.

Build the air pressure to normal. Release the parking brake. Move the vehicle forward at about 5 mph. Apply the brakes firmly with the brake pedal. The vehicle should not pull to one side or the other. It should stop firmly, promptly, and evenly. If it doesn't, the brakes need adjustment.

If you have a trailer hand valve, repeat the procedure and apply the trailer hand valve to test the trailer service brakes.

SEVEN-STEP PRE-TRIP INSPECTION

As you recall, there are seven main steps in this inspection routine. They are:

- approach the vehicle
- raise the hood or tilt the cab and check the engine compartment
- start the engine and inspect inside the cab
- check the lights
- walk all around the vehicle, inspecting as you go
- check the signal lights
- check the brakes

Step One: Vehicle Overview

As you walk towards the vehicle, notice its general condition. Look for damage. Note if the vehicle is leaning to one side. This could mean a flat tire. Cargo may be overloaded or may have shifted. Or, it could be a suspension problem.

Look under the vehicle for fresh oil, coolant, grease, or fuel leaks. Check the area around the vehicle for people, other vehicles, objects, low hanging wires, or limbs. These could become hazards once the vehicle begins to move.

Look over the most recent vehicle inspection report. Drivers typically have to make a vehicle inspection report in writing each day. The vehicle owner then should see that any items in the report that affect safety are repaired. If the mechanic repaired the defects, or determined no repairs were needed, there will be a certification for that on the form.

You should look at the last report to find out what was the matter, if anything. Inspect the vehicle to find out whether problems were fixed, or whether repairs were not needed.

Step Two: Engine Compartment Check

Check that the parking brakes are on and/or wheels chocked. You may have to raise the hood or open the engine compartment door. If you have a tilt cab, secure loose items in the cab before you tilt it. Then they won't fall and break something.

At this site, check the engine oil level. The oil should be above the "Low" or "Add" mark on the dipstick. See that the level of coolant is above the "Low" level line on the reservoir. Check the condition of coolant-carrying hoses.

Check the radiator shutters and winterfront, if your vehicle has one. In cold weather, remove ice from the radiator shutters. Make sure the winterfront is not closed too tightly. If the shutters freeze shut or the winterfront is closed too much, the engine may overheat and stop. Inspect the fan. Make sure the blades are sound and not likely to catch on hanging wires or hoses.

If your vehicle has power steering, check the fluid level and the condition of the hoses. Check the dipstick on the oil tank. The fluid level should be above the "Low" or "Add" mark.

Here's where you check the windshield washer fluid level.

If your battery is located in the engine compartment, perform the battery check now.

If you have an automatic transmission, check the fluid level. You may have to do this with the engine running. Your owner's manual will tell you if that is the case.

Check drive belts for tightness and excessive wear. Press on the center of the belt. The owner's manual will tell you how much slack there should be. Also, if you can easily slide a belt over a pulley, it is definitely too loose or too worn. Look for leaks in the engine compartment. These could be fuel, coolant, oil, power steering fluid, hydraulic fluid, or battery fluid.

Look for cracked or worn insulation on electrical wiring.

Check the compressor for the air brakes. Check the oil supply. If it's belt-driven, check the belt. It should be in good condition. Check belt tightness.

Lower and secure the hood, cab, or engine compartment door.

Next, check any handholds, steps, or deck plates. Remove all water, ice and snow, or grease from handholds, steps, and deck plates that you must use to enter the cab or to move about the vehicle. This will reduce the danger of slipping.

Figure 10-14. Check the air compressor when you're at the engine compartment.

Step Three: Inside the Cab

Get in the cab. Inspect inside the cab. Start the engine. Make sure the parking brake is on. Shift into neutral, or "Park" if your transmission is automatic. Start the engine and listen for unusual noises.

Check the gauge readings. The oil pressure should come up to normal within seconds after the engine is started. The ammeter and/or voltmeter should give normal readings. Coolant temperature should rise gradually until it reaches normal operating range. The engine oil temperature should also rise slowly to normal operating range.

Oil, coolant, and charging circuit warning lights will come on at first. That tells you the lights are working. They should go out right away unless there's a problem.

Make sure your controls work. Check all of the following for looseness, sticking, damage, or improper setting:

- steering wheel
- accelerator ("gas pedal")
- foot brake
- trailer brake (if your vehicle has one)
- parking brake
- retarder controls (if your vehicle has them)
- transmission controls
- interaxle differential lock (if your vehicle has one)
- horn(s)
- windshield wiper and washers
- headlights
- dimmer switch
- turn signal
- four-way flashers
- clearance, identification, and marker light switch(es).

If your vehicle has a clutch, test it now. Depress the clutch until you feel a slight resistance. One to two inches of travel before you feel resistance is normal. More or less than that signals a problem.

Check your mirrors and windshield for the defects described earlier.

Check that you have the required emergency equipment and that it is in good operating condition.

Check for optional items, such as a tire changing kit, and items required by state and local laws, such as mud flaps.

Step Four: Check Lights

Next, check to see that the lights are working. Make sure the parking brake is set, turn off the engine, and take the key with you. Turn on the headlights (on low beams) and the four-way flashers, and get out. Go to the front of the vehicle. Check that the low beams are on and both of the four-way flashers are working. Push the dimmer switch and check that the high beams work. Turn off the headlights and four-way hazard warning flashers. Turn on the parking, clearance, side-marker, and identification lights. Turn on the right-turn signal, and start the "walk-around" part of the inspection.

Step Five: Walk-around Inspection

Walk all around the vehicle, inspecting as you go. Start at the cab on the driver's side. Cover the front of the vehicle. Work down the passenger side to the rear. Cover the rear of the vehicle. Work up the driver's side back to the starting position. Do it this way every time.

Clean all the lights, reflectors, and glass as you go along.

Left Front Side

The driver's door glass should be clean. Door latches or locks should work properly.

Perform a tire, wheel, and rim check at the left front wheel. Perform a suspension system and braking system check. Check the steering parts. Check the air hoses for leaks and breaks. Check the brake assembly. Look for parts that need replacement or repair: a cracked drum or a loose or worn brake lining. Check the slack adjuster to see if it needs adjustment. Drain air tanks if necessary.

Front

Check the condition of the front axle. Perform a check of the steering system parts. You should actually take hold of steering system parts and shake them to say for sure that they are not loose.

Check the windshield. Pull on the windshield wiper arms to check for proper spring tension.

Check the wiper blades for the defects described earlier.

Check the lights and reflectors (parking, clearance and identification, and turn signal lights) at this site. Make sure you have all the required ones as described earlier. They should be clean and working.

Right Front Side

The right front has parts similar to the left front. Perform the same checks. The passenger door glass should be clean. Door latches or locks should work properly. Check the tire, wheel, and rim at the right front wheel. Perform a suspension system and braking system check. Check the steering parts. Check the air hoses for leaks and breaks. Check the brake assembly. Look for parts that need replacement or repair: a cracked drum or a loose or worn brake lining. Check the slack adjuster. Have it adjusted if necessary. Drain air tanks as needed.

For COE trucks, check the primary and safety cab locks here.

Right Side

The fuel tank is located here. Check to see that it is mounted securely, not damaged or leaking. The fuel crossover line must be secure, and not hanging so low that it would be exposed to road hazards. The filler caps must be on firmly. Check the fuel supply. Perform these checks for each fuel tank your vehicle has.

Check all parts you can see at this site. See that the rear of the engine is not leaking. Check for leaks from the transmission. Check the exhaust system parts for defects as described earlier.

Inspect the frame and cross members for bends and cracks.

Electrical wiring should be secured against snagging, rubbing, and wearing.

If your vehicle has a spare tire carrier or rack, check it for damage. It should be securely mounted in the rack. Make sure you have the correct size spare tire and wheel. The spare tire must be in good condition and properly inflated.

Cargo Securement

Check the cargo securement at the right front of the vehicle. It must be properly blocked, braced, tied, chained, and so forth. If you need a header board, make sure it is strong enough and secure. If you have side boards, check them. The stakes must be strong enough for the load, free of damage, and properly set in place.

Make sure you haven't created handling problems for yourself by overloading the front axles.

Any canvas or tarp must be properly secured to prevent tearing and billowing.

If you are hauling an oversized load, have the necessary signs safely and properly mounted. Make sure you have the permits you need to haul this load.

Check that the curbside cargo compartment doors are securely closed, latched, and locked. See that the required security seals are in place.

Right Rear

At this location, check the wheels, rim, tires, brake system, and suspension parts as you did at the right front. Check that all parts are sound, properly mounted and secure, and not leaking. Check the axle. Powered axles should not leak.

Check the lights and reflectors required at this location. They should be clean and working.

Rear

Check the lights and reflectors required at this location. They should be clean and working.

Make sure you have a license plate. It should be clean and securely mounted.

If mud flaps are required, check them now. They should be free of damage and fastened according to whatever regulations apply. If there are no legal guidelines, make sure they are at least well-fastened, not dragging on the ground or rubbing the tires.

Cargo Securement

Check the cargo securement at the right rear of the vehicle. It must be properly blocked, braced, tied, chained, and so forth. Check that the tailboard is

Step 5: Walk-around inspection

A. Left front side: wheel and tire, suspension, brakes, axle, steering, side marker lamp and reflector, door glass, latches and locks, mirrors

B. Front of cab: axle, steering system, windshield, lights and reflectors

C. Right front side: door glass, latches and locks, wheels and tires, suspension, brakes, axle, steering, condition of bed or body, side marker lamp and reflector

D. Right side: fuel tank, exhaust system, frame and cross members, wiring, spare tire, lights and reflectors, mirrors

E. Cargo securement, curbside doors

F. Right rear: wheels and tires, suspension, brakes, axle, lights and reflectors

G. Rear: lights and reflectors, license plate, mudflaps, condition of bed or body, rear doors

H. Cargo securement

I. Left rear and left front: wheels and tires, suspension, brakes, steering, axle, lights and reflectors, battery, condition of bed or body

Figure 10-15. Check the air brake assembly when you inspect the wheel area.

strong enough and secure. If you have end gates, check them. The stakes must be strong enough, free of damage, and properly set in the stake pockets.

Any canvas or tarp must be properly secured to prevent tearing and billowing. Make sure the tarp doesn't cover up your rear lights.

Check to make sure that you haven't distributed the load so as to overload the rear axles.

If you are hauling an oversized load, have the necessary signs safely and properly mounted. Have any lights or flags required for projecting loads. Make sure you have the permits you need to haul this load.

Check that the rear doors are securely closed, latched, and locked.

Left Rear and Front Side

At this location, check the wheels, rim, tires, brake system, and suspension parts just as you did for the right rear and front side. Check that all parts are sound, properly mounted and secure, and not leaking. Check the axle. Powered axles should not leak.

Check the lights and reflectors required at this location. They should be clean and working.

Your vehicle's battery may be mounted here, rather than in the engine compartment. If so, perform the battery check now.

Step Six: Check Signal Lights

Get in the cab and turn off all the lights. Then, turn on the stop lights. Or, have a helper step on the brake pedal while you watch to see if the light goes on.

Now turn on the left-turn signal lights. Then get out and check the left side lights, rear and front.

Step Seven: Check Brakes

Now you'll perform some tests with the engine running and the parking brakes off. Make sure you're on a level surface. Chock the wheels.

Get back in the vehicle. Turn off any lights you don't need for driving. Check to see that you have all the required papers, trip manifests, permits, and so forth. Secure all loose articles in the cab. If

Step 1: Vehicle overview for general condition

Step 2: Engine compartment checks
Fluid levels and leaks
Hoses and belts
Battery
Compressor
Windshield washer
Wiring

Step 3: Inside the cab checks
Parking brake on
Gauge readings
Warning lights
Controls
Emergency equipment
Optional equipment

Step 4: Check lights
Headlights (low and high beams)
Four-way flashers
Parking lights
Clearance lights
Side marker lights
Identification lights
Right-turn signal

Step 5: Walk-around inspection
A. Left front side: wheel and tire, suspension, brakes, axle, steering, side marker lamp and reflector, door glass, latches and locks, mirrors
B. Front of cab: axle, steering system, windshield, lights and reflectors
C. Right front side: door glass, latches and locks, wheels and tires, suspension, brakes, axle, steering, condition of bed or body, side marker lamp and reflector
D. Right side: fuel tank, exhaust system, frame and cross members, wiring, spare tire, lights and reflectors, mirrors
E. Cargo securement, curbside doors
F. Right rear: wheels and tires, suspension, brakes, axle, lights and reflectors
G. Rear: lights and reflectors, license plate, mudflaps, condition of bed or body, rear doors
H. Cargo securement
I. Left rear and left front: wheels and tires, suspension, brakes, steering, axle, lights and reflectors, battery, condition of bed or body

Step 6: Check signal lights

Step 7: Brake check

Figure 10-16. Vehicle Inspection Aid for straight vehicles with air brakes.

they are free to roll around, they could hinder your operation of the controls, or hit you in a crash.

Start the engine. Perform air brake tests, numbers one through four. Then stop the vehicle. Remove the chocks. Perform brake tests five and six.

DRIVING WITH AIR BRAKES

Your air brakes will be there to serve you if you treat them right. You've seen how to maintain and inspect them. It's important that you also know the right way to use them.

Normal Stops

For normal stops, simply push the brake pedal down. Control the pressure so the vehicle comes to a smooth, safe stop. If you have a manual transmission, don't push the clutch in until the engine rpm is close to idle. Once you have stopped you can select a starting gear.

Don't "ride" the brakes. That just draws down your air pressure and heats up your brakes. The only time you would ever want to do this is if your brakes got very wet. Then ride the brakes only for as long as it takes to dry the brakes.

Emergency Stops

Good speed and space management will keep the need for "panic" stops to a minimum. If you do have to brake suddenly, try to maintain steering control. Keep the vehicle in a straight line. You can do this by using "controlled" or "stab" braking. These braking techniques were described in Chapter 7. Remember them?

In controlled braking, you apply the brakes as hard as you can without locking the wheels. Don't turn the steering wheel while you do this. If you need to make a larger steering adjustment or if the wheels lock, release the brakes. Reapply the brakes as soon as you have traction again.

In stab braking, you apply your brakes all the way. Release the brakes when the wheels lock up. As soon as the wheels start rolling, apply the brakes fully again. It can take up to one second for the wheels to start rolling after you release the brakes. If you reapply the brakes before the wheels start rolling, the vehicle won't straighten out.

Air Brakes and Stopping Distance

You need increased stopping distance with air brakes. It takes time for air to flow to the brakes after you have stepped on the pedal. The braking response is not as immediate as it is with hydraulic brakes.

Remember the stopping distance formula? It's

$$\begin{aligned} &\text{perception distance} \\ +\ &\text{reaction distance} \\ +\ &\text{braking distance} \\ \hline =\ &\text{total stopping distance} \end{aligned}$$

You must add the distance taken up by "brake lag" to this formula. At 55 mph on a dry surface, you can travel about 32 feet before the brakes respond to your stepping on the pedal. That would make your total stopping distance over 300 feet—longer than a football field.

Braking on a Downgrade

Brake fade and brake loss are real dangers on a downgrade. It's easy to lose your brakes on a hill, and that's when you really need them, so it's vital that you use them correctly. Start down the hill in a low gear that will give you a lot of engine braking. That way you can use snub braking. Apply the brakes just hard enough to feel the vehicle slow. When the speed has been reduced to about five mph below your safe speed, release the brakes. If your speed rises above the safe level, repeat the procedure.

Above all, don't fan the brakes. Using them hard builds up tremendous heat. Releasing them briefly does not give them enough time to cool off. When you apply them again, you just increase the heat. Brakes won't take too much of this treatment before they expand beyond usefulness, or even burn up.

So again, use a low gear and light steady pressure.

If your brakes are out of adjustment, you'll really notice it on a downgrade. Most long grades offer a "pull-out" at the top of the hill. This is a safe area to the side of the road. Stop, check, and have your brakes adjusted if necessary before heading down. Don't just step on the brakes and decide they're OK. Get out of the vehicle and check them thoroughly.

Low Air Pressure

Heed your low air pressure warning. It means you still have a little air pressure left, and can probably still make a safe stop. Stop and park the vehicle the first chance you get to do so safely. Don't wait until the emergency brakes come on. It's harder to control the vehicle when the spring brakes come on.

As you can see, the idea behind air brakes is not a complicated one. Air brakes are fairly easy to use, maintain, and inspect. The system as a whole is not that complex. It is large, however, and has many parts. So there are many chances for problems to develop. A single problem could cause the whole system to fail. Therefore, if you plan to drive a vehicle with air brakes, you must understand each and every part. You must commit yourself to proper maintenance and thorough inspection. If you do, your air brakes should work dependably and reliably.

PASS POST-TRIP

Instructions: For each true/false test item, read the statement. Decide whether the statement is true or false. If it is true, circle the letter A. If it is false, circle the letter B. For each multiple-choice test item, choose the answer choice—A, B, C, or D—that correctly completes the statement or answers the question. There is only one correct answer. Use the answer sheet provided on page 241.

1. The compressed air in the brake chamber transmits the force exerted by the driver's foot on the brake pedal to the foundation brakes.
   A. True
   B. False

2. When you use brakes hard, the first thing that happens is _____.
   A. the linings become worn
   B. they get out of adjustment
   C. they get hot
   D. they crack

3. If you have an alcohol evaporator, you do not have to drain the air tanks.
   A. True
   B. False

4. If your air compressor fails, _____.
   A. you will have no brakes
   B. the brakes will immediately lock up
   C. gradually decreasing air pressure will continue to be available from the air tanks for a while
   D. air pressure will not be affected at all

5. Front wheel braking is good to have on _____.
   A. dry roads
   B. wet roads
   C. icy roads
   D. all of the above

6. Pushing the brake pedal down when the spring brakes are on will _____.
   A. set the parking brakes
   B. release the parking brakes
   C. damage the brakes
   D. adjust the slack

7. The emergency brake system is a completely separate system and is completely under the driver's control.
   A. True
   B. False

8. The low air pressure warning device should come on before air pressure drops below _____.
   A. 20 psi
   B. 45 psi
   C. 60 psi
   D. 125 psi

9. At 55 mph on a dry surface, the average driver will need more than _____ feet to stop a CMV with air brakes.
   A. 100
   B. 200
   C. 300
   D. 400

10. The best braking technique to use on a downgrade is _____.
    A. snub braking
    B. controlled braking
    C. stab braking
    D. hard braking

CHAPTER 10 ANSWER SHEET

Test Item	Answer Choices				Self - Scoring Correct Incorrect	
1.	A	B	C	D	☐	☐
2.	A	B	C	D	☐	☐
3.	A	B	C	D	☐	☐
4.	A	B	C	D	☐	☐
5.	A	B	C	D	☐	☐
6.	A	B	C	D	☐	☐
7.	A	B	C	D	☐	☐
8.	A	B	C	D	☐	☐
9.	A	B	C	D	☐	☐
10.	A	B	C	D	☐	☐

Cut Here

Chapter 11

Vehicle Combinations

In this chapter, you will learn about:

- coupling and uncoupling a single semitrailer
- coupling and uncoupling doubles
- inspecting vehicle combinations
- pulling trailers safely

To complete this chapter you will need:

- a dictionary
- a pencil or pen
- blank paper, a notebook, or an electronic notepad
- colored pencils, pens, markers, or highlighters
- a CDL preparation manual from your state Department of Motor Vehicles, if one is offered
- the Federal Motor Carrier Safety Regulations pocketbook (or access to U.S. Department of Transportation regulations, Parts 383, 393, and 396 of Subchapter B, Chapter 3, Title 49, Code of Federal Regulations)
- the owner's manual for your vehicle, if available

PASS PRE-TRIP

Instructions: Read the statements. Decide whether each statement is true or false. If it is true, circle the letter A. If it is false, circle the letter B.

1. In a triple combination, the heaviest trailer should be in the middle.
   A. True
   B. False

2. The pre-trip inspection of a double or triple combination should include draining the converter dolly air reservoir.
   A. True
   B. False

3. A fully loaded tractor-trailer is 10 times more likely to roll over in a crash than an empty one.
   A. True
   B. False

If you plan to pull one or more trailers with your vehicle, you will have to take your CDL test in that vehicle. You'll be tested on your knowledge of coupling and uncoupling. You'll have to show you can inspect the combination. This is true whether you're pulling a single trailer, semitrailer, doubles, or triples.

You'll have to pass the Knowledge Test all CDL applicants must take. You must show you have additional knowledge on combination vehicles. Then, once you pass the Skills Test in a "representative vehicle," you'll have a CDL with an "A" code. You'll be licensed to drive Group A ("combination") vehicles.

If you want to pull doubles and triples, you're not done yet. You'll need the doubles/triples endorsement. You'll not only have to take the Skills Test while pulling a trailer. You'll also have to answer additional knowledge questions about pulling doubles and triples.

In this chapter, we'll cover the material drivers need to get a CDL for combination vehicles. If you plan to haul only a single trailer, that's the only part of this chapter you will need. If you want the doubles/triples endorsement, you should complete the whole chapter.

Remember, FMCSR Part 383 states that drivers of tractor-semitrailer combinations must know the correct way to couple and uncouple a tractor and semitrailer. They must know why and how to inspect the vehicle combination.

This chapter begins with coupling and uncoupling a single semitrailer. Toward the end of this you'll find the inspection routine for a vehicle combination.

COUPLING A SINGLE SEMITRAILER

Coupling and uncoupling aren't hard procedures, but for safety's sake, they must be done right.

What's involved in coupling? To put it very simply, you're going to back the tractor up to the trailer so the coupling assemblies connect. Then you must supply electricity to the trailer so the lights will work. If you have air brakes, you must supply the trailer with air. Also, you must make sure you can control the trailer from the tractor.

Slow and steady wins the race here. Follow the procedures step by step every time. Use the rear-view mirrors. Know your equipment. You have to know the width of the tractor as compared to the width of the trailer. Then remember that the center of the fifth wheel is always in the center of the tractor frame and the kingpin is always in the center of the front of the trailer.

Inspect Area

Before you begin any coupling procedure, walk the area around the trailer and tractor. Look for anything in your path that could damage the tractor or trailer. Boards lying on the ground can fly up when popped from the ground by a tire. Nails, glass, or other objects can damage a tire. Make sure the way is clear before you begin the first stages of alignment.

Inspect Vehicles

Check the coupling devices on the tractor and the trailer. Look for damaged or missing parts. Inspect the tractor frame and the fifth wheel mounting. There should be no cracked or bent parts. The mounting should be secure. Make sure the trailer kingpin isn't bent or broken.

Lubricate the fifth wheel. Lubrication reduces friction between the fifth wheel and the trailer. That gives you better steering control.

Pre-position the fifth wheel. It should be tilted down (toward the rear of the tractor). The locking jaws should be open.

Stabilize Vehicles

Work on the most level ground you can find if you have a choice about it. Uneven ground will make your task just that much harder. Apply the spring brakes. As you move the tractor under the trailer, it can move the trailer. Having the brakes on will keep the trailer from rolling backward.

Some older trailers don't have spring brakes. If yours doesn't, put chocks at the rear of your trailer tires. Perhaps you're not sure if you have spring brakes or not. You can tell just by looking at the brakes. Find the service brake chamber. Look for the spring brake chamber "piggybacking" on the service brake chamber. Or, look at the number of air lines going into the brake chamber. Spring brakes will have two air lines, service brakes have only one. Either way, if you don't have spring brakes, use chocks to keep your vehicle from moving.

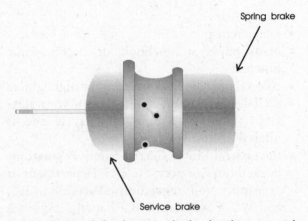

Figure 11-1. Look for the spring brake chamber mounted on the service brake chamber.

Align Tractor

A proper coupling requires you to center the kingpin in the fifth wheel within a small margin of error. Before you back, you must align the tractor and trailer precisely. If they don't, you'll have to move the tractor or trailer before you can complete the coupling.

Place the tractor so the trailer kingpin is as near to the center of the fifth wheel V-slot as possible. Locate the center of the trailer by using its sides as a gauge in your rear-view mirrors. As you straighten the tractor in front of the trailer, the corners of the trailer will appear evenly in the mirrors. If there is an unequal amount of the trailer in one mirror, you are too far to the other side.

Don't try to back under the trailer at an angle. You could damage the landing gear or push the trailer sideways.

Back Slowly

If you back slowly you can steer the tractor in the desired direction to align the fifth wheel with the kingpin. Keep backing until the fifth wheel just touches the trailer. Don't hit the trailer!

Align Trailer

Put on the parking brake and put the transmission in neutral. Go out and compare the level of the fifth wheel with the height of the kingpin. If the trailer is too far below the fifth-wheel level, the tractor may strike and damage the nose of the trailer. If the trailer is higher than the fifth-wheel level, the trailer will come over the fifth wheel when you try to back under it. You could damage the rear of the tractor that way. The trailer should be low enough that it is raised slightly by the tractor when the tractor backs under it.

Incorrect alignment - trailer too low
Incorrect alignment - trailer too high
Correct alignment - trailer level with fifth wheel

Figure 11-2. Aim for a good vertical alignment.

If you are either too high or two low, you will have to use the landing gear to raise or lower the trailer to the fifth-wheel level. It isn't all that easy to roll up a loaded trailer.

The landing gear crank is hinged and swings under the trailer to a latch. The latch secures it to the frame while the trailer is in motion. If the crank handle were allowed to swing freely while the trailer is moving, it could damage a nearby vehicle or passing pedestrian. Always secure the crank handle when you're done using it.

Connect Air Lines

The first step of the actual coupling of the tractor and trailer is to connect the air supply lines. First, check the rubber seals on both connections. If one is worn or cracked, have it replaced immediately.

Otherwise, you might end up with a service line air leak you wouldn't notice until you put on the brakes.

There are two air supply lines: the service brake line and the emergency brake line. These are almost always colored red for emergency and blue for service. The connections at the front of the trailer will usually be painted the color of the air hose that should be connected to them. Secure each air supply line to the color-matched trailer connection.

If you cross the air lines on a new trailer with spring brakes, you will not be able to release the trailer brakes. If you cross the air lines on an old trailer without spring brakes, you could drive off and not have any braking power on the trailer.

Lock Trailer Brakes

After you return to the tractor, charge the trailer air supply by pushing in the red trailer air supply knob. When pressure is normal, apply the trailer parking brakes by pulling out the trailer air supply knob. This puts on the trailer brakes to keep it from moving. Release the tractor brakes by pushing in the yellow tractor parking knob.

Back Under Trailer

Put the transmission in the lowest reverse gear and back—slowly. Keep backing until the tractor comes into contact with the trailer. You will feel a definite bump. Don't bump the kingpin too hard. Continue backing slowly until progress is stopped by the kingpin locking into the fifth wheel.

Check Connection

Raise the landing gear slightly. Check the connection by pulling forward very slowly. If the tractor will not move, the connection is complete. If it does move, stop immediately and back again.

Put the transmission in neutral. Put the parking brakes on. Shut off the engine. Take the key with you so someone else can't move the truck while you are under it.

Get out of the tractor and check to see that the fifth wheel locking jaw is closed around the trailer kingpin. To do this you must look under the front of the trailer at the fifth wheel. Use a flashlight if it's too dark to see clearly. If the jaw is closed you will see it locked securely around the back of the kingpin. There should be no space between the upper and lower fifth wheel. If there is space, the

CHAPTER 11 ANSWER SHEET

Test Item	Answer Choices				Self - Scoring Correct Incorrect	
1.	A	B	C	D	☐	☐
2.	A	B	C	D	☐	☐
3.	A	B	C	D	☐	☐
4.	A	B	C	D	☐	☐
5.	A	B	C	D	☐	☐
6.	A	B	C	D	☐	☐
7.	A	B	C	D	☐	☐
8.	A	B	C	D	☐	☐
9.	A	B	C	D	☐	☐
10.	A	B	C	D	☐	☐

Cut Here

Chapter 12

Tank Vehicle Endorsement

In this chapter, you will learn about:

- the causes of cargo surge
- the effects of cargo surge on vehicle handling
- how to prevent cargo surge
- the braking response of tank vehicles
- baffled and compartmented tank vehicles
- the different types of tank vehicles
- liquid cargo density and cargo surge
- tank emergency systems
- the retest and marking requirements for DOT specification vehicles

To complete this chapter, you will need:

- a dictionary
- a pencil or pen
- blank paper, a notebook, or an electronic notepad
- colored pencils, pens, markers, or highlighters
- a CDL preparation manual from your state Department of Motor Vehicles, if one is offered
- the Federal Motor Carrier Safety Regulations pocketbook (or access to U.S. Department of Transportation regulations, Parts 383, 393, and 396 of Subchapter B, Chapter 3, Title 49, Code of Federal Regulations)
- the owner's manual for your vehicle, if available

PASS PRE-TRIP

Instructions: Read the statements. Decide whether each statement is true or false. If it is true, circle the letter A. If it is false, circle the letter B.

1. The difference between cargo tanks and portable tanks is that portable tanks may be loaded or unloaded while off the vehicle.
   A. True
   B. False

2. Liquid surge can push a stopped truck into an intersection.
   A. True
   B. False

3. Forward-and-backward surge is a big problem with smooth bore tanks.
   A. True
   B. False

A tank vehicle is a vehicle used to transport cargo in bulk. You'll see tanks carrying lime, and you'll see tanks carrying milk.

As far as commercial driver licensing is concerned, though, "tanks" mean vehicles carrying liquids and gases in bulk. This definition is given in FMCSR Part 383.

Part 383 further defines a tank vehicle as a permanently attached tank, or a portable tank able to hold 1,000 gallons or more. That is, you can have a straight truck-type tanker. You can have a semitrailer tanker. You can have a portable tank on a flatbed trailer. Permanent tanks are loaded and unloaded while still on the vehicle. Portable tanks may be loaded or unloaded while off the vehicle.

As you know by now, you need a Tank Vehicle Endorsement on your CDL to transport liquids in bulk. This chapter will help you get that endorsement.

EFFECTS OF LIQUID LOADS ON VEHICLE HANDLING

It takes special knowledge and skill to haul bulk liquids. This cargo presents two handling problems:

- high center of gravity
- liquid surge

High Center of Gravity

You recall that "high center of gravity" means that much of the load's weight is carried high up off the road. This makes the vehicle top-heavy and rollover more likely. Rollover is particularly likely with liquid tankers. Tests have shown that tankers can turn over at the speed limits posted for curves. Take highway curves and ramps well below the posted speeds.

Liquid Surge

Liquid surge results from movement of the liquid in partially filled tanks. This movement can have bad effects on handling. For example, when the vehicle is coming to a stop, the liquid will surge back and forth. When the wave hits the end of the tank, it tends to push the truck in the direction in which the wave is moving. If the truck is on a slippery surface like ice, the wave can shove a stopped truck out into an intersection.

Free-flowing lightweight liquids like water and milk tend to slosh more than thicker liquids. Thicker liquids like corn syrup tend to ride better than free-flowing liquids. The surging back and forth of any liquid in a tanker can cause serious driving problems.

The less you move the liquid around, the less effect liquid surge will have. So you must make all your movements—turning, shifting, stopping— gradually and slowly.

BRAKING RESPONSE OF TANKS

The brakes on most vehicles work best when the vehicle is fully loaded. The weight of the load gives you more traction. When the vehicle is empty, or bobtailing, it takes longer to stop. You could need as much as twice the stopping distance. Also, the brakes are more likely to lock up when you make an emergency stop in an empty vehicle.

The worst case would be a vehicle with a partial, liquid load. First, your vehicle does not have the traction it would have if it were full. Second, the surge factor is worse with a partial load than a full load.

The surge factor is at its worst in a tanker that is 80 percent full. This is because there is enough liquid to be quite heavy. At the same time, there is enough space for it to surge. If the tanker is 90 percent full, there is more liquid and more weight, but not enough space for it to move around. If the tanker is 40 percent full, there is plenty of space. However, there is not enough liquid and weight to throw the tanker too far out of control.

So, with a partial load, you lose the advantage of traction you would have with a full load. Then, the surging of the liquid can be so forceful, it can overcome the stopping power of your brakes. Your vehicle could travel quite a distance before it comes to a complete stop.

Avoid braking in turns. You must drive slowly and carefully at all times. That way, if you must use the brakes, you can do so gradually. This reduces the effect of liquid surge. You can keep the vehicle under control as you stop.

BAFFLES AND COMPARTMENTS

Some tankers are one long cylinder inside. These are called "smooth bore" or tanks. The smooth bore tanker is designed to carry one particular

Figure 12-1. Liquid surge in a tank vehicle.

cargo at a time. Because it is a long hollow tube with no sharp corners, it is easy to load, unload, and clean.

A problem is there's nothing inside to slow down the flow of the liquid. Therefore, forward-and-backward surge is very strong. Smooth bore tanks are usually those that transport food products (milk, for example). That means you must be aware of the surge factor. You must be very careful when driving smooth bore tanks, especially when starting and stopping.

Some liquids are heavier than others. That is, an amount of one liquid will weigh more than the same amount of another. This is due to density. You'll find liquid densities discussed in greater detail later in this chapter. For now, know that

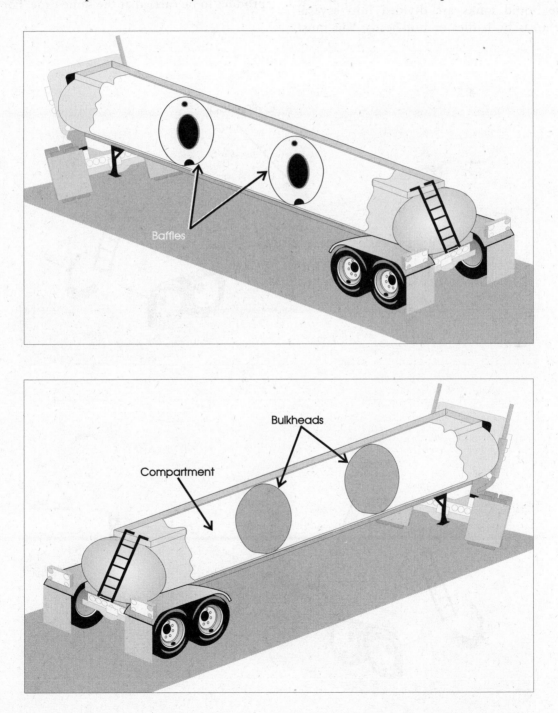

Figure 12-2. The baffles in the trailer in the top picture control the movement of the liquid cargo. The compartments in the trailer in the bottom picture completely separate different types of liquids.

when you have a heavy liquid in your tanker, the tanker should be either more or less than 80 percent full. As you just read, at 80 percent, 20 percent of the tank is left empty for movement within the tank. If you are more than 80 percent full, there is less empty space for movement. If you have less liquid, the surge factor is also lessened because there's simply less liquid to move.

Some liquid tanks are divided into several smaller areas by baffles or bulkheads. You must pay attention to weight distribution when loading and unloading the smaller areas. Don't put too much weight on the front or rear of the vehicle.

Bulkheads

Sometimes tankers are divided into compartments by bulkheads. These allow more than one type of product to be carried at the same time. For exam-

Figure 12-3. Cylindrical and elliptical are the two basic shapes you will see most often in liquid tankers.

ple, a compartmented tanker would allow you to haul both diesel fuel and gasoline in one trip.

Some tankers have double-walled bulkheads. The law requires that diesel fuel and gasoline be divided by a double bulkhead.

Bulkheads also help to control the surge factor somewhat.

Baffles

Baffled liquid tanks also have bulkheads in them. Baffles are dividers that simply break up the tank area into smaller areas. There is a hole at the top of the baffle that allows air movement through the trailer. The hole on the bottom allows the liquid to flow through for unloading. The middle hole is big enough that a person can crawl inside for cleaning. A tanker may have several baffles.

The baffles help to control the forward-and-backward liquid surge. However, side-to-side surge can still occur. This can cause a rollover. Be extremely cautious (slow and careful) in taking curves or making sharp turns with a partially or fully loaded liquid tanker.

TYPES OF TANKS

In general, liquid tankers are either elliptical or cylindrical in shape. The elliptical is egg-shaped at the end and has the lower center of gravity. It's more stable on the road. The elliptical shape cuts down the surge factor.

The cylindrical is round. It's considered the strongest and most versatile. There are also variations of these shapes since the liquids they haul have differing needs for drainage and weight distribution. For example, the double conical is a kind of cylindrical tanker.

Within these two classes, there are many different types of tankers. This is because a tanker has design and construction features that suit it to haul a particular liquid. Some tanks are lined (cladded). This protects the tank from corrosive cargo. Some tanks are heated or cooled. Others are insulated. That helps to keep the cargo within a temperature range without actually heating or cooling it. Still other tanks hold the cargo under pressure.

LIQUID DENSITY AND CARGO SURGE

Some liquids weigh more than others. That is, an amount of one liquid can weigh more than the same amount of another. The heavier liquid has a higher density.

The higher the density of the liquid, the less the cargo surge will be. A high density liquid will be less likely to move in the first place. This is because of inertia.

 Remember inertia? If not, review Chapter 8.

It would take a lot of force to overcome the inertia of a high density liquid.

A small amount of a high density liquid can be very heavy. You can't load much of it into the tanker without being overweight. So you will have a lower center of gravity.

On the other hand, it is fairly easy to get a light liquid sloshing around.

The density of plain water is 8.3 pounds per gallon.

DRIVING TANKS

A tanker on the road is most stable when it is empty. A tanker that is 80 percent full is the least stable.

Except for a high center of gravity, a tanker is somewhat stable when it is full. However, you will rarely fill your tank completely full. Liquids expand as they warm up. You must leave room for the liquid to expand. This is called outage. Different liquids expand by different amounts. So, each liquid requires a different amount of outage. You must know the outage requirement when hauling liquids in bulk. You'll get this information from your dispatcher. You may also have an outage chart in the driver's manual your employer gives you.

Your employer may also want you to know about innage. This is the depth of liquid in the tank. The measurement is taken from the surface of the liquid to the bottom of the tank.

Also, a full tank of dense liquid (such as some acids) may exceed legal weight limits. For that reason you may often only partially fill tanks with heavy liquids. The amount of liquid to load into a tank depends on:

- the amount the liquid will expand in transit, and
- the weight of the liquid, and
- legal weight limits

How will you know the level of liquid in your tank? Your vehicle is required to have a liquid level sensing device. A probe inside the tank is wired to a controller. You'll usually find the controller on the curb side of the vehicle near other operator controls.

You have read several general cautions now about driving carefully when transporting liquids. Here are some specific guidelines.

Never Tailgate

This is always a dangerous practice, but it is much more dangerous with a liquid load. You've seen what can happen in a panic stop. Cargo surge adds to the stopping distance. A collision is almost always bound to result.

Shifting

When upshifting, always release the clutch after the surge has hit the rear of the tank.

Ramps

Always slow down and downshift before entering a freeway entrance or exit ramp. This risk of a rollover is very great on a ramp. A slow speed in the curve will reduce this risk.

Downgrades

Always downshift at the top of a long hill or mountain. Downshift before you start down the grade. Use the snub braking technique to control your speed.

You know by now that you should not fan the brakes on a downgrade. This is especially important with liquid loads. Pumping or fanning the brakes causes the vehicle to rock. This increases the liquid surge.

Evasive Action

You know you should never make sharp or sudden changes in direction at high speed. This is even more important when hauling liquids because of the surge factor and high center of gravity.

If you drop off the edge of the pavement, never return abruptly to the roadway. Get the vehicle under control and reduce your speed. If possible, avoid using the brakes until your speed has dropped to about 20 mph. Then brake very gently to avoid skidding on a loose surface. If the shoulder is clear, stay on it until your vehicle has come to a stop. Then you can safely bring the vehicle back onto the roadway.

If you are doing a good job of speed and space management, you should not have to take evasive action in the first place.

Adverse Conditions

On slippery roads, nearly all vehicles lose traction. This is even worse when you have a liquid load. The liquid surge itself is enough to cause your vehicle to lose traction. You may have to stop driving and wait out the weather, whereas you might have gone on with a different type of load.

Figure 12-4. Outage.

Uncoupling

Let the load settle before you uncouple your trailer. If you don't, liquid surge could cause the landing gear to collapse.

EMERGENCY SYSTEMS

Cargo tanks are designed to reduce the chance of accidental leaks. If the tank becomes damaged, design features work to keep the cargo from leaking out. For example, fittings and attachments that don't themselves hold any cargo are attached to the tank in a special way. They're designed so that if they break off, cargo won't leak out. The rear bumper protects the tank and piping from rear-end collisions. Filling, manhole, and inspection openings are protected from being damaged in a vehicle rollover. Safety devices prevent the manhole and fill covers from opening fully when the tank is pressurized.

Most cargo tanks are also equipped with emergency systems that help keep the cargo from leaking out if there's a major accident. Some systems operate automatically. Others must be operated by the driver.

Piping that isn't protected from accidental damage must have a stop-valve and a shear section.

Stop Valves

A stop valve is a valve that stops the flow of lading (the cargo). You'll find stop valves on the tank loading and unloading outlets. These are held in the closed position by their own energy supply. When they're closed, the cargo is kept inside the tank.

The valves can be internal or external. Internal valves are self-closing. Their power supply is inside the tank. External valves self-close in emergencies, such as a fire or broken hose. (During normal operations, they can be operated manually.) The power for external self-closing stop valves is located outside the tank.

Each valve has a remote control that is located more than 10 feet from the valve. A cable links the control to the valve. This is a part of the emergency system the driver can operate manually. You operate the cable by a lever or other control. You'll usually find this lever in an operator's cabinet on the curb side of the vehicle. You may also find an emergency release trip at the road side toward the front of the vehicle.

Cargo tanks that carry flammable, pyrophoric, oxidizing, or poisonous liquids must have manual or mechanical controls for the stop valves. The stop valves must also have controls that will respond to heat, in case of fire. Thermal valves will close before the temperature gets above 250 degrees Fahrenheit.

Shear Sections

A shear section is a "sacrificial" device. That means it will fail under pressure.

You have already seen one example of a "sacrificial" device. A fuse is such a device. It fails under a load, and thereby protects another device.

A shear section will break away under pressure. In a rollover, the weight of the vehicle and cargo will press on a section of the vehicle not meant to bear so much weight. The shear section will break off under this pressure. This will preserve the important part of a pipe and its attachment to the tank, preventing a leak. In other words, the shear section will break before the pipe will.

You'll find the shear section outside the stop valve but inside the accident damage protection device.

Pressure Relief Systems

Cargo tanks also have pressure relief systems. They keep the tank from bursting or collapsing from too much or too little pressure. This helps keep the lading from leaking or escaping if the vehicle rolls over or is hit.

There's a primary and a secondary pressure relief system. The primary system has at least one reclosing valve. The secondary system has another valve that will back-up or assist the primary valve. These systems will be marked with the pressure at which they're set to discharge and with the flow rate. (You'll also see the manufacturer's name and the model number.)

Which of these devices your vehicle will have and where they are located depends on the tank's specification. Check the owner's manual for your own vehicle if you're not certain of what you have or where it is.

Rupture disc with rain shield

Overturn guard

Pressure gauge

Shut-off valve

Safety relief valve

Figure 12-5. Tank vehicle safety features.

Portable Tank Emergency Systems

Portable tanks don't have all the emergency systems that cargo tanks do. Here are the features they do have.

The outlets of portable tanks that carry liquefied compressed gas have excess-flow valves. That is, the outlet valves are rated for flow by the manufacturer. Once the flow rate exceeds this limit, the excess-flow valve will close automatically. Portable tanks will have safety relief valves that work automatically. Filling and discharge lines will have manually operated shut-off valves.

RETEST AND MARKING REQUIREMENT

Hazardous materials may only be hauled in "authorized" vehicles. The DOT has set specifications for the design and construction of vehicles that will haul hazmat. These specifications state what material can be used to build the tank. A corrosive, heavy, or radioactive material calls for a different design and different construction materials than a flammable one does. These specifications also provide guidelines for designing and building tanks that will carry hazardous materials under pressure or at a certain temperature.

A tank that meets DOT specifications is "authorized" to carry hazmat. Regulations in title 49 CFR Parts 178 and 180 state that DOT specification tanks must be retested. These parts set the retest schedule. The regulations further state that DOT specification tanks must be marked with retest information. As the driver, you won't usually be involved in testing tanks. You must know how to read the markings, though, so you can comply with the cargo tank regulations when you operate one.

Retest

Title 49 CFR Part 180 deals with the manufacture of cargo tanks. It also covers the operation, maintenance, repair, and requalification of all specification cargo tanks. It includes improved standards for inspecting and testing tanks.

PASS BILLBOARD

Cargo and portable tanks may be built to DOT specifications. If so, they receive a DOT specification code number. Coded tankers are those that have been approved to haul hazardous liquids. As you know by now, you can't haul a placarded load of hazardous liquids without a Hazardous Materials Endorsement.

Cargo tanks are numbered in the 300s and 400s. These are:

- MC 300
- MC 301
- MC 303
- MC 304
- MC 305
- MC 306
- MC 307
- MC 310
- MC 311
- MC 312
- MC 330
- MC 331
- MC 338
- MC 406
- MC 407
- MC 412

Portable tanks are numbered:

- 51
- 56
- 57
- 60
- IM 101
- IM 102

Cargo Tank Specifications

MC 300 and 301 Tanks. These tanks are no longer built, but some may still be in service. They are made of mild steel or mild steel, high-tensile steel, or stainless steel combined. They are used mainly for transporting flammable or poisonous liquids.

MC 303, 304, and 305 Tanks. Tanks meeting this specification are no longer built. However, some are still in service. MC 303 tanks are made of welded ferrous alloy (high-tensile steel). They can also be made of stainless steel. They are used mainly to haul flammable or poisonous liquids.

MC 304 tanks are made of mild steel, welded ferrous alloy or stainless steel and aluminum. They also carry flammable or poisonous liquids. These tanks were built to keep liquids under a pressure of 25 psi.

MC 305 tanks are built of aluminum alloys. They carry flammable or poisonous liquids at atmospheric pressure.

MC 306 Tanks. MC 306 tanks are made of aluminum or stainless steel. They carry flammable liquids and combustible fuels like No. 2 diesel. They also carry flammable solvents and non-regulated chemicals. They carry all these liquids at low or atmospheric pressure.

MC 307 Tanks. MC 307 tanks are "general chemical trailers." They are made of stainless steel and aluminum. They hold flammable liquids with vapor pressure of at least 25 psi. This is a moderate pressure, but it's higher than what MC 306 tanks can handle. They also carry poisonous and flammable liquids that are also corrosive or oxidizing.

MC 310 and 311 Tanks. These tanks are no longer built, but may still be in service. MC 310 and 311 tanks are made of steel and stainless steel. They haul mainly corrosive liquids.

MC 312 Tanks. MC 312 tanks are made of steel and stainless steel. They transport corrosive liquids, oxidizers, organic peroxides, and poisonous liquids, as well as some solids.

MC 312 tanks are used to carry hydrogen peroxide. Mild steel, copper, and brass won't stand up to hydrogen peroxide, so these tanks must be pure aluminum, or aluminum/magnesium alloys. Some are stainless steel.

This is a high pressure tanker.

MC 330 Tanks. These tanks are no longer built, but may still be in service. They are made of steel, and are mainly for hauling compressed gases.

MC 331 Tanks. These are seamless steel. They are used mainly to haul compressed gases.

MC 338 Tanks. MC 338 tanks are insulated, and built with a design pressure of 25.3 to 500 pounds per square inch gauge (psig). They are used mainly to haul cryogenic liquids.

 The pressure of liquids and gases is measured with a manometer. The measurement is stated as "pounds per square inch gauge" (psig).

TOFC Tanks. A TOFC tank is used for railroad flat car service (piggyback). "TOFC" stands for Tank On Flat Car. This is an MC 307 or 312 tank made of stainless steel with a design pressure of 35 psi.

Non-spec Tanks. "Non-spec" tanks are not built to any one of the US DOT MC specifications. They transport non-regulated loads.

MC 406, 407, and 412 Tanks. These tanks are all designed to haul cargo under pressure.

Portable Tanks

Specification 51. These are steel portable tanks. They can be seamless or welded, or both. They have a design pressure of between 100 psig and 500 psig, and carry mainly corrosive liquids.

Specification 56. These are metal portable tanks with a maximum GWR of 7,000 pounds.

Specification 57. These metal portable tanks can hold between 110 and 660 gallons.

Specification 60. These are welded steel cylindrical portable tanks. Sometimes they are lined.

IM 101 and 102. These are steel portable tanks. Sometimes they are lined. They are designed to carry liquids for intermodal transport.

Tanks are inspected and tested two ways. One is a visual inspection of both the outside and inside of the tank. The other tests the tank for leaks. Some tanks are pressure-tested. This can be a pneumatic or hydrostatic test. Yet another test measures the thickness of the metal that the tank is made of.

Figure 12-6 shows the inspection and retest schedule for most tanks.

MC 330 and MC 331 cargo tanks in sodium metal service don't have to be pressure-tested. Certain uninsulated lined or clad cargo tanks also don't have to be pressure-tested. These are tanks designed to haul cargo at a pressure of less than 15 psig. These must, however, get an external visual inspection and a lining inspection at least once each year.

Marking

The month and year of the last test or inspection, and what type of test or inspection was done, is marked on the tank itself. Or, it may be stamped on the certification plate. You may see these abbreviations:

- V for external visual inspection and test
- I for internal visual inspection
- P for pressure retest
- L for lining test
- K for leakage test
- T for thickness test

For example, the marking "10-95, P, V, L" would tell you that in October 1995, the cargo tank received and passed a pressure retest, external visual inspection and test, and a lining inspection.

Portable Tanks

Portable tanks are also inspected, retested, and marked. The schedule is given in Title 49 CFR Part 180. These tanks are at least pressure-tested and visually inspected. Some are also tested to see how well they hold up to vibration and being dropped.

Test or Inspection	Cargo Tank Configuration, and Service	Period	Test or Inspection	Cargo Tank Configuration, and Service	Period
Inspections			**Tests**		
External Visual	All cargo designed tanks to be loaded by vacuum with full opening rear head	six months	Leakage	MC 330 and MC 331 cargo tanks in chlorine service	two years
	All other cargo tanks	one year		All other cargo tanks except MC 338	one year
Internal Visual	All insulated cargo tanks except MC 330, MC 331, MC 338	one year	Pressure (hydrostatic or pneumatic)	All cargo tanks that are insulated with no manhole or insulated and lined, except MC 338	one year
	All cargo tanks transporting lading corrosive to the tank	one year		All cargo tanks designed to be loaded by vacuum with full opening rear head	two years
	All other cargo tanks except MC 338	five years		MC 330 and MC 331 cargo tanks in chlorine service	two years
				All other cargo tanks	five years
Lining/Cladding	All lined or clad cargo tanks transporting lading corrosive to the tank	one year	Thickness over entire tank	All unlined cargo tanks in corrosive service except MC 338	two years

Figure 12-6. Inspection and retest schedule.

Figure 12-7. A tanker with testing and retest markings.

Briefly, the testing and inspection schedule is as follows:

- Specification 51 once every five years
- Specification 56 and 57 once every two and one-half years. Specification 60 tanks are tested at the end of the first four-year period after the original test. Then they are tested at least once every two years up to a total of 12 years of service. After that, Specification 60 portable tanks are retested once a year.

The date of the most recent retest is marked on the tank, on or near the metal certification plate.

Hauling bulk liquids can be dangerous work. That's not because of the type of liquid. After all, what could be more harmless than milk or water? It's the handling problems the liquid cargo creates that make hauling bulk liquids such a challenge. Even the most simple maneuvers must be made with extreme caution when you have a liquid load.

Of course, some liquid loads are hazardous. Bulk liquid tanks are often filled with dangerous substances that can explode, burst into flame, even kill if not handled properly. To transport these, you not only need a Tank Vehicle Endorsement but also a Hazardous Materials Endorsement. That's the subject of the next chapter.

PASS POST-TRIP

Instructions: For each true/false test item, read the statement. Decide whether the statement is true or false. If it is true, circle the letter A. If it is false, circle the letter B. For each multiple-choice test item, choose the answer choice—A, B, C, or D—that correctly completes the statement or answers the question. There is only one correct answer. Use the answer sheet provided on page 279.

1. The difference between cargo tanks and portable tanks is that portable tanks may be loaded or unloaded while off the vehicle.
   A. True
   B. False

2. When taking a curve with a loaded tanker, the best way to prevent rolling is by traveling _____.
   A. at a speed above the posted limit
   B. at the posted speed limit
   C. at a speed below the posted limit
   D. with the brakes on

3. Liquid surge can push a stopped truck into an intersection.
   A. True
   B. False

4. The brakes on a bulk liquid tanker work best when the vehicle is _____.
   A. fully loaded
   B. partly loaded
   C. empty
   D. bobtailing

5. Forward-and-backward surge is a big problem with smooth bore tankers.
   A. True
   B. False

6. Baffles help control _____ in a tanker.
   A. the high center of gravity
   B. side-to-side surge
   C. forward-and-backward surge
   D. weight distribution

7. The density of liquid cargo affects _____.
   A. weight distribution
   B. cargo surge
   C. stopping distance
   D. all of the above

8. Outage is _____.
   A. the flow rate of an outlet
   B. allowing room for liquid cargo to expand
   C. a vacuum failure
   D. completely emptying a tank

9. When upshifting, always release the clutch _____ the surge has hit the rear of the tank.
   A. before
   B. during
   C. after
   D. unless

10. When you see a tanker marked "12-89, K," you know _____.
    A. it's authorized for chlorine service
    B. it had a leakage test
    C. it's carrying food products
    D. it's not a DOT specification tank

CHAPTER 12 ANSWER SHEET

Test Item	Answer Choices				Self - Scoring Correct Incorrect
1.	A	B	C	D	☐ ☐
2.	A	B	C	D	☐ ☐
3.	A	B	C	D	☐ ☐
4.	A	B	C	D	☐ ☐
5.	A	B	C	D	☐ ☐
6.	A	B	C	D	☐ ☐
7.	A	B	C	D	☐ ☐
8.	A	B	C	D	☐ ☐
9.	A	B	C	D	☐ ☐
10.	A	B	C	D	☐ ☐

Cut Here

Chapter 13

Hazardous Materials Endorsement

In this chapter you will learn about:

- hazardous materials regulations
- handling hazardous materials
- hazardous materials emergencies
- hazardous materials emergency response procedures

To complete this chapter you will need:

- a dictionary
- a pencil or pen
- blank paper, a notebook, or an electronic notepad
- colored pencils, pens, markers, or highlighters
- a CDL preparation manual from your state Department of Motor Vehicles, if one is offered
- the Federal Motor Carrier Safety Regulations pocketbook with Hazardous Materials Compendium (or access to U.S. Department of Transportation regulations, Parts 171, 172, 173, 177, 178, 180, 383, 392, and 397 of Title 49, Code of Federal Regulations)
- the owner's manual for your vehicle, if available

PASS PRE-TRIP

Instructions: Read the statements. Decide whether each statement is true or false. If it is true, circle the letter A. If it is false, circle the letter B.

1. A written plan is something you must apply for before making a trip with explosives.
   A. True
   B. False

2. Hazardous materials markings can be a label, tag, or sign.
   A. True
   B. False

3. In addition to a special license and training, you may need a special permit from the federal, state, or local government to haul hazardous materials.
   A. True
   B. False

Hazardous materials present a risk to health, safety, and property. This is especially true when they are being transported. If you plan to drive a vehicle with a placarded load of hazardous materials, you must have a Hazardous Materials Endorsement on your CDL.

There's only one exception to this. You don't need a hazardous materials endorsement to operate a vehicle with a hazmat load that is not placarded. When would a hazmat load not need placards? Title 49 CFR Section 177.823 lists three conditions:

- the vehicle is escorted by a representative of a state or local government
- the carrier has permission from the Department of Transportation, or
- the vehicle must be moved to protect life or property

At all other times, a vehicle with hazmat must have placards.

HAZARDOUS MATERIALS REGULATIONS

Hazardous materials handled improperly in transport can injure or kill people. Regulations exist to prevent this. The point of the regulations is to:

- contain the material
- communicate the risk
- assure safe drivers and equipment

Containment

To protect drivers and others, the rules tell shippers how to package safely. Similar rules tell drivers how to load, transport, and unload bulk tanks. These are containment rules.

Communication

Shippers must warn drivers and others about a material's hazardous qualities. They put warning labels on packages and describe materials in a way that clearly warns of the risk. There are rules for drivers too. They must warn others if there is an accident or a leak. Placards are another way to communicate the risk.

Safe Drivers and Equipment

As the driver, you must complete a Transportation Security Administration security screening. If you have a CDL and want to upgrade to one with a hazmat endorsement, you must complete this screening. In addition, you must complete this screening to renew a hazmat endorsement you may already have. Hazmat endorsements must be renewed every five years so that this screening may take place.

Your state will administer the screening. Your state must provide the TSA with a driver's fingerprints, criminal history, alien status, and information from CDLIS and international databases going back seven years.

The TSA requires that you provide proof of citizenship or immigration status. Proof should include one document from List A and one document from List B, both of which follow:

List A: ONE Document Is Acceptable from the Following Forms of Identification

- Unexpired U.S. Passport (book or card)—demonstrates U.S. Citizenship
- Unexpired Enhanced Tribal Card (ETC)—demonstrates U.S. Citizenship
- Unexpired Merchant Mariner Document (MMD)—designates U.S. Citizenship
- Unexpired Free and Secure Trade (FAST) Card—designates U.S. Citizenship
- Unexpired NEXUS Card—designates U.S. Citizenship
- Unexpired Secure Electronic Network for Travelers Rapid Inspection (SENTRI) Card—designates U.S. Citizenship
- Unexpired U.S. Enhanced Driver's License (EDL)—designates U.S. Citizenship
- Permanent Resident Card (I-551), often referred to as a "Green Card"—demonstrates LPR status
- Unexpired Foreign Passport AND immigrant visa with I-551 annotation of "Upon Endorsement Serves as Temporary Evidencing Permanent Resident of 1 Year"—demonstrates LPR status
- Unexpired Re-entry Permit (I-327)—demonstrates LPR status

Figure 13-1. Placards on vehicles communicate the risk of hazardous materials transport.

*At least two documents from List B are required if you do not have a document from List A. The documents must include:
1) a valid photo ID, and
2) a document that meets citizenship requirements. For example, the combination of a driver's license and a U.S. Social Security card contains a photo ID, but does not demonstrate citizenship status and is not a valid combination. However, the combination of a valid driver's license and a U.S. birth certificate would meet the document requirements for enrollment.

List B: You MUST Have at Least ONE Document from Each Category Below for a Total of TWO Documents

The names on all documents MUST MATCH with your application name, unless you provide a valid proof of name change*

(*Photo ID + Proof of U.S. Citizenship + Name Change Document {if needed} = Valid Combination*)

Valid Photo ID/Valid Proof of Citizenship
- *Unexpired* driver's license issued by a state or an outlying possession of the United States
- *Unexpired* photo ID card issued by a state or an outlying possession of the United States. This must include a state or state agency seal or logo (such as a state university ID)
- U.S. military ID card or U.S. retired military ID
- U.S. military dependent's card
- Native American tribal document with photo
- *Unexpired* Merchant Mariner License (MML) bearing an official raised seal, or a certified copy
- *Unexpired* Department of Homeland Security (DHS)/Transportation Security Administration (TSA) Transportation Worker Identification Credential (TWIC)
- *Unexpired* Merchant Mariner Credential (MMC)

Valid Proof of Citizenship
- Original or certified copy of birth by a state, county, municipal possession of the United States, bearing an official seal
- U.S. Certificate of Citizenship
- U.S. Certificate of Naturalization
- U.S. Citizen Identification Card
- Consular Report of Birth Abroad

- Certification of Report of Birth Abroad
- Expired U.S. passport within 12 months of expiration**

*Valid Proof of Name Change (if needed)
Original or Certified Copy of a Court Ordered Name Change Document (to include marriage certificates and divorce decrees) if the names on your photo ID and citizenship status document do not exactly match.
**An expired U.S. passport may not be presented by itself. It must be presented with at least one other List B document (and a name change document if needed). You may provide a second List B document, or one of the following: Voter's card, U.S. Social Security card, U.S. military discharge papers (DD-214), or a Department of Transportation (DOT) medical card.

You must pass a written test about transporting hazardous materials. To pass the test, you must know how to:

- recognize shipments of hazardous materials
- safely load shipments
- correctly placard your vehicle
- safely transport shipments

Learn the rules and follow them. Following the rules reduces the risk of injury from hazardous materials. Taking shortcuts by breaking rules is unsafe. Rule breakers can be fined and put in jail.

Inspect your vehicle before and during each trip. Law enforcement officers may stop and inspect your vehicle. They can also check your shipping papers. They will look for a hazardous materials endorsement on your driver's license.

You can see that nearly everyone involved in the transport of hazardous materials has responsibilities.

Shipper

The shipper sends products from one place to another by truck, railroad, ship, or airplane. Shippers use the hazardous materials regulations to decide the product's:

- proper shipping name
- hazard class
- identification number

- correct packaging
- correct label and markings
- correct placard

Shippers also package the materials and label and mark the package. They prepare the shipping paper and supply placards. Shippers certify on the shipping paper that they have prepared the shipment according to the rules. Exceptions to this are if you are pulling cargo tanks supplied by you or your employer, or if these materials and supplies are being transported by the carrier who owns them.

Carrier

Carriers take the shipment from the shipper to its destination. They check that the shipper correctly named, labeled, and marked the shipment. They refuse improper shipments. Carriers report accidents and incidents involving hazardous materials to the proper government agency.

Driver

You, the driver, make sure all who have been involved with the hazardous material—the packagers, loaders, shippers, and carriers—have done their job. You check that the shipper has identified, marked, and labeled the product. You refuse leaking shipments. You placard your vehicle when loading, if needed.

You make your best effort to transport the shipment safely and without delay. You follow all special rules about transporting hazardous material. Also, you keep hazardous materials shipping papers in the proper place.

Your responsibilities as a driver transporting hazardous materials are to:

- recognize a hazardous materials shipment
- identify the hazards the shipment presents
- communicate the danger to others
- know what to do in an emergency

How do you fulfill these responsibilities? To answer that, you must know the hazards materials regulations. As you know, all CDL drivers must know these regulations, even if they don't plan to haul hazmat. That way, they can recognize a hazardous materials load. They can determine if they are licensed to transport that load or not.

The hazardous materials regulations you must know are:

- Title 49 CFR Part 397 (found in the FMCSR)
- Title 49 CFR Parts 171, 172, 173, 177, and 178 (the Hazardous Materials Regulations, or HMR)

FMCSR PART 397

Some of the hazardous materials regulations are found in FMCSR Part 397. You read about them in Chapter 5. Here's a very brief review. These regulations cover:

- state and local laws
- attendance of motor vehicles
- parking
- routes
- fires
- smoking
- fueling
- tires
- instructions and documents

State and Local Laws

Remember "higher standard of care?" When there are two or more sets of regulations, you should follow the strictest set. Local hazmat regulations may be more strict than the federal regulations. If so, you would follow the local regulations.

Attendance of Motor Vehicles

With few exceptions, a vehicle hauling Division 1.1, 1.2, or 1.3 explosives must never be abandoned. There must always be a qualified person with the vehicle. This is called "attendance." You "attend" the vehicle when you are in the vehicle, awake, and not in the sleeper. If you are within 100 feet of the vehicle and have a clear view of it, you are also attending the vehicle.

A "qualified" person is someone the carrier has put in charge of attending the vehicle. To be qualified, you must be informed about the hazmat in the vehicle. You must know what to do in an emergency. You must be authorized and able to move the vehicle.

A vehicle with explosives may sometimes be left unattended, if:

- the vehicle is parked in a safe haven, or on a construction or survey site
- the lawful bailee of the explosives knows they are explosive and what to do in an emergency

 The "lawful bailee" is the person who is officially in charge of or responsible for the explosives.

- the vehicle is in clear sight of the bailee, or is in a safe haven

There is one reason why you may leave a vehicle with other kinds of hazmat unattended. That's if you must leave the vehicle to perform some maintenance, put out warning devices, or some other necessary part of your driving job.

Parking

Never park with Division 1.1, 1.2, or 1.3 explosives within five feet of the traveled part of the road. Unless your work requires it, do not park within 300 feet of

- a bridge, tunnel, or building,
- a place where people gather, or
- an open fire

If you must park to do your job, do so only briefly. Don't park on private property unless the owner is aware of the danger. Someone must always watch the parked vehicle. You may let someone else watch it for you only if your vehicle is

- on the shipper's property, or
- on the carrier's property, or
- on the consignee's property

You can, of course, leave your vehicle unattended in a safe haven.

You may park a placarded vehicle (not carrying explosives) within five feet of the traveled part of the road only if your work requires it. Do so only briefly. Someone must always watch the vehicle when parked on a public roadway or shoulder. Do not uncouple a trailer and leave it with hazardous material on a public street. Do not park within 300 feet of an open fire.

Routing

Vehicles hauling hazardous cargo don't always follow the easiest and fastest highways. Instead, hazmat routing must avoid roads that go through heavily populated areas. The only exception to this is when there is no other possible way to get where you're going.

For Division 1.1, 1.2, or 1.3 explosives, the carrier or driver must have a written route plan. Usually the carrier writes up the plan. You may have to do it yourself if you start your trip from somewhere other than your home terminal.

This written plan must include curfews and permits from those cities that require them. Any such permit must be applied for prior to the trip.

The written plan may list certain hours of the day when a vehicle hauling hazmat may travel through a city. Some cities have ordinances as to what time of day hazardous materials are allowed to pass through them. Other cities require permits that must be applied for in advance. More and more cities and states are passing laws that deal with hazardous materials.

Fires

You must not park a vehicle with hazmat within 300 feet of open fire. Don't even drive past one unless you are sure you can do so without stopping.

Smoking

Vehicles with hazardous cargo must be kept away from flames. This includes flames used to light cigarettes. So, smoking is not allowed within 25 feet of a vehicle carrying Class 1 materials, Class 5 materials, or flammable materials classified as Division 2.1, Class 3, Divisions 4.1 and 4.2. It's also not permitted around an empty tank motor vehicle that has been used to transport Class 3, flammable materials, or Division 2.1 flammable gases, which when it was loaded, was required to be marked or placarded.

Fueling

Special care must be taken when fueling a vehicle loaded with hazardous cargo. Turn the engine off first. Then be sure that someone is at the nozzle throughout the fueling process, controlling the flow.

Tires

A tire fire could be especially dangerous when you're hauling hazmat. Therefore, frequent tire inspections are required en route. If you have dual tires, check them at the start of each trip and when you park. Check the tires at the start of each trip and when you park. Check for proper tire inflation.

Figure 13-2. When hauling hazmat, check dual tires at the start of each trip and every time you park.

If a tire is low, flat, or leaking, you must get it repaired before going any further. If your check shows you have a hot tire, you must remove it. Place it at a safe distance from your vehicle. An overheated tire can burst into flame. Then inspect your vehicle until you find why the tire overheated in the first place. Get the problem fixed before you continue to drive.

Instructions and Documents

If you're hauling Division 1.1, 1.2, or 1.3 explosives, your carrier must give you certain instructions and documents. You must have a copy of FMCSR Part 397. You must get written instructions on what to do in an emergency or if you are delayed. These instructions must include the names and telephone numbers of people to contact about the emergency or delay. You must also get written information about the nature of the explosives you're transporting. The instructions must also tell you what precautions to take in case of fire, accidents, or leaks.

You must sign a receipt for these documents. The carrier keeps the receipt on file for a year.

When you get these documents, you must keep them with you. You must know everything they contain and obey the instructions.

Figure 13-3. Vehicles carrying hazardous waste must be marked.

TITLE 49 CFR PART 171

Title 49 CFR Part 171 states the DOT requirements for the transport of hazardous materials and waste by rail car, aircraft, and vessel. The definition of "transportation" is broad. It includes pretransportation activities like filling hazardous materials packaging, loading hazardous materials, and reviewing shipping papers. It also covers interstate, intrastate, and foreign motor vehicle transport. We'll mention the rail, air, and vessel regulations only when they also have to do with motor vehicle transport. This part also covers the transport of flammable cryogenic liquids in portable tanks and cargo tanks. Last, this part states requirements for manufacturing, marking, maintaining, repairing, and testing hazmat packaging.

General

Hazmat may not be transported in commerce unless it's been properly classed, described, packaged, marked, labeled, and prepared for shipment the way the regulations require.

Hazardous waste may not be hauled in a vehicle that isn't marked as follows:

- the legal name or trade name of the private carrier operating the vehicle
- the motor carrier identification number (a number with the letters USDOT) issued by the FMCSA
- the name of the person operating the vehicle, if that's not the carrier, accompanied by the operating carrier

When hazardous waste is delivered, the entire shipment must be delivered. If the shipment is to be transferred to another carrier, the entire shipment must be transferred. That is to say, you can't deliver some of it and dump the rest. You could be fined, even jailed, for discharging hazardous waste anywhere but the place named on the manifest.

Definition of Terms

This part contains general information and definitions used in other hazmat regulations. Here's a brief rundown of some that relate to transporting hazardous materials by motor vehicle.

"Approved" means approval issued or recognized by the Department of Transportation.

"Atmospheric gases" means argon, krypton, neon, nitrogen, oxygen, and xenon.

"Btu" means British thermal unit. It's a measurement of heat energy.

"Bulk packaging" includes a transport vehicle or freight container in which hazardous materials are loaded with no other container. Such a vehicle can hold more than 119 gallons of liquid, 882 pounds of solid, or 1,000 pounds (water capacity) of gas.

"C" means Celsius or Centigrade. It's one scale used for measuring temperature.

"Cargo tank" means any tank permanently attached to or forming a part of any motor vehicle. A straight truck with a tank cargo compartment would fit this definition. It also means any bulk liquid or compressed gas packaging not permanently attached to any motor vehicle. An example would be a tank semitrailer. Because of its size, construction, or the way it's attached to a motor vehicle, it can be loaded or unloaded without being removed from the motor vehicle. Cylinders are not cargo tanks. (Cargo tanks are discussed in more detail in Chapter 12.)

"Carrier" means a person engaged in the transportation of passengers or property by land or water, as a common, contract, or private carrier. It also covers civil aircraft.

"Combustible liquid" is defined in 173.120 (and later in this chapter).

"Compressed gas" is defined in Part 173.115 (and later in this chapter).

"Consumer commodity" means a material that is packaged and distributed for retail sale for use by individuals. The material is meant for personal care or household use. This term also includes drugs and medicines.

"Corrosive material" is defined in Part 173.136. It's also described in more detail later in this chapter.

"Cryogenic liquid" is super-cold liquid. It's further defined in Part 173.115.

"Cylinder" means a pressure vessel designed for pressures higher than 40 psia (you'll find "psia" defined later in this section). A portable tank or cargo tank is not considered a cylinder.

"Designated facility" means a hazardous waste treatment, storage, or disposal facility that has been named on the manifest by the generator (creator of the waste).

"DOD" means the U.S. Department of Defense.

"EPA" means U.S. Environmental Protection Agency.

"Etiologic agent" is defined in Part 173.134 (and later in this chapter).

"Explosives" are defined in Part 173.50.

"°F" means degrees Fahrenheit. It's another scale for measuring temperature.

"Filling density" refers to how full tankers and cylinders should be loaded with bulk liquids and compressed gases. These are defined in Parts 173.304, 173.314, 173.315, 173.316, 173.318, and 173.319 (or review Chapter 12).

"Flammable gas," "flammable liquid," and "flammable solid" are defined in Part 173 (and later in this chapter).

"Flash point" means the lowest temperature at which a substance gives off flammable vapors. These vapors will ignite if they come in contact with a spark or flame. The flash point of liquids is given in Part 173.120.

"Freight container" means a reusable container with a volume of 64 cubic feet or more. It's designed and built so it can be lifted with its contents intact. It's mainly used to hold packages (in unit form) during transport.

"Fuel tank" means a tank other than a cargo tank used to transport flammable or combustible liquid. It's also a tank that holds compressed gas used to fuel the transport vehicle it's attached to, or equipment on that vehicle. This is different from, say, a tank semitrailer that transports fuel as cargo.

"Gas poisonous by inhalation" is defined in Part 173.115.

"Gross weight" means the weight of packaging plus the weight of its contents.

"Hazardous material" means a substance or material, including a hazardous substance, that the Secretary of Transportation judges to pose an unreasonable risk to health, safety, and property when transported in commerce.

"Hazardous substance" means a material listed in the Appendix to Part 172.101. This appendix lists how much of the material, in one package, is considered hazardous. If the hazmat is in a mixture or solution, the solution is measured to see how much of it is hazmat. This measurement is compared against a table of RQ (reportable quantities). In short, some solutions and mixtures have enough hazmat to be hazardous. Others don't.

Solutions/Mixture Concentration By RQ pounds (kilograms)	Table Weight Percent	PPM (parts per mil)
5000 (2270)	10	100,000
1000 (454)	2	20,000
100 (45.4)	0.2	2,000
10 (4.54)	0.02	200
1 (0.454)	0.002	20

"Hazardous waste" means any material that is subject to the Hazardous Waste Manifest Requirement of the U.S. Environmental Protection Agency, specified in 40 CFR Part 262.

"ICAO" means International Civil Aviation Organization.

"Intermodal container" means a freight container designed and built to be used in two or more modes of transport.

"Intermodal portable tank" or "IM portable tanks" means a specific class of portable tanks designed mainly for international intermodal use.

"Irritating material" is further defined in Part 173.132(a) (and later in this chapter).

"Limited quantity" means the maximum amount of a hazardous material for which there is a specific labeling and packaging exception. In other words, some amounts of hazmat don't have to be labeled or packaged according to the usual regulations. That's a limited quantity of that hazmat. There are no exceptions for poison-by-inhalation materials.

"Marking" means putting the descriptive name, instructions, cautions, weight, or specification marks required by these regulations on outer containers of hazmat.

"Mixture" means a material composed of more than one chemical compound or element.

"Mode" means any of the following transportation methods: rail, highway, air, or water.

"Motor vehicle" includes a vehicle, machine, tractor, trailer, or semitrailer, or any combinations of these. This term assumes the vehicle is driven or drawn by mechanical power, is on the highway, and is transporting passengers or property. It doesn't refer to vehicles used on rail. It also doesn't include a trolley bus running on a fixed overhead electric wire and carrying passengers.

"Name of contents" means the proper shipping name specified in Part 172.101.

"N.O.S." means not otherwise specified.

"Non-bulk packaging" means a package smaller than the capacities stated for "bulk packaging."

"Operator" means a person who controls the use of an aircraft, vessel, or vehicle.

"Organic peroxide" is further defined in Part 173.128.

"ORM" means Other Regulated Materials. It is defined in Part 173.144.

"Outage" or "ullage" means the amount by which a packaging falls short of being full of liquid. It's usually stated in percent by volume. "Outage" was discussed in Chapter 12. Refer to that chapter for more details about outage.

"Outer packaging" means the outermost enclosure used to transport a hazardous material. This is other than a freight container.

"Overpack" means an enclosure that is used by a single consignor to provide protection or convenience in handling of a package or to combine two or more packages. "Overpack" does not include a freight container. Overpack has a special meaning when used to refer to packaging specified by Part 178.

"Oxidizer" or "oxidizing material" is defined in 173.127 (and later in this chapter).

"Packaging" means the assembly of one or more containers and any other part needed to comply with the minimum packaging requirements of this subchapter. It includes containers (other than freight containers or overpacks), portable tanks, cargo tanks, tank cars, and multi-unit tank car tanks. Radioactive materials are covered in Part 173.403.

"Poisonous material" other than a gas is defined in Part 173.132.

"Portable tank" means any packaging (except a cylinder having a 1,000-pound or less water capacity) designed to be loaded into or on or temporarily coupled to a transport vehicle or ship. These tanks are equipped with skids, mounting, or other parts that make mechanical handling possible. Not included in this definition is any cargo tank, tank car, multi-unit tank car tank, or trailers that carry 3AX, 3AAX, or 3T cylinders.

"Preferred route" or "Preferred highway" is a highway for shipment of "highway route controlled quantities" of radioactive materials. These routes are named by state routing agencies. When there is no other option (as described in Part 177.103), any interstate system highway can be named a preferred route.

"Proper shipping name" means the name of the hazardous material shown in Roman print (not italics) in Part 172.101.

"P.s.i." or "psi" means pounds per square inch.

"P.s.i.a." or "psia" means pounds per square inch absolute.

What's the difference between psi and psia? Psi is a measurement taken using atmospheric pressure as a yardstick. Psia uses vacuum (or zero pressure) as a reference point.

"P.s.i.g." or "psig" means pounds per square inch gauge. That's a measurement of fluid or gas pressure taken with a gauge called a manometer.

"Pyrophoric liquid" is defined in Parts 173.124(b) (and later in this chapter).

Hazardous Substances Other than Radionuclides	
Paraformaldehyde	1000 (454)
Paraldehyde	1000 (454)
Parathion	10 (4.54)
PCBs	1 (0.454)
PCNB	100 (45.4)
Pentachlorobenzene	10 (4.54)
Pentachloroethane	10 (4.54)
Pentachloronitrobenzene	100 (45.4)
Pentachlorophenol	10 (4.54)
1,3-Pentadiene	100 (45.4)
Perchloroethylene	100 (45.4)
Perchloromethyl mercaptan @	100 (45.4)
Phenacetin	100 (45.4)
Phenanthrene	5000 (2270)
Phenol	1000 (45.4)
Phenol, 2-chloro-	100 (45.4)

Figure 13-4. Part of the list of Hazardous Substances Other than Radionuclides.

"Radioactive materials" are defined in Part 173.403.

"Reportable Quantity" (RQ) means the quantity specified in Column 2 of the table in Part 172.101, for any material identified in Column 1.

"Shipping paper" means a shipping order, bill of lading, manifest, or other shipping document serving the same purpose. These documents must have the information required by Subpart C of Part 172.

"Solution" means any uniform liquid mixture of two or more chemical compounds or elements that won't separate while being transported under normal conditions.

"Spontaneously combustible materials (solid)" means a solid substance that may heat up or ignite by itself while being transported under normal conditions. This includes sludges and pastes. It also includes solids that will heat up and ignite when exposed to air.

"SCF" (standard cubic foot) means one cubic foot of gas measured at 60°F and 14.7 psia.

"Technical name" means a recognized chemical name currently used in scientific and technical handbooks, journals, and texts. Some generic descriptions are used as technical names. These are "organic phosphate," "organic phosphorus compound mixture," "methyl parathion," and "parathion."

"TOFC" means trailer-on-flat-car.

"Transport vehicle" means a cargo-carrying vehicle such as an automobile, van, tractor, truck, semitrailer, tank car, or rail car used to transport cargo by any mode. Each cargo-carrying body is a separate transport vehicle.

"United States" means the fifty states, the District of Columbia, the Commonwealth of Puerto Rico, the Virgin Islands, American Samoa, or Guam.

"Viscous liquid" means a liquid material that has a measured viscosity in excess of 2500 centistokes at 25 degrees Centigrade (77 degrees Fahrenheit). Viscosity is determined using procedures in ASTM Method D 445-72 "Kinematic Viscosity of Transparent and Opaque Liquids (and the Calculation of Dynamic Viscosity)" or ASTM Method D 1200-70 "Viscosity of Paints, Varnishes, and Lacquers by Ford Viscosity Cup."

 "Viscosity" is a measurement of a liquid's tendency to resist flowing. A liquid with a high viscosity doesn't flow as easily as one with a low viscosity.

"Volatility" refers to how fast materials evaporate and become vapor.

That's a partial list of terms defined in Part 171.8. You should be aware of the official definition of what is hazardous, as well as the meaning of other terms used in the business of transporting hazardous materials. Should you run into other terms for which you need definitions, look in Part 171.8.

This part contains other regulations you must know if you plan to haul hazmat. Some of them are mainly of interest to shippers, carriers, and employers. We'll cover the ones the driver should know. If you are a carrier or employer as well as a driver, you should inform yourself of all the hazardous materials regulations.

Keep this in mind as well. State and local governments may have their own hazmat regulations. You must know the regulations of every local area in which you plan to transport hazardous materials.

North American Shipments

Part 171.12 deals with North American shipments. Shipments to or from Mexico must comply with the regulations in this subchapter.

Canada has its own hazmat regulations. These are the Transportation of Dangerous Goods or TDG regulations. They're similar to DOT hazmat regulations. Canadian shipments that meet TDG requirements usually also meet DOT hazmat regulations. Sometimes, special action is required.

Read Title 49 CFR Parts 171.12, 171.22, and 171.23 in depth if you handle Canadian hazardous materials shipments.

Reporting Hazardous Materials Incidents

Carriers are responsible for reporting hazardous materials incidents. Since the driver is the one on the scene, your employer will likely need your help with this. You may be given special instructions or duties regarding hazardous materials incidents such as leaks and spills.

TITLE 49 CFR PART 172

This part includes the Hazardous Materials Table. Here you will also find information on how to understand and communicate the danger. This is done through shipping papers and manifests, package marking, labels, and placards. This part of the HMR also tells about special provisions, emergency response, and training requirements.

The Hazardous Materials Table lists hazardous materials, along with their description, proper shipping name, and class. It lists the label, packing group, marking, and placards for each material.

The hazmat table also shows if a material is to be transported by truck, rail, air, or vessel. All this information helps to communicate the hazard presented by the material—and prevent trouble. You'll use this table to:

- decide if the material is regulated for transport by truck
- determine if the proper shipping name has been used on shipping papers and package markings
- identify the material's hazard class
- find the proper identification number
- find the packing group
- determine if the label is correct
- determine if the correct package was used

You'll find part of the table in Figure 13-5.

Column 1 of the table tells you if a hazardous material is regulated for truck transport. This is done by codes.

The letter "A" means the transport of the hazmat is regulated when done by air. "W" marks hazmat that will be restricted when transported by vessel. The letter "D" identifies proper shipping names appropriate only for domestic shipments, while "I" is for international commerce. The letter "G" identifies proper shipping names for which one or more technical names of the hazardous material must be entered. They will then be shown in parentheses, in association with the basic description.

Some materials are regulated because they are "RQ"—reportable quantity. If a certain amount of the material is spilled or released into the environment, the EPA wants to know about it. The EPA determines the quantity. When material is shipped in this quantity, it is regulated, even though it may not be when shipped in a lesser quantity.

The plus sign (+) in column 1 shows that the proper shipping name and hazard class for the entry has been fixed and can't be changed. In other words, this is the name to use whether or not the material meets the definition of that class.

 The different hazard classes were first discussed in Chapter 5. You've also just seen them mentioned in the definitions section of Part 171. Each class is defined in greater detail in different parts of the HMR. You'll find most of them in Part 173.

In column 2 you'll find the proper shipping name. Entries are in alphabetical order. Names shown in regular type are proper shipping names. Use these names to determine whether the shipper has used the proper names on shipping papers and packages. Names shown in slanted type (italics) are not proper shipping names.

When hazmat is shipped in a mixture or solution, the proper shipping name itself may identify the material as a solution or mixture. Or you may see the word "solution" or "mixture." Either the exact concentration or the range of concentration will be stated.

You may see "N.O.I." or "N.O.I.B.N." "N.O.I." stands for "not otherwise indexed." "N.O.I.B.N." and "N.O.S." stand for "not otherwise indexed by name." An example of when this type of entry might be used would be a mixture of flammable liquids. No specific product shipping name can

§172.101 Hazardous Material Table									
Symbols	Hazardous materials descriptions and proper shipping names	Hazard class or Division	Identification Numbers	Packing Group	Label(s) Required (if not excepted)	Special provisions	(8) Packaging Authorizations (§ 173.***)		
							Exceptions	Non-bulk packaging	Bulk packaging
(1)	(2)	(3)	(4)	(5)	(6)	(7)	(8A)	(8B)	(8C)
——	Poisonous, solids, self heating, n.o.s ...	6.1	UN3124	1	POISON, SPONTANEOUSLY COMBUSIBLE	A5__	None	211	241

Note: Columns 9 and 10 do not apply to transportation by highway.

Figure 13-5. Part of the Hazardous Materials Table.

be established, so this mixture might be listed as "Flammable Liquid N.O.S."

Column 3 gives the hazard class or division. The hazard class gives you an idea about the type of danger presented by the material. It's easy to guess the danger presented by something like "detonators for ammunition." However, if you are hauling "cymenes" and don't know what that is, the table will help. You'll learn that this is a Class 3 material, and so is a flammable liquid.

If you find "Forbidden" in column 3 for something you are to transport, contact your employer or dispatcher immediately. A "Forbidden" item may not be transported.

Some materials fit into more than one class. Then, the number of the class that presents the highest danger should be used. Part 173.2 will help you to decide how to classify such a material. Part 173.2a lists the classes from the highest danger to the least danger.

Some materials will always have the hazards of, and therefore the classification of, a single class. These are:

- Class 1 (explosive) material that meets any other hazard class or division as defined in this part shall be assigned a division in Class 1
- Division 5.2 (organic peroxide) material that meets the definition of any other hazard class or division shall be classed as Division 5.2
- Division 6.2 (infectious substance) material that also meets the definition of another hazard class or division, other than Class 7, or that also is a limited quantity Class 7 material, shall be classed as Division 6.2
- material that meets the definition of a wetted explosive in Part 173.124(a)(1) of this subchapter (Division 4.1). Wetted explosives are either specifically listed in the Hazardous Materials Table or are approved by the Associate Administrator.
- a limited quantity of a Class 7 (radioactive) material that meets the definition for more than one hazard class or division shall be classed in accordance with Part 173.423. It's classed for the additional hazard, packaged to conform with the requirements specified in Part 173.421, and offered for transportation in accordance with the requirements that apply to the hazard for which it is

classed. A limited quantity Class 7 (radioactive) material that is classed other than Class 7 is excepted from some of the requirements if the entry "Limited quantity radioactive material" appears on the shipping paper in association with the basic description.

Materials that meet the definition of other classes but that are poisonous when inhaled require special marking, labeling, placarding, and shipping paper descriptions.

You may find a letter after some of the entries in column 3. For example, those labeled "detonators for ammunition" have the letter B after the hazard class number. These letters refer to compatibility groups and segregation requirements. These relate to loading requirements. You'll learn more about segregation later in this chapter.

Hazmat will be listed by a technical name or a generic name. Some items on the table are hazardous wastes. Either the name will identify the material as hazardous waste, or the word "waste" will be used with the name.

Column 4 lists the proper identification number that must be on the packaging or shipping paper, bulk and non-bulk packages, portable tanks, and cargo tanks. Materials for international shipment will have a UN number. Materials with an NA number can't be shipped outside the United States, except to Canada.

Column 5 names the section of Part 173 that describes the packing requirements for the entry. The packing group is chosen by the degree of danger presented by the material. Compare the packing group entry on the table with the entry on the shipping papers. Note that Class 2 (Gases), Class 7 (Radioactive material), Combustible liquids, and ORM-D materials do not have packing groups.

Use column 6 to check that the packages have the proper labels. You may see more than one label listed. The first label listed indicates the main hazard. Other labels indicate secondary hazards. All the labels listed must be displayed.

Column 7 lists any special provisions, such as packaging requirements, that may apply to the entry. The entries in column 7 are codes. You'll find what the codes stand for in Part 172.102. In some states, codes containing the letter "H" refers to a special provision that applies only to transportation by highway. A code containing the letter "N" refers to a special provision that applies only to non-bulk packaging requirements, while "B" codes are for bulk-packaging requirements. A code containing the letter "T" refers to a special provision that applies only to transportation in IM portable tanks. Codes with the letter "W" refer to a special provision that applies only to transportation by water; "R" codes are for transport by rail, and "A" codes are for air transport.

Column 8 will help you to be sure that the shipper has put the hazmat in the proper package for truck transport. There are three segments to column 8. Put "173" in front of any three-digit number that you find in any of these segments. That gives you the number of the federal regulation part that provides additional information. In segment A of column 8, the entry refers to packaging exceptions. In segment B of column 8, the entry refers to authorized non-bulk packaging. Segment C lists those sections that authorize bulk packing.

The final columns, columns 9 and 10, refer to shipments regulated when transported other than by truck. Column 9 lists quantity limits for transport aboard aircraft or railcar. Column 10 refers to requirements for water transport.

Another list that's used is the List of Hazardous Substances and Reportable Quantities. It's appendix A to the hazmat table. As you've learned, the DOT and EPA want to know about spills or leaks of some products in certain quantities. This list names those products and their "reportable quantities," or RQ. You may see RQs on the shipping paper.

Some items have more than one name. The other name is listed in the "Synonyms" column on the list.

Shipping Papers and Manifests

Being able to recognize a hazardous materials shipment is the first step in handling it correctly and safely. All licensed CMV drivers must be able to recognize a hazardous materials shipment. One way to do this is by the shipping paper and manifest listings. Filling out the shipping paper is mainly the responsibility of the shipper. As the driver, you must know how to read it to know what you're carrying. Part 172 states how hazardous materials are to be described on the shipping paper. This covers all hazardous materials (other than those for air or water transport, and ORM-D unless it is for transport by air or water).

Shipping Papers

Not all shipping papers are alike. When it comes to hazardous materials, though, they all must have certain information:

- the proper shipping name from column 2 on the Hazardous Materials Table
- the hazard class or division from column 3 on the Hazardous Materials Table
- the identification number from column 4 on the Hazardous Materials Table
- the packing group from column 5 on the Hazardous Materials Table
- total quantity by weight, volume, or whatever is appropriate for the material
- an emergency response telephone number for each hazardous material, or one number if it will cover all the hazmat listed

Some shipping papers may include both hazardous and non-hazardous shipments. In such cases, the hazardous material must be described first. Or, it can be highlighted in a different color from the other entries. Another option is to place an "X" in the "HM" (hazardous materials) column before the shipping name. You may see the letters RQ instead of X if the item is not hazardous but is a reportable quantity. If the hazardous material is hazardous waste, the shipper must put the word "waste" on the paper, before the shipping name.

Figure 13-6 is a sample shipping paper. Note that there are page numbers that tell whether there is more than one page. The total number of pages appears on the first page.

In column 1 of each entry, you'll see the quantity.

Column 2 has the description of the hazardous product. This includes the proper shipping name, hazard class, and identification number, in that order. The proper shipping name from column 2 of the Hazardous Materials Table should always be used. Then comes the hazard class from column 3 of the table. That's followed by the ID number from the Hazardous Materials Table, column 4.

Sometimes this name doesn't give much of a clue as to the nature of the materials or wastes. So, descriptive terms are added. This could be "ignitability," "corrosivity," or "reactivity." These terms are called ICR terms (perhaps you can guess why). Other descriptive terms may limit the transport of certain materials to a particular DOT specification tank.

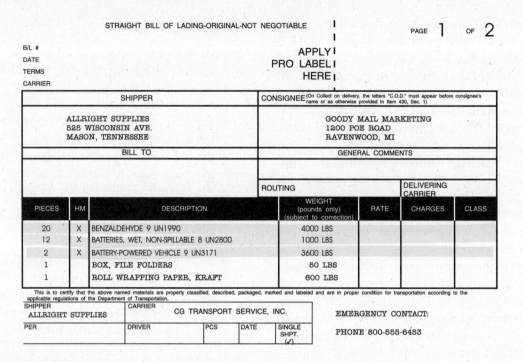

Figure 13-6. Sample shipping paper.

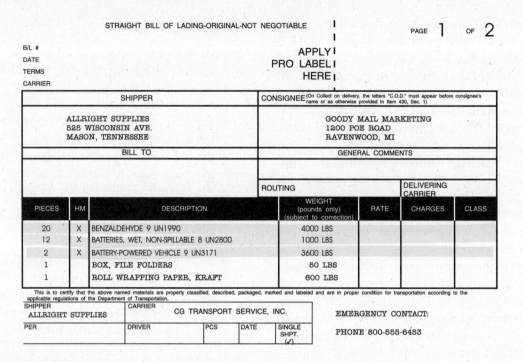

Cargo and portable tanks may be built to DOT specifications. If so, they receive a DOT specification code number. Coded tankers are those that have been approved to haul hazardous liquids. Refer to Chapter 12 for more details on DOT specifications for tanks.

You may also see a note that alerts you to special dangers. Examples are "dangerous when wet" and "poison inhalation hazard." "Inhalation hazard" tells you that you can be poisoned by simply breathing in the hazardous material or its vapors. Knowing that, you would be able to protect yourself if it leaked or spilled.

Shipping papers must have entries for unusual circumstances. A shipment made under a DOT exemption must be marked "DOT-E" (before October 1, 2007) or "DOT-SP" (after October 1, 2007) followed by the exemption number that was assigned. The basic description of limited quantity of a hazmat must be followed by the words "Limited Quantity" (or the abbreviation "LTD. QTY.").

Information for radioactive material must include the name of the radionuclide, its physical and chemical form, and its activity in curies, milli-curies, or microcuries (these are all measurements of radioactivity). Also, the words "Highway Route Controlled Quantity" must appear, along with the category label and the transport index for each Yellow II or Yellow III package.

Some packages contain only the remains of a hazardous material. In that case, no quantity is listed. Still, these remains can be hazardous themselves. The description on the shipping paper will then read "Residue: Last contained..." with the name of the hazardous material that was in the package and the letters "RQ."

The last column for the entry gives the weight. On the bottom right of this shipping paper, you'll find the emergency contact phone number. You can see that it is clearly marked as an emergency contact number, as required by law.

Last, you'll find the shipper's certification on the shipping paper. This is the shipper's statement that the shipment was prepared according to regulations.

Manifest

Manifests are used for transporting hazardous wastes. The shipper prepares the manifest, dates, and signs it. If the shipper is not the one who created the waste, whoever did must sign and date the manifest. The first carrier involved in the transport of the waste also signs and dates it. A copy of the manifest must be signed by each carrier who transports the waste. The facility receiving the waste dates and signs the copy.

A copy of the manifest with all the dates and signatures goes to each person representing each carrier transporting the waste. One of those could be you, the driver. A copy also goes to the person who represents the facility that receives the waste. Last, the manifest copy is returned to the shipper or generator (creator) of the waste, and all the carriers. Your employer will keep the manifest on file for three years. This sets up a "paper trail" of all the steps and stops in the transport of the waste.

"Waste" must be entered before the proper shipping name on the manifest. The manifest will also include this information:

- document number
- generator's U.S. EPA 12-digit identification number
- total number of pages used to complete the manifest, and any continuation pages
- name, mailing address, and emergency contact phone number of the generator
- name and identification number of the first transporter who will transport the waste, plus names and identification numbers of any additional transporters
- special handling instructions
- shipper's name, mailing address, phone number, and Environmental Protection Agency (EPA) identification number
- name and EPA identification number of each carrier
- name, address, and EPA identification number of the designated facility (plus an alternate facility, if given)
- description of the material
- quantity (by units of weight or volume)
- type and number of containers loaded on the vehicle

Marking

Every hazmat package, freight container, and transport vehicle must be marked as described in this part of Title 49 CFR. Most of the marking requirements are the shipper's responsibility. They are different for bulk and non-bulk packages. Since the markings can be important to you, you should know something about them.

Remember the definition of bulk and non-bulk packaging? "Bulk packaging" includes a transport vehicle or freight container in which hazardous materials are loaded with no other container, such as an inner lining. Such a vehicle can hold more than 119 gallons of liquid, 882 pounds of solid, or 1,000 pounds (water capacity) of gas. "Non-bulk packaging" means a package smaller than the capacities stated for "bulk packaging."

Marking must be long-wearing, in English, and printed on or attached to the surface of the package. Markings can also be put on a label, tag, or sign. They must stand out against the background color. They must not be hidden by other labels or fixtures. They must be placed away from other markings such as advertisements.

"ORM" stands for "Other Regulated Materials," as you now know.

Packages of radioactive materials may be marked "Type A" or "Type B." These stand for different levels of hazard.

Packages of liquid hazardous materials are marked with arrows to show you how to keep the package upright. That way it's less likely to leak. Arrows may be used along with or instead of words.

Tanks

Hazardous materials may not be carried in portable or cargo tanks or tank cars unless they are marked. They must be marked at least on each side with the UN identification number specified for the cargo to be hauled. Portable tanks holding over 1,000 gallons and cargo tanks must also be marked on each end. If the tractor hides the front of the cargo tank, the tractor should be marked. The name of the owner or shipper must be displayed on a portable tank carrying hazmat.

The shipper is supposed to give the carrier the necessary placards with these identification numbers if the tank isn't already marked. Orange panels with four-inch high black numbers can be used instead of diamond-shaped placards.

The name of the material may have to be marked on the tank. If so, it must be in letters at least two inches high. Both sides of the tank must be marked. This is required when the tank will be carrying certain Class 2 materials such as flammable and non-flammable gas and cryogenic liquid. "QT" and "NQT" markings are required for MC 330 and MC 331 cargo tanks. The letters stand for "Quenched and Tempered" or "Not Quenched and Tempered." This describes the type of metal used to build the tank.

Cargo tanks carrying more than one hazmat must be marked on two sides with the ID number of each one. The markings should be in the same order as the compartments in which the material is being carried. If an "Elevated Temperature Material" is the cargo, the tank must be marked on each side and both ends with the word "Hot."

Labels

You know that the packages holding hazardous materials must be labeled. This is required by Title 49 CFR Part 172 with few exceptions. Special labels are used for this. Shippers are responsible for labeling packages. You, the driver, must be able to recognize the labels and check the shipping papers to make sure that the shipment is prepared properly.

Labels are not used on compressed gas cylinders that are not overpacked. Instead, the label is placed on a hang tag hung around the neck of the cylinder. Or, a decal may be used. The cylinders themselves may be stamped as holding compressed gas. Compressed gas cylinders that are permanently mounted on a vehicle don't need labels. ORM packages don't need labels. Neither do packages of combustible liquids. Packages with low activity radioactive materials don't need labels if they're hauled in a special vehicle used only by the consignor. Cargo tanks and single unit tank cars don't need labels.

Cargo tanks don't need labels if they are placarded.

What if a package contains more than one type of hazmat? In some cases, the package must have more than one label.

Even empty packages may have to have labels. When a package is empty, any hazardous material shipping name and identification number markings, any hazard warning labels or placards, and any other markings indicating that the material is hazardous (e.g., RQ, Inhalation Hazard) should be removed, obliterated, or securely covered in transportation. If they aren't, then labels are still needed unless the packaging is not visible in transportation and the packaging is loaded by the

shipper and unloaded by the shipper or consignee. Empty packages aren't merely empty. They are:

- unused
- cleaned of residue and purged of vapors to remove any potential hazard
- refilled with a material that is not hazardous to such an extent that any residue remaining in the packaging no longer poses a hazard, or
- contain only the residue of an ORM-D material, a Division 2.2 non-flammable gas, other than ammonia, anhydrous, and with no subsidiary hazard, at an absolute pressure less than 280 kPa (40.6 psia); at 20°C (68°F); and any material contained in the packaging does not meet the definitions for a hazardous substance, a hazardous waste, or a marine pollutant.

A non-bulk packaging containing only the residue of a hazardous material covered by Table 2 does not have to be included in determining the applicability of the placarding requirements, and is not subject to the shipping paper requirements of this subchapter when collected and transported by a contract or private carrier for reconditioning, remanufacture, or reuse. (You'll find Table 2 later in this chapter). The description on the shipping paper for a packaging containing the residue of a hazardous material may include the words "Residue: Last Contained . . ." along with the basic description of the hazardous material last contained in the packaging.

A package that contains the remains of an elevated temperature material may remain marked in the same manner as when it contained a greater quantity of the material even though it no longer meets the definition for an elevated temperature material.

DOT 106 and 110 tanks must be labeled on each end.

There are three different "Radioactive" labels for different levels of radioactivity. White I is the lowest level. Next comes Yellow II. The highest level is Yellow III.

Hazmat package labels are diamond-shaped and four inches square. They have a solid black line border. The labels show the class of hazardous materials to which the package belongs. Any numbers that might be on the labels are part of a worldwide system used to identify hazardous materials. Each number stands for a different type of hazmat. Figure 13-7 shows the hazmat labels and placards.

DOT CHART 15
Hazardous Materials Markings, Labeling and Placarding Guide

U.S. Department of Transportation

Pipeline and Hazardous Materials Safety Administration

Refer to 49 CFR, Part 172:

Marking - Subpart D

Labeling - Subpart E

Placarding - Subpart F

NOTE: This document is for general guidance only and should not be used to determine compliance with 49 CFR, Parts 100-185.

HAZARDOUS MATERIALS MARKINGS

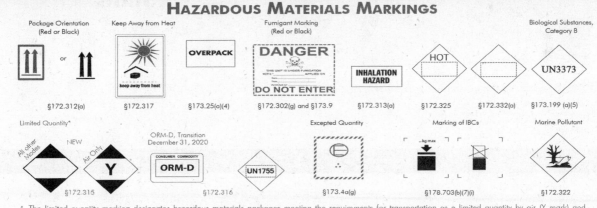

Package Orientation (Red or Black)	Keep Away from Heat		Fumigant Marking (Red or Black)				Biological Substances, Category B
§172.312(a)	§172.317	§173.25(a)(4)	§172.302(g) and §173.9	§172.313(a)	§172.325	§172.332(a)	§173.199 (a)(5)

Limited Quantity*		ORM-D, Transition December 31, 2020		Excepted Quantity	Marking of IBCs	Marine Pollutant
§172.315		§172.316		§173.4a(g)	§178.703(b)(7)(i)	§172.322

* The limited quantity marking designates hazardous materials packages meeting the requirements for transportation as a limited quantity by air (Y mark) and packages meeting the requirements for transport as a limited quantity by surface modes (no Y). A Y-marked package meeting the requirements for transport by air may be transported by all modes. In some instances packages bearing the surface mark (no Y) may also be acceptable for transport by air provided the packages meet all relevant requirements for air transport (for example UN0012, UN0014, or UN0055).

Hazardous Materials Warning Labels
Actual label size: at least 100 mm (3.9 inches) on all sides

CLASS 1 Explosives: Divisions 1.1, 1.2, 1.3, 1.4, 1.5, 1.6

§172.411

* Include compatibility group letter.
** Include division number and compatibility group letter.

CLASS 2 Gases: Divisions 2.1, 2.2, 2.3

§172.405(b), §172.415, §172.416, §172.417

CLASS 3 Flammable Liquid

§172.419

CLASS 4 Flammable Solid, Spontaneously Combustible, and Dangerous When Wet: Divisions 4.1, 4.2, 4.3

§172.420, §172.422, §172.423

CLASS 5 Oxidizer, Organic Peroxide: Divisions 5.1 and 5.2

§172.426, §172.427

CLASS 6 Poison (Toxic), Poison Inhalation Hazard, Infectious Substance: Divisions 6.1 and 6.2

§172.323, §172.405(c), §172.429, §172.430, §172.432

For Regulated Medical Waste (RMW), an Infectious Substance label is not required on an outer packaging if the OSHA Biohazard marking is used as prescribed in 29 CFR 1910.1030(g). A bulk package of RMW must display a BIOHAZARD marking.

CLASS 7 Radioactive

§172.436, §172.438, §172.440, §172.441

CLASS 8 Corrosive

§172.442

CLASS 9 Miscellaneous Hazardous Material

§172.446

Cargo Aircraft Only

§172.448

Empty Label

EMPTY

§172.450

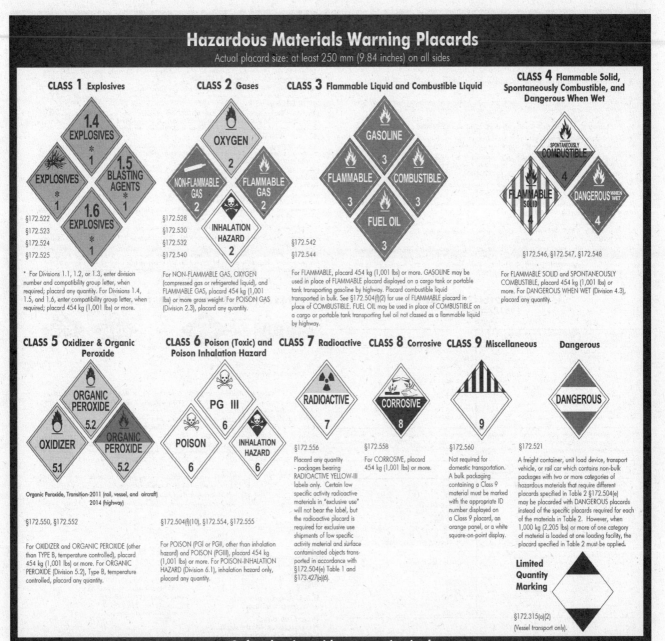

Hazardous Materials Warning Placards

Actual placard size: at least 250 mm (9.84 inches) on all sides

CLASS 1 Explosives

§172.522
§172.523
§172.524
§172.525

* For Divisions 1.1, 1.2, or 1.3, enter division number and compatibility group letter, when required; placard any quantity. For Divisions 1.4, 1.5, and 1.6, enter compatibility group letter, when required; placard 454 kg (1,001 lbs) or more.

CLASS 2 Gases

§172.528
§172.530
§172.532
§172.540

For NON-FLAMMABLE GAS, OXYGEN (compressed gas or refrigerated liquid), and FLAMMABLE GAS, placard 454 kg (1,001 lbs) or more gross weight. For POISON GAS (Division 2.3), placard any quantity.

CLASS 3 Flammable Liquid and Combustible Liquid

§172.542
§172.544

For FLAMMABLE, placard 454 kg (1,001 lbs) or more. GASOLINE may be used in place of FLAMMABLE placard displayed on a cargo tank or portable tank transporting gasoline by highway. Placard combustible liquid transported in bulk. See §172.504(f)(2) for use of FLAMMABLE placard in place of COMBUSTIBLE. FUEL OIL may be used in place of COMBUSTIBLE on a cargo or portable tank transporting fuel oil not classed as a flammable liquid by highway.

CLASS 4 Flammable Solid, Spontaneously Combustible, and Dangerous When Wet

§172.546, §172.547, §172.548

For FLAMMABLE SOLID and SPONTANEOUSLY COMBUSTIBLE, placard 454 kg (1,001 lbs) or more. For DANGEROUS WHEN WET (Division 4.3), placard any quantity.

CLASS 5 Oxidizer & Organic Peroxide

Organic Peroxide, Transition-2011 (rail, vessel, and aircraft) 2014 (highway)

§172.550, §172.552

For OXIDIZER and ORGANIC PEROXIDE (other than TYPE B, temperature controlled), placard 454 kg (1,001 lbs) or more. For ORGANIC PEROXIDE (Division 5.2), Type B, temperature controlled, placard any quantity.

CLASS 6 Poison (Toxic) and Poison Inhalation Hazard

§172.504(f)(10), §172.554, §172.555

For POISON (PGI or PGII, other than inhalation hazard) and POISON (PGIII), placard 454 kg (1,001 lbs) or more. For POISON-INHALATION HAZARD (Division 6.1), inhalation hazard only, placard any quantity.

CLASS 7 Radioactive

§172.556

Placard any quantity - packages bearing RADIOACTIVE YELLOW-III labels only. Certain low specific activity radioactive materials in "exclusive use" will not bear the label, but the radioactive placard is required for exclusive use shipments of low specific activity material and surface contaminated objects transported in accordance with §172.504(e) Table 1 and §173.427(a)(6).

CLASS 8 Corrosive

§172.558

For CORROSIVE, placard 454 kg (1,001 lbs) or more.

CLASS 9 Miscellaneous

§172.560

Not required for domestic transportation. A bulk packaging containing a Class 9 material must be marked with the appropriate ID number displayed on a Class 9 placard, an orange panel, or a white square-on-point display.

Dangerous

§172.521

A freight container, unit load device, transport vehicle, or rail car which contains non-bulk packages with two or more categories of hazardous materials that require different placards specified in Table 2 §172.504(e) may be placarded with DANGEROUS placards instead of the specific placards required for each of the materials in Table 2. However, when 1,000 kg (2,205 lbs) or more of one category of material is loaded at one loading facility, the placard specified in Table 2 must be applied.

Limited Quantity Marking

§172.315(a)(2)
(Vessel transport only).

Safety begins with communication!

General Guidelines on Use of Warning Labels and Placards

LABELS

See 49 CFR, Part 172, Subpart E, for complete labeling regulations.

- The Hazardous Materials Table [§172.101, Col. 6] identifies the proper label(s) for the hazardous material listed.
- Any person who offers a hazardous material for transportation MUST label the package, if required [§172.400(a)].
- Labels may be affixed to packages when not required by regulations, provided each label represents a hazard of the material contained in the package [§172.401].
- For labeling mixed or consolidated packages, see §172.404.
- The appropriate hazard class or division number must be displayed in the lower corner of a primary and subsidiary hazard label [§172.402(b)].
- For classes 1,2,3,4,5,6, and 8, text indicating a hazard (e.g., "CORROSIVE") is NOT required on a primary or subsidiary label. The label must otherwise conform to Subpart E of Part 172 [§172.405].
- Labels must be printed on or affixed to the surface of the package near the proper shipping name marking [§172.406(a)].
- When primary and subsidiary labels are required, they must be displayed next to each other [§172.406(c)].
- For a package containing a Division 6.1, PG III material, the POISON label specified in §172.430 may be modified to display the text PG III instead of POISON or TOXIC. Also see §172.405(c).
- The ORGANIC PEROXIDE label [§172.427] indicates that organic peroxides are highly flammable. Use of the ORGANIC PEROXIDE label eliminates the need for a flammable liquid subsidiary label. The color of the border must be black and the color of the flame may be black or white.

PLACARDS

See 49 CFR, Part 172, Subpart F, for complete placarding regulations.

- Each person who offers for transportation or transports any hazardous material subject to the Hazardous Materials Regulations must comply with all applicable requirements of Subpart F [§172.500].
- Placards may be displayed for a hazardous material, even when not required, if the placarding otherwise conforms to the requirements of Subpart F of Part 172 [§172.502(c)].
- For other than Class 7 or the DANGEROUS placard, text indicating a hazard (e.g., "FLAMMABLE") is not required. Text may be omitted from the OXYGEN placard only if the specific ID number is displayed on the placard [§172.519(b)(3)].
- For a placard corresponding to the primary or subsidiary hazard class of a material, the hazard class or division number must be displayed in the lower corner of the placard [§172.519(b)(4)].
- Except as otherwise provided, any bulk packaging, freight container, unit load device, transport vehicle or rail car containing any quantity of material listed in Table 1 must be placarded [§172.504].
- When the aggregate gross weight of all hazardous materials in non-bulk packages covered in Table 2 is less than 454 kg (1,001 lbs), no placard is required on a transport vehicle or freight container when transported by highway or rail [§172.504(c)].
- Notes: See §172.504(f)(10) for placarding Division 6.1, PG III materials.
- Placarded loads require registration with USDOT. See §107.601 for registration regulations.
- The new ORGANIC PEROXIDE placard became mandatory 1 January 2011 for transportation by rail, vessel, or aircraft and becomes mandatory 1 January 2014 for transportation by highway. The placard will enable transport workers to readily distinguish peroxides from oxidizers [§172.552].

PLACARDING TABLES
[§172.504(e)]

TABLE 1

Category of material (Hazard Class or division number and additional description, as appropriate)	Placard name
1.1	EXPLOSIVES 1.1
1.2	EXPLOSIVES 1.2
1.3	EXPLOSIVES 1.3
2.3	POISON GAS
4.3	DANGEROUS WHEN WET
5.2 (Organic peroxide, Type B, liquid or solid, temperature controlled.)	ORGANIC PEROXIDE
6.1 (Materials poisonous by inhalation (see §171.8))	POISON INHALATION HAZARD
7 (Radioactive Yellow III label only)	RADIOACTIVE[1]

[1] RADIOACTIVE placard also required for exclusive use shipments of low specific activity material and surface contaminated objects transported in accordance with §173.427(b)(4) and (5) or (c) of the subchapter.

TABLE 2

Category of material (Hazard Class or division number and additional description, as appropriate)	Placard name
1.4	EXPLOSIVES 1.4
1.5	EXPLOSIVES 1.5
1.6	EXPLOSIVES 1.6
2.1	FLAMMABLE GAS
2.2	NON-FLAMMABLE GAS
3	FLAMMABLE
Combustible Liquid	COMBUSTIBLE
4.1	FLAMMABLE SOLID
4.2	SPONTANEOUSLY COMBUSTIBLE
5.1	OXIDIZER
5.2 (Other than organic peroxide, Type B, liquid or solid, temperature controlled)	ORGANIC PEROXIDE
6.1 (Other than materials poisonous by inhalation)	POISON
6.2	(None)
8	CORROSIVE
9	Class 9 (See §172.504(f)(9))
ORM-D	(None)

IDENTIFICATION NUMBER DISPLAYS

§172.332

Appropriate placard must be used with orange panel.

IDENTIFICATION NUMBER MARKINGS ON ORANGE PANELS OR APPROPRIATE PLACARDS MUST BE DISPLAYED ON: (1) Tank Cars, Cargo Tanks, Portable Tanks, and other Bulk Packagings; (2) Transport vehicles or freight containers containing 4,000 kg (8,820 lbs) in non-bulk packages of only a single hazardous material having the same proper shipping name and identification number loaded at one facility and transport vehicle contains no other material, hazardous or otherwise; and (3) transport vehicles or freight containers containing 1,000 kg (2,205 lbs) of non-bulk packages of materials poisonous by inhalation in Hazard Zone A or B. See §§172.301(a)(3), 172.313(c), 172.326, 172.328, 172.330, and 172.331.

§172.527

Square white background required for placard for highway route controlled quantity radioactive material and for rail shipment of certain explosives and poisons, and for flammable gas in a DOT 113 tank car (§172.507 and §172.510).

This Chart is available online at the following link:
http://phmsa.dot.gov/hazmat

U.S. Department of Transportation

Pipeline and Hazardous Materials Safety Administration

USDOT/PHMSA/OHMIT/PHH-50
1200 New Jersey Avenue, SE
Washington, D.C. 20590
Phone: (202) 366-4900
Email: training@dot.gov

PHH50-0143-0214

Figure 13-7. General Guidelines on Use of Warning Labels and Placards.

Placards

Placards are required by the regulations in Part 172. A placard is similar to a label. However, a placard is attached to the outside of the vehicle to show clearly that it contains a load of hazardous materials. The placard for a certain material will be of the same color and wording as its label. Look at Figure 13-8.

You will check to make sure that you have the right placard or placards for the load.

Placards go on each end and each side of the vehicles.

Figure 13-8. How to properly affix placards to a vehicle.

When more than one type of hazmat is being hauled, the vehicle must have more than one type of placard. A single placard reading "Dangerous" is enough when two or more non-bulk packages of material Placard Table 2 are hauled together under these conditions:

- the total weight of any single hazardous material loaded at a single facility doesn't exceed 2,205 pounds
- the cargo isn't being hauled in portable tanks, cargo tanks, or tank cars

When more than one division placard is required for Class 1 materials, you only need the placard for the lowest division number.

Tank vehicles used to haul any hazardous materials must have placards at all times, even when empty. After the tank has been completely cleaned, or reloaded with material that doesn't need placards, the placards can come off. Empty non-bulk packages don't need placards.

If your shipping paper shows your cargo presents a "poison-inhalation hazard," your vehicle must have "Poison" placards on each side and each end, as well as the class placard.

The law requires the shipper to provide the carrier with the right placards for the load. The only exception is if the vehicle is already correctly placarded.

As you have seen, most vehicles must be placarded on all four sides. Here are some that don't:

- tanks with valves, fittings, regulators, or gauges on one end that would hide the placard don't have to placarded on that end
- portable tanks able to hold less than 1,000 gallons need to be placarded on only opposite sides

You've also seen that cargo tanks and portable tanks that were placarded for hazardous materials must still be placarded when emptied. Placards may be removed only when the tank is completely cleaned, or when it's reloaded with a material not needing placards.

There are additional placarding exceptions:

When more than one division placard is required for Class 1 materials on a transport vehicle, rail car, freight container, or unit load device, only the placard representing the lowest division number must be displayed.

A FLAMMABLE placard may be used in place of a COMBUSTIBLE placard on a cargo tank or portable tank or a compartmented tank car that contains both flammable and combustible liquids.

A NON-FLAMMABLE GAS placard is not required on a transport vehicle that contains non-flammable gas if the transport vehicle also contains flammable gas or oxygen and it is placarded with the required FLAMMABLE GAS or OXYGEN placards.

OXIDIZER placards are not required for Division 5.1 materials on freight containers, unit load devices, or transport vehicles that also contain Division 1.1 or 1.2 materials and that are placarded with EXPLOSIVES 1.1 or 1.2 placards.

For transportation by transport vehicle or rail car only, an OXIDIZER placard is not required for Division 5.1 materials on a transport vehicle, rail car, or freight container that also contains Division 1.1 or 1.2 explosives and is placarded with EXPLOSIVES 1.1 or 1.2 placards.

The EXPLOSIVE 1.4 placard is not required for those Division 1.4 Compatibility Group S (1.4S) materials that are not required to be labeled 1.4S.

For domestic transportation of oxygen or compressed oxygen, or refrigerated liquid, the OXYGEN placard may be used in place of a NON-FLAMMABLE GAS placard.

For domestic transportation, a POISON INHALATION HAZARD placard is not required on a transport vehicle or freight container that is already placarded with the POISON GAS placard.

For domestic transportation, a Class 9 placard is not required. A bulk packaging containing a Class 9 material must be marked with the appropriate identification number displayed on a Class 9 placard, an orange panel, or a white-square-on-point display configuration as required by subpart D of this part.

For Division 6.1, Packing Group III materials, a POISON placard may be modified to display the text "PG III" below the mid-line of the placard.

For domestic transportation, a POISON placard is not required on a transport vehicle or freight container required to display a POISON INHALATION HAZARD or POISON GAS placard.

Otherwise, placards must be placed so they can be seen from all directions the vehicle faces. When you're pulling a trailer, one side faces the rear of the tractor or trailer in front of it. That side doesn't need a placard, since no one can see it anyway when the vehicles are coupled.

Placards must be securely attached. They must be clear of ladders, pipes, doors, and tarps that could hide them. They must be placed high enough on the vehicle so the wheels don't spray dirt or water on them. They must be at least three inches away from any other marking on the vehicle. They must be maintained in good condition so they can always be read clearly. Make sure the placard holder doesn't hide any part of the placard except maybe the borders.

Like labels, some placards may include the UN identification number. This should be in the lower corner of the diamond. Placarding requirements are summed up on pages 301–302. Note that the materials in Table 1 (Figure 13-9) must always be placarded as shown in the table. Materials in Table 2 (Figure 13-10) don't have to be placarded when the gross weight of all hazardous materials is less than 1,000 pounds.

TITLE 49 CFR PART 173

This part includes definitions of hazardous materials for the purpose of transporting them. It also gives the requirements for preparing hazardous materials shipments. Inspecting, testing, and retesting requirements are given for those involved in these procedures. Most of the requirements in this part are of interest to shippers. We'll discuss the ones that are important to you, the driver.

Hazardous materials classes are listed in order from most to least dangerous:

- Class 7 (radioactive materials, other than limited quantities)
- Division 2.3 (poisonous gases)
- Division 2.1 (flammable gases)
- Division 2.2 (non-flammable gases)
- Division 6.1 (poisonous liquids), Packing Group I, poisonous-by-inhalation only
- a material that meets the definition of a pyrophoric material
- a material that meets the definition of a self-reactive material
- Class 3 (flammable liquids), Class 8 (corrosive materials), Division 4.1 (flammable solids), Division 4.2 (spontaneously combustible materials), Division 4.3 (dangerous when wet materials), Division 5.1 (oxidizers), or Division 6.1 (poisonous liquids or solids other than Packing Group I, poisonous-by-inhalation)
- Combustible liquids
- Class 9 (miscellaneous hazardous materials)

Fumigated Trucks

Trucks and trailers sometimes haul cargo that has been fumigant or treated with poisonous liquid, solid, or gas. Such vehicles must be placarded with a special "Fumigant" placard. These vehicles may not be transported until the vehicle has been aired out and no longer presents a danger.

Standard Requirements for Packages

In the definition section, you learned that some hazardous materials react dangerously with water, air, heat, or flame—even each other. These materi-

TABLE 1		
Category of material (Hazard class or division number and additional description, as appropriate)	**Placard name**	**Placard design section reference (§)**
1.1	EXPLOSIVES 1.1	172.522
1.2	EXPLOSIVES 1.2	172.522
1.3	EXPLOSIVES 1.3	172.522
2.3	POISON GAS	172.540
4.3	DANGEROUS WHEN WET	172.548
5.2 (Organic peroxide, Type B, liquid or solid, temperature controlled)	ORGANIC PEROXIDE	172.552
6.1 (Material poisonous by inhalation (see §171.8 of this subchapter))	POISON INHALATION HAZARD	172.555
7 (Radioactive Yellow III label only)	RADIOACTIVE[1]	172.556

[1]RADIOACTIVE placard also required for exclusive use shipments of low specific activity material and surface contaminated objects transported in accordance with §173.427(b)(4) and (5) or (c) of the subchapter.

RADIOACTIVE placards are also required for: All shipments of unpackaged LSA-I material or SCO-I; all shipments required by §§173.427, 173.441, and 173.457 of this subchapter to be operated under exclusive use; and all closed vehicles used in accordance with §173.443(d).

Figure 13-9. Table 1.

als come in packages that prevent such reactions. These are marked with DOT package specification marks.

You'll use column 8 of the hazmat table (located on page 291) to make sure that materials are packaged in the proper packaging for truck transport.

Qualification, Maintenance, and Use Of Tanks

Cargo and portable tanks used to haul hazardous materials must meet DOT specifications. Tanks must also meet inspection, retest, and marking requirements. The month and year of the most recent test are stamped into the metal of each tank. Or, it may be stamped on or near the metal certification plate.

Retest and marking of tanks is discussed in more detail in Chapter 12. That chapter also includes the retest schedule for cargo and portable tanks.

Portable tanks that have become worn out or damaged must be retested. So must tanks that have not been used to transport hazardous materials for

a year. Portable tanks must be loaded onto trucks so that no part of the tank sticks out or overhangs.

Hazardous materials that will react with each other must not be loaded together in the same cargo tank.

Qualification, Maintenance, and Use Of Cylinders

Cylinders are built to specification just like tanks. DOT numbers show what the cylinder may be used for. Refer to Figure 13-11 for more details.

Cylinders are also tested. Most of them are retested every five years. Specification 3HT cylinders are retested every three years. Retests are not required for Specification 3C, 4C, and 4L cylinders. The cylinder will be marked with the month and year of the test.

Definitions and Preparation

The remainder of Part 173 has details about the hazardous materials themselves. These include definitions and packaging descriptions that are mostly of interest to shippers. What most driv-

TABLE 2		
Category of material (Hazard class or division number and additional description, as appropriate)	**Placard name**	**Placard design section reference (§)**
1.4	EXPLOSIVES 1.4	172.523
1.5	EXPLOSIVES 1.5	172.524
1.6	EXPLOSIVES 1.6	172.525
2.1	FLAMMABLE GAS	172.532
2.2	NON-FLAMMABLE GAS	172.528
3	FLAMMABLE	172.542
Combustible liquid	COMBUSTIBLE	172.544
4.1	FLAMMABLE SOLID	172.546
4.2	SPONTANEOUSLY COMBUSTIBLE	172.547
5.1	OXIDIZER	172.550
5.2 (Other than organic peroxide, Type B, liquid or solid, temperature controlled)	ORGANIC PEROXIDE	172.552
6.1 (Other than material poisonous by inhalation)	POISON	172.554
6.2	(None)	
8	CORROSIVE	172.558
9	Class 9 (see §172.504(f)(9))	172.560
ORM-D	(None)	

(f) *Additional placarding exceptions.*

(1) When more than one division placard is required for Class 1 materials on a transport vehicle, rail car, freight container, or unit load device, only the placard representing the lowest division number must be displayed.

(2) A FLAMMABLE placard may be used in place of a COMBUSTIBLE placard on—

(i) A cargo tank or portable tank.

(ii) A compartmented tank car which contains both flammable and combustible liquids.

(3) A NON-FLAMMABLE GAS placard is not required on a transport vehicle which contains non-flammable gas if the transport vehicle also contains flammable gas or oxygen and it is placarded with FLAMMABLE GAS or OXYGEN placards, as required.

(4) OXIDIZER placards are not required for Division 5.1 materials on freight containers, unit load devices, transport vehicles, or rail cars which also contain Division 1.1 or 1.2 materials and which are placarded with EXPLOSIVES 1.1 or 1.2 placards, as required.

Figure 13-10. Table 2.

(5) For transportation by transport vehicle or rail car only, an OXIDIZER placard is not required for Division 5.1 materials on a transport vehicle, rail car, or freight container which also contains Division 1.5 explosives and is placarded with EXPLOSIVES 1.5 placards, as required.

(6) The EXPLOSIVE 1.4 placard is not required for those Division 1.4 Compatibility Group S (1.4S) materials that are not required to be labeled 1.4S.

(7) For domestic transportation of oxygen, compressed or oxygen, refrigerated liquid, the OXYGEN placard in §172.530 of this subpart may be used in place of a NON-FLAMMABLE GAS placard.

(8) For domestic transportation, a POISON INHALATION HAZARD placard is not required on a transport vehicle or freight container that is already placarded with the POISON GAS placard.

(9) For Class 9, a CLASS 9 placard is not required for domestic transportation, including that portion of international transportation, defined in §171.8 of this subchapter, which occurs within the United States. However, a bulk packaging must be marked with the appropriate identification number on a CLASS 9 placard, an orange panel, or a white square-on-point display configuration as required by subpart D of this part.

(10) For Division 6.1, PG III materials, a POISON placard may be modified to display the text "PG III" below the mid line of the placard.

(11) For domestic transportation, a POISON placard is not required on a transport vehicle or freight container required to display a POISON INHALATION HAZARD or POISON GAS placard.

(g) For shipments of Class 1 (explosive materials) by aircraft or vessel, the applicable compatibility group letter must be displayed on the placards, or labels when applicable, required by this section. When more than one compatibility group placard is required for Class 1 materials, only one placard is required to be displayed, as provided in paragraphs (g)(1) through (g)(4) of this section. For the purposes of paragraphs (g)(1) through (g)(4), there is a distinction between the phrases *explosive articles* and *explosive substances*. *Explosive article* means an article containing an explosive substance; examples include a detonator, flare, primer, or fuse. *Explosive substance* means a substance contained in a packaging that is not contained in an article; examples include black powder and smokeless powder.

(1) Explosive articles of compatibility groups C, D, or E may be placarded displaying compatibility group E.

(2) Explosive articles of compatibility groups C, D, or E, when transported with those in compatibility group N, may be placarded displaying compatibility group D.

(3) Explosive substances of compatibility groups C and D may be placarded displaying compatibility group D.

(4) Explosive articles of compatibility groups C, D, E, or G, except for fireworks, may be placarded displaying compatibility group E.

Figure 13-10. (cont'd.)

Cylinders made in compliance with-	Used exclusively for-
DOT-3A, DOT-3AA, DOT-3A480X, DOT-4AA480	Anhydrous ammonia of at least 99.95% purity.
DOT-3A, DOT-3AA, DOT-3A480X, DOT-3B, DOT-4B, DOT-4BA, DOT-4BW	Butadiene, inhibited, which is commercially free from corroding components.
DOT-3A, DOT-3A480X, DOT-3AA, DOT-3B, DOT-4AA480, DOT-4B, DOT-4BA, DOT-4BW	Cyclopropane which is commercially free from corroding components.
DOT 3A, DOT 3AA, DOT 3A480X, DOT 4B, DOT 4BA, DOT 4BW, DOT 4E	Chlorinated hydrocarbons and mixtures thereof that are commercially free from corroding components.
DOT-3A, DOT-3AA, DOT-3A480X, DOT-3B, DOT-4BA, DOT-4BW, DOT-4E	Fluorinated hydrocarbons and mixtures thereof which are commercially free from corroding components.
DOT-3A, DOT-3AA, DOT-3A480X, DOT-3B, DOT-4B, DOT-4BA, DOT-4BW, DOT-4E	Liquified hydrocarbon gas which is commercially free from corroding components.
DOT-3A, DOT-3AA, DOT-3A480X, DOT-3B, DOT-4B, DOT-4BA, DOT-4BW, DOT-4E	Liquified petroleum gas that meets the detail requirements limits in Table 1 of ASTM 1835, Standard Specification for Liquefied Petroleum (LP) Gases (incorporated by reference; see Sec. 171.7 of this subchapter) or an equivalent standard containing the same limits.
DOT-3A, DOT-3AA, DOT-3B, DOT-4B, DOT-4BA, DOT-4BW, DOT-4E	Methylacetylene-propadiene, stabilized, which is commercially free from corroding components.
DOT-3A, DOT-3AA, DOT-3B, DOT-4B, DOT-4BA, DOT-4BW	Anhydrous mono, di, trimethylamines which are commercially free from corroding components.
DOT4B240, DOT-4BW240	Ethylene imine, inhibited.

Figure 13-11. Chart of cylinder use (from Title 49 CFR 180.209).

ers need to know about the hazardous materials themselves was covered in Chapter 6, and in the "definitions" section of this chapter. What follows are some other important points of information not covered in Chapter 6.

Explosives. Explosives are chemical compounds, mixtures, or devices that explode. Division 1.1 explosives are the most dangerous. Division 1.2 explosives are less dangerous. They don't explode. Instead, they burn rapidly. Of the three, Division 1.6 explosives present the least danger. They are the least dangerous of all. They're not likely to explode by accident.

Leaking or damaged packages of explosives are forbidden. So are loaded firearms. Other explosives forbidden for transport are:

- An explosive mixture or device containing a chlorate and also containing: an ammonium salt, including a substituted ammonium or quaternary ammonium salt; or an acidic substance, including a salt of a weak base and a strong acid
- propellants that are unstable, condemned, or deteriorated
- nitroglycerin, diethylene glycol dinitrate, or any other liquid explosives not specifically authorized by this subchapter
- fireworks that combine an explosive and a detonator, or fireworks containing yellow or white phosphorus
- a toy torpedo, the maximum outside dimension of which exceeds 23 mm (0.906 inch), or a toy torpedo containing a mixture of potassium chlorate, black antimony (antimony sulfide), and sulfur, if the weight of the explosive material in the device exceeds 0.26 g (0.01 ounce)
- an explosive article with its means of initiation or ignition installed, unless otherwise approved

Don't transport these hazardous materials. Explosives can be very dangerous if not handled properly. The packages may be marked with special instructions and warnings. Examples are "This Side Up" and "Do Not Store Or Load With Any High Explosive." These warnings help all those involved in the shipment to handle the explosives safely.

Hazard zones. Certain materials always present an inhalation danger. The degree of danger is described by its hazard zone rating. Hazard Zone A is the most dangerous, while Hazard Zone D is the least.

Flammable, combustible, and pyrophoric liquids. A flammable liquid is one with a flash point that is not more than 140 degrees Fahrenheit, or any material in a liquid phase with a flash point at or above 100 degrees Fahrenheit that is intentionally heated and offered for transportation or transported at or above its flash point in a bulk packaging. A combustible liquid has a flash point at or above 140 degrees and below 200 degrees Fahrenheit. Liquids with higher flash points can still burn. They are not termed flammable or combustible in this setting. Still, you would not use "non-flammable" or "non-combustible" markings on your vehicle when hauling these materials.

A pyrophoric liquid is one that will ignite by itself within five minutes of coming into contact with the air.

The flash points determine the packing group (column 5 on the hazmat table).

Flammable solids, oxidizers, and organic peroxides. A flammable solid is a solid material, other than an explosive, that can cause a fire. The fire can start from friction. Or, the material might retain heat from manufacturing or processing. This heat can start a fire. These materials may also burn when combined with water.

Oxidizers throw off oxygen. This in turn causes other materials to burn.

Organic peroxides are not all that dangerous by themselves. But they do release a lot of oxygen. Around a spark or flame, they become very dangerous. Having organic peroxides near a fire is like adding gasoline to the flames. Sparks from your vehicle's electric system or friction from an overheated tire could start a fire. Organic peroxides could turn a small fire into a major disaster. That makes them dangerous to transport.

Corrosive materials. A corrosive is a solid or liquid that harms human skin on contact. Corrosives can dissolve metal and other materials, too. In fact, corrosion rates are determined by the material's effect on steel. Still, it's the damage to human skin that is used in the definition.

Gases. Compressed gases are held under pressure. When in the container, compressed gases have an absolute pressure of more than 40 psi (that is, 40 psia) at 68 degrees Fahrenheit.

Compressed gas is said to be flammable if:

- a mixture of 13 percent or less will form a flammable mixture when combined with air
- it passes an American Society for Testing and Materials explosives test for flammability

Compressed gas in solution. A compressed gas in solution is a nonliquefied compressed gas that is dissolved in a solvent.

Cryogenic liquid is a coolant gas. It will boil at minus 130 degrees Fahrenheit when it's at 14.7 psi absolute.

This class of hazardous materials also includes refrigerant gases and dispersant gases. These are compressed gases. Some are flammable, and some are non-flammable.

Title 49 CFR Part 173 lists filling densities for transporting compressed gases in cargo and portable tank containers. Filling densities were covered in Chapter 12.

Poisons, irritating materials, etiologic agents, and radioactive materials. There are two divisions of poison: 6.1 and 6.2. Poison Division 6.1 is a material other than a gas. Of the two divisions, 6.1 is the most dangerous. Just a small amount in the air can kill. Poison Division 6.2 are biohazards.

Irritating materials are liquid or solid. When exposed to air or flames, they give off dangerous fumes.

Etiologic agents are microorganisms (germs). They cause disease.

Radioactive materials give off dangerous rays. Some radioactive materials give off strong rays. Others are weak. Different type packages will be used based on the type of radioactive material they are to contain.

Other regulated materials. "Other regulated materials" are those that don't meet any of the other definitions. Still, they are dangerous when transported in commerce. So, they must be regulated to protect the public. ORM-D is an ordinary consumer item. It's dangerous in transport because of its form, amount, or because of the way it's packaged.

Part 173 contains other regulations and exceptions for a variety of materials, such as nitric acid, wet batteries, chemical kits, matches, asbestos, cigarette lighters, fire extinguishers—the list goes on. As a driver hauling hazmat, you should be familiar with Part 173 as it relates to the cargo you're carrying.

TITLE 49 CFR PART 177

Part 177 lists more requirements for private, common, or contract carriers for the transport of hazardous materials by motor vehicle.

General Requirements

Carriers must comply with state and federal regulations. They must instruct their employees about these regulations and how to comply with them.

Packages, vehicles, documents, shippers, carriers, and drivers must all meet the requirements of Title 49 CFR Parts 170 to 189, and 390 to 397 (the FMCSR).

Shipping paper accessibility. Shipping papers must have the shipper's certification. They must be marked differently from shipping papers for regular cargo. Or, the hazmat shipping papers can be placed on the top of a stack of cargo documents.

Drivers must carry these shipping papers so they are easy to get. When you're at the vehicle's controls, the shipping paper must be within your easy reach when you're wearing a seat belt. They can also be kept in the holder mounted on the inside of the driver's door. They must be where they can be easily seen by someone looking into the cab.

When you're not at the vehicle's controls, the shipping paper must be in the holder or on the driver's seat. These requirements are so that authorities can get to the shipping papers in case of an accident, or for an inspection.

Loading and Unloading

General requirements. Like any other cargo, hazardous materials packages must be loaded securely. Never load hazardous materials on a pole trailer. Don't you smoke or let anyone nearby smoke while loading and unloading explosives, flammable liquids, solids or compressed gas, or oxidizers. Don't let any fire or flame get near these hazardous materials. That includes matches, lighters, cigars, and pipes, as well as cigarettes. Keep the hand brake on at all times when loading and unloading hazardous materials.

Don't use any tools that could puncture, dent, or damage hazmat packages.

You must be aware of the temperature of the hazmat containers and their contents and prevent any increase. Some materials must be maintained at a specific temperature called the control temperature. These are transported in vehicles specially designed for that purpose.

A cargo tank must be attended by a qualified person at all times when it is being loaded. The person responsible for loading the cargo tank is also responsible for seeing that it is attended.

A cargo tank must be attended by a qualified person at all times when it is being unloaded, too. This is not necessary when the cargo tank is on the consignee's property. This responsibility also ends if the power unit has been separated from the cargo tank and removed. When the job of transporting the materials is complete, the carrier is no longer responsible for them. This includes having to attend the unloading.

The meaning of "attendance" here is not quite the same as in FMCSR Part 397. Remember what that was? Here, you must have a clear view of the vehicle. You must be qualified. This term, too, has a specific meaning. It means that you must know about the danger and know emergency procedures. You must be authorized and able to move the vehicle. The difference with hazmat is you must be within 25 feet of the vehicle to attend it.

Some hazardous materials may not be loaded together with other hazardous materials. The prohibited combinations are listed in the Segregation and Separation Chart. Figure 13-12 shows some examples.

Keep cargo tank manholes and valves closed while driving.

You may not use a cargo heater when you transport certain hazardous materials. When you're hauling explosives, you have to go farther. You must drain or remove the heater fuel tank. Then you must disconnect the heater's power source. This is so that there is no chance the heater will be used at all, even by mistake.

Explosives. Don't load explosives with the engine running. Don't use metal tools when you handle explosives. Don't roll the packages. Don't throw them or drop them. Keep packages of explosives away from sparks, flames, even the heat of exhaust gases. If you tarp a load of explosives, use rope or wire tiedowns.

Don't load Division 1.1 or 1.2 explosives into combinations of more than two cargo carrying vehicles. You may also not load Division 1.1 or 1.2 explosives when one of your trailers is a full trailer with a wheel base shorter than 184 inches. Also, if one of your vehicles is a cargo tank with placards, you may not load Division 1.1 or 1.2 explosives. You can't transport Division 1.1 or 1.2 explosives if your other cargo is any of these:

- explosive substances, N.O.S., Division 1.1A (explosive) material (Initiating explosive),
- packages of Class 7 (radioactive) materials bearing "Yellow III" labels,
- Division 2.3 (poisonous gas) or Division 6.1 (poisonous) materials, or
- hazardous materials in a portable tank or a DOT specification 106A or 110A tank

Check the inside of the vehicle. Don't load explosives if there are sharp bolts, screws, nails, or the like sticking out. They could puncture the packages of explosives. The floors must be tight, and lined to keep dust, powder, or vapor from leaking. The lining must not be made of iron or steel.

Don't load detonators with Division 1.1, 1.2, 1.3, 1.4, or 1.5 explosives unless the detonators are specially packaged for this.

Protect the cargo. Load explosives so they are completely contained in the vehicle, or covered by a tarp. They should not stick out at any point. If your vehicle has a tailgate, you must be able to close it securely. Make sure any other cargo that makes up the load won't damage the explosives.

You may transfer explosives from one container or vehicle to another while on the public highway only in an emergency. If such an emergency occurs, you must remember to put out your warning devices.

Flammable liquids. Stop the engine. Load and unload flammable liquids with the engine off. You

Class or division		Notes	1.1 1.2	1.3	1.4	1.5	1.6	2.1	2.2	2.3 gas zone A	2.3 gas Zone B	3	4.1	4.2	4.3	5.1	5.2	6.1 liquids PG I zone A	7	8 liquids only
Segregation Table for Hazardous Materials																				
Explosives	1.1 and 1.2	A	*	*	*	*	*	X	X	X	X	X	X	X	X	X	X	X	X	X
Explosives	1.3		*	*	*	*	*	X		X	X	X		X	X	X	X	X		X
Explosives	1.4		*	*	*	*	*	O		O	O	O		O				O		O
Very insensitive explosives	1.5	A	*	*	*	*	*	X	X	X	X	X	X	X	X	X	X	X	X	X
Extremely insensitive explosives	1.6		*	*	*	*	*													
Flammable gases	2.1		X	X	O	X				X	O							O	O	
Non-toxic, non-flammable gases	2.2		X			X														
Poisonous gas Zone A	2.3		X	X	O	X		X				X	X	X	X	X	X			X
Poisonous gas Zone B	2.3		X	X	O	X		O				O	O	O	O	O	O			O
Flammable liquids	3		X	X	O	X				X	O					O		X		
Flammable solids	4.1		X			X				X	O							X		O
Spontaneously combustible materials	4.2		X	X	O	X				X	O							X		X
Dangerous when wet materials	4.3		X	X		X				X	O							X		O
Oxidizers	5.1	A	X	X		X				X	O	O						X		O
Organic peroxides	5.2		X	X		X				X	O							X		O
Poisonous liquids PG I Zone A	6.1		X	X	O	X		O				X	X	X	X	X	X			X
Radioactive materials	7		X			X		O												
Corrosive liquids	8		X	X	O	X				X	O		O	X	O	O	O	X		

Figure 13-12. Segregation and Separation Chart.

Instructions for using the Segregation Table for Hazardous Materials are as follows:

(1) The absence of any hazard class or division or a blank space in the table indicates that no restrictions apply.

(2) The letter "X" in the table indicates that these materials may not be loaded, transported, or stored together in the same transport vehicle or storage facility during the course of transportation.

(3) The letter "O" in the table indicates that these materials may not be loaded, transported, or stored together in the same transport vehicle or storage facility during the course of transportation unless separated in a manner that, in the event of leakage from packages under conditions normally incident to transportation, commingling of hazardous materials would not occur. Notwithstanding the methods of separation employed, Class 8 (corrosive) liquids may not be loaded above or adjacent to Class 4 (flammable) or Class 5 (oxidizing) materials; except that shippers may load truckload shipments of such materials together when it is known that the mixture of contents would not cause a fire or a dangerous evolution of heat or gas.

(4) The "*" in the table indicates that segregation among different Class 1 (explosive) materials is governed by the compatibility table.

(5) The note "A" in the Notes column of the table means that, notwithstanding the requirements of the letter "X," ammonium nitrate (UN 1942) and ammonium nitrate fertilizer may be loaded or stored with Division 1.1 (explosive) or Division 1.5 materials.

(6) When the §172.101 table or §172.402 of this subchapter requires a package to bear a subsidiary hazard label, segregation appropriate to the subsidiary hazard must be applied when that segregation is more restrictive than that required by the primary hazard. However, hazardous materials of the same class may be stowed together without regard to segregation required for any secondary hazard if the materials are not capable of reacting dangerously with each other and causing combustion or dangerous evolution of heat, evolution of flammable, poisonous, or asphyxiant gases, or the formation of corrosive or unstable materials.

DO NOT LOAD . . .	IN THE SAME VEHICLE WITH . . .
Division 6.1 or 2.3 (POISON or poisonous inhalation hazard) labeled material	animal or human food unless the poison package is overpacked in an approved way. Foodstuff is anything you swallow. However, mouthwash, toothpaste, and skin creams are not foodstuff.
Division 2.3 (POISONOUS) Zone A or 6.1 PG1 Zone A	oxidizers, flammables, corrosives, organic peroxides.
Charged storage batteries	Division 1.1 explosives.
Class 1 detonating primers	any other explosives unless in authorized containers or packaging.
Division 6.1 cyanides or cyanide mixtures	acids, corrosive materials, or other acidic materials that could generate hydrogen cyanide. Cyanides are materials with the letters CYAN as part of their shipping name. For example: Acetone Cyanohydrin, Silver Cyanide, Trichloroisocyanuric acid.
Nitric acid (Class B)	Other corrosive liquids in carboys, unless separated from them in an approved way.

Figure 13-12. (cont'd.)

may only have the engine running if you need it to run a pump.

Guard against static. You must have a ground if the flammable liquids are in separate metal containers.

 Review Chapter 6 for an explanation of grounding. Otherwise, static electricity might create enough of a spark to ignite the flammable liquid.

Close manholes and valves. Do not drive a cargo tank carrying flammable liquid with the manhole cover or valves open. Make sure all liquid discharge systems are free of leaks.

Flammable solids and oxidizers. Protect the cargo. As with explosives, flammable solids and oxidizers must be completely contained and secured in the vehicle, or covered by a tarp. If your vehicle has tailgates, you must be able to close and secure them. You should have no part of the cargo sticking out.

Keep the cargo dry. Flammable solids and oxidizers may be especially dangerous when wet.

Guard against heat. This type of cargo can ignite or explode if it gets hot. Make sure you have room around the packages for air to circulate. This helps keep them from overheating. Also, it reduces the chance of friction between the packages creating heat and starting a fire.

Load bagged ground, crushed, granulated, or pulverized charcoal (known as charcoal screening) so that the bags are laid horizontally and piled so that there will be spaces for effective air circulation. Those spaces shall not be less than 3.9 inches wide. Maintain air space between the rows. Don't pile the bags; and air spaces shall be maintained between rows of bags. Bags should be no closer than 5.9 inches from the top of any motor vehicle with a closed body.

Don't load nitrates in an all-metal vehicle other than a closed one of aluminum or aluminum alloy.

Corrosive liquids. Nitric acid must be loaded on the floor of the vehicle. Don't load packages of nitric acid on top of anything else.

You may load such containers of corrosive liquids higher than one tier, but only if the containers are in a protective crate or box. Don't load them so high that the stack is unstable. Make sure the floor is even so these containers won't tip over and break. You might need a false floor to provide a level surface.

All storage batteries containing any electrolyte must be loaded so that all such batteries will be protected against any other lading falling onto or against them. Protect and insulate battery terminals against short circuits.

Compressed Gases. Start with a flat surface. Compressed gas cylinders must have a flat, level surface. Your vehicle might have racks designed to carry compressed gas cylinders. In that case, you don't have to be concerned about the floor.

Secure cylinders in an upright position. Strap them in, or block and brace them in place. The same rules apply to portable tanks.

There are special rules for cylinders of hydrogen and cryogenic liquids. You may only transport these in special racks. You may only have a certain amount in your vehicle at one time. You must never enter a tunnel when you have these cylinders on your vehicle. Stop before crossing a railroad if your vehicle carries any amount of chlorine.

Only private and contract carriers are allowed to transport these materials. Then, the cargo must travel directly from origin to destination.

Load and unload these materials with the engine off. You may only have it on if you need it to run a pump. Then, you must turn it off before you disconnect the filling or discharge lines. If your vehicle has shut-off valves in the discharge end of the delivery hose, you may leave the engine running.

Figure 13-13. Close the cargo tank liquid discharge valve, except when loading and unloading.

You must have a gas mask when you're hauling chlorine in a cargo tank. Also, you must have an emergency kit to control leaks. Before you couple or uncouple your tank, you must detach any loading and unloading connections. Never leave the tank uncoupled from the tractor without chocking it first. Always close the liquid discharge valves on cargo tanks. The only time you should have them open is during loading and unloading. The unloading of these vehicles is done under close attendance by a qualified person.

Avoid delays. You may haul flammable cryogenic liquid in a package that holds more than 125 gallons (of water). When you do, you must be extra careful to avoid trip delays. Should you be delayed and notice a rise in pressure, get to a remote and safe location. Then vent the tank to relieve the excess pressure.

For each shipment of this type, you must make a written record of the cargo tank pressure and the outside temperature. Make this record at these times:

- at the start of each trip
- right before and after any manual venting
- at least once every five hours
- when you reach your destination

When you transport flammable cryogenic liquid in a cargo tank, the pressure must not exceed the marked rated hold time (MRHT). You must complete your trip from start to finish within the one-way travel time (OWTT). You'll find these figures marked on the tank. Your trip may take longer than the OWTT if you can stop and get the tank equilibrated. This is a pressure-balancing operation that may only be done where cryogenic liquids are loaded and unloaded. It's performed under tight controls.

Poisons. You must load arsenic only at places where the poisonous dust won't get into the air and hurt people. You must never do this on a public highway or in a public place.

You may not use a vehicle that had arsenic in it for anything else until it's been completely cleaned.

You may not haul a Division 2.3 (poisonous gas) or Division 6.1 (poisonous) material if there is any interconnection between packaging.

Never load materials labeled POISON or POISON INHALATION HAZARD with other cargo meant to be eaten by people or animals. The only exception is when the poison is overpacked in a dust-proof and liquid-tight package.

Radioactive material. The number of packages of radioactive materials you can have in your vehicle is controlled by a transport index number. You must not load more than 50.

Some radioactive packages are labeled "Yellow II" or "Yellow III." Load these according to the separation distances table shown below, Figure 13-14.

Neither you nor anyone else should be in a vehicle with radioactive materials unless they must.

Don't load fissile Class 7 materials with other fissile radioactive shipments. Load them at least 20 feet from other "radioactive" packages.

Separation and Segregation. As you saw earlier, you must not load certain combinations of hazardous materials. Refer to Figure 13-12 to see what some of these are.

Shipments in Transit, Accidents

Delays in delivery. When you're hauling hazardous materials, avoid delays in making delivery.

Total transport index	Minimum separation distances in feet to nearest undeveloped film for various times of transit					Minimum distance in feet to area of persons, or minimum distance in feet from dividing partition of cargo compartments
	Up to 2 hours	2-4 hours	4-8 hours	8-12 hours	Over 12 hours	
None	0	0	0	0	0	0
0.1 to 1.0	1	2	3	4	5	1
1.1 to 5.0	3	4	6	8	11	2
5.1 to 10.0	4	6	9	11	15	3
10.1 to 20.0	5	8	12	16	22	4
20.1 to 30.0	7	10	15	20	29	5
30.1 to 40.0	8	11	17	22	33	6
40.1 to 50.0	9	12	19	24	36	7

Note: The distance in the table must be measured from the nearest point on the packages of radioactive materials.

Figure 13-14. Separation distances table.

Disabled vehicle. In spite of your best efforts, your vehicle could break down en route. If this happens, make an extra special effort to protect your load of hazmat. Protect others from your load. Make every attempt to move the vehicle out of harm's way.

Broken packages. If you find broken or leaking packages en route, you may try to repair them if it will be safe to do that. You may send them on to the destination or back to the shipper in a salvage drum. If you do repair or repackage the hazmat, you must do such a good job that the hazmat is now safe to transport. The repaired package must not leak and spoil other cargo. Mark the repaired package clearly with the consignee's name.

If you can't repair the package, you must find a safe place to store the hazmat as quickly as possible. Don't dispose of it yourself.

Emergency stops. When hauling certain hazardous materials, you must not stop on the traveled part of the highway for any reason except for normal traffic stops. The hazardous materials in question are:

- flammable liquids and solids
- oxidizers
- corrosives
- compressed gases
- poisons

If you do stop, you must put out your warning devices.

If your vehicle is a cargo tank carrying flammable liquids or flammable compressed gases, you must do the same. This is true even if the vehicle is empty.

Put out your warning devices if you stop for any reason other than a normal traffic stop while hauling Division 1.1, 1.2, and 1.3 explosives.

Vehicle repair and maintenance. You may not use heat, flames, or devices that produce sparks to repair or maintain the cargo area or fuel system of your vehicle when you have a placarded load. No one is allowed to work on the vehicle inside a building unless the cargo area and fuel system are closed and not leaking. While the work is being done, there must be someone able to move the vehicle immediately if that becomes necessary. The vehicle must be removed from the building as soon as the work is done.

Special rules apply when your vehicle has Division 1.1, 1.2, or 1.3 explosives, or Class 3 (flammable liquids) or Division 2.1 (flammable gases). In that case, any source of flames, sparks, or glowing heat inside the building must be turned off.

Your cargo tank must be free of gas before it can be welded or repaired with a flame-producing device. This applies to cargo tanks that transport Class 3 or Division 6.1 hazmat.

TITLE 49 CFR PART 178

The regulations in Part 178 deal with shipping containers. They set specifications for manufacturing and testing containers used in hazardous materials transportation. In this part, a shipping container can be anything from one carboy to an entire cargo tank.

Most of the regulations in this part are of concern to manufacturers and shippers. We'll go into detail on those of particular interest to the driver. As always, though, you should be thoroughly familiar with all the regulations that relate to your driving job.

Part 178 requires manufacturers to mark authorized containers with a DOT specification. This includes not only portable and cargo tanks, but cylinders, drums, and so forth. These containers may also be marked with the UN symbols and packaging identification codes you've already read about.

The last section of Chapter 12 covered the design, construction, retesting, and marking of portable and cargo tanks in detail. We won't repeat that information here. If you plan to haul hazardous materials in these, you need a Tank Vehicle Endorsement. If you haven't already, read Chapter 12.

In this section, you'll find information about other hazmat containers that the driver needs to know.

Carboys, Jugs, and Drums

The DOT specification code for most carboys, jugs, and drums begins with the number 1, followed by a letter. These containers will be marked with the DOT specification code. You may find other markings, such as the manufacturer's name and the date of manufacture. You will find the capacity of the container marked on the outside as well. Markings may be printed or stamped on the container. You may also find them on a metal plate attached to the container.

These containers are tested when they are first made. The retesting requirements are different from the ones that apply to portable and cargo tanks. So you won't usually find a retest marking on them.

Inside Containers and Linings

The DOT specification code for inside containers and linings begins with the number 2, followed by a letter. Other markings include the manufacturer's name, date of manufacture, and capacity.

Cylinders

The DOT specification code for most cylinders is the number 3 or 4, plus one or two letters, and possibly some more numbers. Other markings include the service pressure and a serial number. You may also find the official mark of the official who inspected the cylinder, and the date of the test.

DOT specification requirements for compressed gas cylinders include pressure relief device systems. Most cylinders are retested for service pressure every five years. Some may be retested every 10 years instead. They're also inspected internally and externally. Then they're marked with the retest date and the retester's identification number. Figure 13-15 shows one way this marking may appear. You may also find this information near the serial number.

Figure 13-15. Cylinder markings.

Portable Tanks

Portable tanks are DOT Specification 51, 56, 57, 60, IM 101, or IM 102.

Chapter 12 has more information on portable tank construction, retesting, and marking.

Cargo Tanks

Cargo tanks are DOT specification MC, followed by numbers.

Chapter 12 has more information on cargo tank construction, retesting, and marking.

General Packaging

General packaging is DOT Specification 7A. In addition to this code, you'll see the marking "USA DOT 7A Type A."

OTHER HAZARDOUS MATERIALS REGULATIONS

Title 49 CFR Part 179 describes the specifications for tanks that are to be mounted on or form part of a tank car and that transport hazardous materials in commerce. Some tank cars may have markings in addition to the ones you've already read about. The requirements for these markings are specified in this part. If you are pulling tank cars, you may wish to read this part to learn more about the construction, maintenance, repair, testing, and safety features of these vehicles.

Title 49 CFR Part 180 describes requirements pertaining to the maintenance, reconditioning, repair, inspection, and testing of cylinders, cargo tanks, and tank cars. These are requirements in addition to those contained in Parts 107, 171, 172, 173, and 178.

Title 49 CFR Part 392 deals with the driving of vehicles. Much of Part 392 was covered in Chapter 6. There is one section of this part that has to do with hauling hazardous materials, though. It tells you what to do at railroad grade crossings. These rules apply when your vehicle is placarded:

- Division 1.1
- Division 1.2 or 1.3
- Division 2.3 Poison gas
- Division 4.3
- Class 7
- Class 3 Flammable
- Division 5.1
- Division 2.2
- Division 2.3 Chlorine
- Division 6.1 Poison
- Division 2.2 Oxygen
- Division 2.1
- Class 3 Combustible liquid
- Division 4.1
- Division 5.1
- Division 5.2
- Class 8
- Division 1.4

This also applies any time you haul any amount of chlorine. Cargo tanks used for hazardous materials, whether full or empty, must also be brought to a stop before crossing railroad tracks.

You must not cross such a grade without stopping first. Stop within 50 feet of the track, but not any closer than 15 feet. Listen and look in both directions for an oncoming train. Make certain no train is approaching. When it is safe to proceed, you may cross the track. You must be in a gear that will let you get all the way across the track without changing gears. This is because you must not shift gears while crossing the track.

You need not stop at:

- a streetcar crossing or railroad tracks used exclusively for industrial switching purposes within a business district as defined in Part 390.5
- a railroad grade crossing when a police officer or crossing flagman directs traffic to proceed
- a railroad grade crossing controlled by a functioning highway traffic signal transmitting a green signal that, under local law, permits the CMV to proceed across the railroad tracks without slowing or stopping
- an abandoned railroad grade crossing that is marked with a sign indicating that the rail line is abandoned
- an industrial or spur line railroad grade crossing marked with an official sign reading "Exempt"

HAZARDOUS MATERIALS HANDLING

Many of the regulations you just read tell you how to handle hazardous materials safely. When you know and comply with these regulations, you can feel sure you are handling hazardous materials properly.

To review, here are some of the key issues in handling hazmat.

Forbidden Materials and Packages

Some materials are so hazardous, they must never be transported by common carrier by motor vehicle. Nitroglycerin is one example. If an item is "forbidden," it will be listed that way in column 3 (Hazard Class) of the Hazardous Materials Table.

Leaking or damaged packages of explosives are forbidden. So are loaded firearms. Don't transport these hazardous materials.

Loading and Unloading Materials

Do all you can to protect containers of hazardous materials. Don't use any tools that might damage containers or other packaging during loading. Don't use hooks.

Before loading or unloading, set the parking brake. Make sure the vehicle will not move.

Many products are more hazardous in the heat. Load hazardous materials away from heat sources.

Watch for signs of leaking or damaged containers. Do not transport leaking packages. Depending on the material, you, your truck, and others could be in danger.

Don't smoke! When loading hazardous materials, keep fire away. Don't let people smoke nearby. Never smoke around explosives, oxidizers, or flammables.

Secure packages against movement. Make sure containers don't move around in transit. Brace them so they will not fall, slide, or bounce around. Be very careful when loading containers that have valves or other fittings.

Don't open any package between the points of origin and destination. Never transfer hazardous products from one package to another. You may empty a cargo tank, but do not empty any other package while it is on the vehicle.

The rules usually forbid the use of cargo heaters, including automatic cargo heaters or air conditioner units. Unless you have read all the related rules, don't load the explosives, flammable liquids, and flammable gases in a cargo space that has a heater.

Use closed cargo space. You cannot have overhang or tailgate loads of explosives, flammable solids, and oxidizers. You must load these hazards into a closed cargo space unless all packages are:

- fire and water resistant, or
- covered with a fire and water resistant tarp.

Before loading or unloading any explosive, turn your engine off. Then check the cargo space. You must disable cargo heaters. Disconnect heater power sources and drain heater fuel tanks. There must be no sharp points that might damage cargo. Look for bolts, screws, nails, broken side panels, and broken floor boards.

Use a floor lining with Division 1.1, 1.2, or 1.3 explosives. The floors must be tight and the liner must not contain steel or iron.

Use extra care to protect explosives. Never use hooks or other metal tools. Never drop, throw, or roll the shipment. Protect explosive packages from other cargo that might cause damage.

Do not transfer a Division 1.1, 1.2, or 1.3 explosive from one vehicle to another on a public roadway except in an emergency. If safety requires an emergency transfer, set out red warning reflectors, flags, or electric lanterns. You must warn other highway users.

Never transport damaged packages of explosives. Do not take a package that shows any dampness or oily stain.

You might load breakable containers of corrosive liquids by hand. If so, load them one by one. Keep them right side up. Do not drop or roll the containers. Load them onto an even floor surface.

Load charged storage batteries so their liquid won't spill. Keep them right side up. Make sure other cargo won't fall against or short-circuit them.

If your vehicle doesn't have racks to hold cylinders, the cargo space floor must be flat. If not in a rack, the cylinders must be held upright or braced lying down flat, or in boxes that will keep them from turning over.

Cargo Segregation

Some types of hazardous materials should never be put with other types in the same load.

Do not transport Division 1.1 or 1.2 explosives in triples. Do not transport this class of explosives in vehicle combinations if:

- there is a placarded cargo tank in the combination, or
- the other vehicle in the combination contains initiating explosives, radioactive materials labeled "Yellow III," Division 2.3 (poison gas) or Division 6.1 (poison) or hazardous materials in a portable tank, DOT 106A or 110A tank.

Do not load nitric acid above any other product. Never load corrosive liquids next to or above:

- Class 4 (flammable)
- Class 5 (oxidizing)

Never transport Poison Division 6.1 or irritating materials in containers with interconnections. Never load a package labeled "Poison," "Poison Gas," or "Irritant" in the driver's cab or sleeper. Never load these materials with food meant for humans or animals.

Some packages of radioactive materials bear a number called the transport index. This is the amount of radiation that surrounds each package and passes through packaging nearby. The shipper prints the package's transport index on the label. The total transport index of all packages in a single vehicle must not exceed 50. There are also rules as to how long and how close you can load radioactive products to people, animals, or film.

The regulations name other materials you must keep apart. Refer to the Segregation and Separation Chart (see Figure 13-12) when in doubt about what's allowed.

Attendance and Safe Havens

You can leave your vehicle unattended in a safe haven. A safe haven is a government-approved place for parking unattended vehicles loaded with explosives.

Otherwise, someone must always be "attending" the vehicle. The person watching a placarded vehicle must:

- be in the vehicle, awake and not in the sleeper berth, or within 100 feet of the vehicle and within clear view of it,
- be aware of the hazards,
- know what to do in emergencies, and
- be able to move the vehicle if needed.

Parking

Never park with Division 1.1, 1.2, or 1.3 explosives within five feet of the traveled part of the road. Unless your work requires it, do not park within 300 feet of:

- a bridge, tunnel, or building,
- a place where people gather, or
- an open fire.

If you must park to do your job, do so only briefly.

Don't park on private property unless the owner is aware of the danger. Someone must always watch the parked vehicle. You may let someone else watch it for you only if your vehicle is

- on the shipper's property, or
- on the carrier's property, or
- on the consignee's property.

You may park a placarded vehicle (not carrying explosives) within five feet of the traveled part of the road only if your work requires it. Do so only briefly. Someone must always watch the vehicle when parked on a public roadway or shoulder. Do not park within 300 feet of an open fire.

Routes

Some states and counties require permits to transport hazardous material or waste. They may limit the routes you can use. Local rules about routes and permits change often. As the driver, it's your job to find out if you need permits or must use special routes. Make sure you have all needed papers before starting.

If you work for a carrier, ask your dispatcher about route limits or permits. If you are an independent and are planning a new route, check with state agencies where you plan to travel. Some localities prohibit transportation of hazardous materials through tunnels, over bridges, or other roadways. Check before you start.

When your vehicle is placarded, avoid heavily populated areas, crowds, tunnels, narrow streets, and alleys. Take other routes, even if inconvenient, unless there is no other way. Never drive a placarded vehicle near open fires unless you can safely pass without stopping.

If transporting Division 1.1, 1.2, or 1.3 explosives, you must have a written route plan and follow that plan. Carriers prepare the route plan in advance and give the driver a copy. You may plan the route yourself if you pick up the explosives at a location other than your employer's terminal. Write out the plan in advance. Keep a copy of it with you while transporting the explosives. Deliver shipments of explosives only to authorized persons or leave them in locked rooms designed for explosives storage.

A carrier must choose the safest route to transport placarded radioactive material. After choosing the route, the carrier must tell the driver about the radioactive materials and show the route to be taken.

EMERGENCY EQUIPMENT

Protecting the Public

You know that any time you stop on the highway (other than a normal traffic stop), you must warn others by using your flashers and reflective devices. This is true no matter what type of load you have. When your load is hazardous materials, you must take special steps to warn other highway users and prevent accidents from happening.

Emergency stops. When hauling certain hazardous materials, you must not stop on the traveled part of the highway for any reason except for normal traffic stops. The hazardous materials in question are:

- flammable liquids and solids
- oxidizers
- corrosives
- compressed gases
- poisons

If you do stop, you must put out your warning devices.

If your vehicle is a cargo tank carrying flammable liquids or flammable compressed gases, you must do the same. This is true even if the vehicle is empty.

Put out your warning devices if you stop for any reason other than a normal traffic stop while hauling Division 1.1, 1.2, or 1.3 explosives.

You can only transfer explosives and flammable liquids from one container or vehicle to another in an emergency. Put out your warning devices and protect the scene if you must make this transfer.

Fighting Hazardous Material Fires

You might have to control minor truck fires on the road. The power unit of placarded vehicles must have a fire extinguisher rated 10 B:C or more. However, unless you have the training and equipment to do so safely, don't fight hazardous material fires. Dealing with hazardous material fires requires special training and protective gear.

When you discover a fire, send someone for help. You may use the fire extinguisher to keep minor truck fires from spreading to cargo before firefighters arrive. Feel trailer doors to see if they are hot before opening them. If so, you may have a cargo fire.

Don't open the doors. That could let air in and make the fire flare up. Without air, many fires only smolder. That does less damage than a fire in full flame.

If your cargo is already on fire, it is not safe to fight the fire. Keep the shipping papers with you to give to emergency personnel as soon as they arrive. Warn other people of the danger and keep them away.

Emergency Equipment for Loading and Unloading

Vehicles that use a pump to load and unload may have a manual by-pass. Manual by-passes control spills caused by excess pressure. Excess pressure can in turn cause hoses to rupture, disconnect, or separate from fittings.

Cargo tanks also have manual emergency valve shut-off controls. This is discussed in greater detail in Chapter 12.

Emergency Equipment for Tank Vehicles

When you transport chlorine in cargo tanks you must have an approved gas mask in the vehicle. You must also have an emergency kit for controlling leaks in dome cover plate fittings on the cargo tank.

EMERGENCY RESPONSE PROCEDURES

As you know, shippers must list an emergency response telephone number on the shipping paper. This number can be used by emergency responders to obtain information about any hazardous materials involved in a spill or fire.

Shippers also must provide emergency response information to the motor carrier for each hazardous material being shipped. The emergency response information must be able to be used away from the motor vehicle and must provide information on how to safely handle incidents involving the material. It must include information on the shipping name of the hazardous materials, risks to health, fire, explosion, and initial methods of handling spills, fires, and leaks of the materials.

Such information can be on the shipping paper or some other document that includes the basic description and technical name of the hazardous material. Or, it may be in a guide book such as the *Emergency Response Guidebook* (ERG). Motor carriers may keep an ERG on each vehicle carrying hazardous materials.

You, the driver, must provide the emergency response information to any federal, state, or local authority responding to a hazardous materials incident or investigating one.

There are some general rules to follow whenever you're involved in a hazardous materials accident. However, different hazardous cargos call for different responses.

Specific Emergency Procedures

Many states have specific emergency response guidelines. You should become familiar with what your state requires.

Explosives. If your vehicle breaks down or is in an accident while carrying explosives, warn others of the danger. Keep bystanders away. Do not allow smoking or open fire near the vehicle.

Remove all explosives before pulling apart vehicles involved in a collision. Place the explosives at least 200 feet from the vehicles and occupied buildings. If there is a fire, warn everyone of the danger of explosion. Stay a safe distance away.

Flammable liquids. If you are transporting a flammable liquid and have an accident or your vehicle breaks down, prevent bystanders from gathering. Warn people of the danger. Keep them from smoking.

Never transport a leaking cargo tank farther than needed to reach a safe place. If safe to do so, get off the roadway. Don't transfer flammable liquid from one vehicle to another on a public roadway except in an emergency.

Flammable solids and oxidizers. If a flammable solid or oxidizing material spills, warn others of the fire hazard. Do not open smoldering packages of flammable solids. Remove them from the vehicle if you can safely do so. Gather and remove any broken packages if safe to do so. Also remove unbroken packages if it will decrease the fire hazard.

Corrosives. If corrosives spill or leak in transit, be careful to avoid further damage or injury when handling the containers.

If further transportation of a leaking tank would be unsafe, get off the road. If safe to do so, try to contain any liquid leaking from the vehicle. Keep spectators away from the liquid and its fumes. Do everything possible to prevent injury to other highway users.

Compressed gases. If compressed gas is leaking from your vehicle, warn others of the danger. Only permit those involved in removing the hazard or wreckage to get close. You must notify the shipper of the compressed gas of any accident.

Unless you are fueling machinery used in road construction or maintenance, do not transfer a flammable compressed gas from one tank to another on any public roadway.

Poisons. You must protect yourself, other people, and property from harm. Remember that many products classed as poison are also flammable. If you think a leaking poison liquid or gas might be flammable, take the added precautions needed for flammable liquids or gases. Do not allow smoking, open flame, or welding. Warn others of the hazards of fire, inhaling vapors, or coming into contact with the poison.

A vehicle involved in a leak of Division 2.3 or Division 6.1 must be checked for stray poison before being used again.

If a Division 6.2 (infectious substances) package is damaged in handling or transportation, you should immediately contact your supervisor. Packages that appear to be damaged or show signs of leakage should not be accepted.

Radioactive materials. If a leak or broken package involves radioactive material, tell your dispatcher or supervisor as soon as possible. If there is a spill, or if an internal container might be damaged, do not touch or inhale the material.

Fire and Flames

Fire and flames can be a real hazard when you are hauling hazardous materials. Even the smallest spark can start a fire or cause an explosion. Never drive a placarded vehicle near open fires unless you can safely pass without stopping.

You might break down and have to use stopped vehicle signals. Use reflective triangles or red electric lights. Never use burning signals, such as flares or fusees, around a tank used for flammable liquid or flammable gas. This is true whether the vehicle is loaded or empty. It's also true for vehicles loaded with Division 1.1, 1.2, or 1.3 explosives, or flammable liquids or gases.

Don't smoke. When you are loading hazardous materials, keep fire away. Don't let people smoke nearby. Never smoke around explosives, oxidizers, or flammables.

General Emergency Procedures

As a professional driver, your job at the scene of an accident is to keep people away from the area. Limit the spread of material, if you can do so safely. Communicate the danger to emergency response personnel.

Follow these steps:

1. Check to see that your driving partner is OK
2. Keep shipping papers with you
3. Keep people far away and upwind
4. Warn others of the danger
5. Send for help
6. Follow your employer's instructions

Cargo Leaks

If you discover a cargo leak, identify the material by using shipping papers, labels, or package location. Don't touch any leaking material. Under the stress of handling an accident or leak, you may forget your cargo is hazardous. You could injure yourself this way.

Do not try to identify material or find the source of a leak by smell. Many toxic gases destroy one's sense of smell. They can injure or kill you even if they don't smell. Do not eat, drink, or smoke around a leak or spill.

If hazardous material is spilling from your vehicle, do not move it any more than safety requires.

You may move off the road and away from places where people gather if doing so results in greater safety. Only move your vehicle if you can do so without danger to yourself or others.

Never continue driving with hazardous material leaking from your vehicle to find a phone booth, truck stop, help, or similar reason. Remember that the carrier pays for the cleanup of contaminated parking lots, roadways, and drainage ditches. The costs are huge. So don't leave a lengthy trail of contamination. If hazardous material is spilling from your vehicle, park it. Secure the area and stay there.

Send someone else for help. When sending someone for help, give that person:

- a description of the emergency
- your exact location and direction of travel
- your name, the carrier's name, and the name of the community or city where your terminal is located
- the shipping name, hazard class, and ID number of the material, if you know them

This is a lot for someone to remember. It is a good idea to write it all down for the person you send for help. The emergency response team must know these things to find you and to handle the emergency. They may have to travel miles to get to you. This information will help them to bring the right equipment the first time, without having to go back for it. Never move your vehicle if doing so will cause contamination or damage the vehicle. Keep downwind and away from roadside rests, truck stops, cafes, and businesses.

Never try to repack leaking containers. Although it is sometimes legal to do so, it must be done right. Unless you have been told otherwise, don't try it. Call your dispatcher or supervisor for instructions. If you need to, call emergency personnel.

National Response Center

The National Response Center helps coordinate emergency response to chemical hazards. They are a resource to the local police and firefighters. The person in charge of a vehicle involved in an accident may have to phone the National Response Center. This call will be in addition to any made to police or firefighters.

You or your employer must phone when any of the following occur as a direct result of a hazardous materials incident:

- A person is killed.
- A person receives injuries requiring hospitalization.
- Estimated carrier or other property damage exceeds $50,000.
- The general public is evacuated for one or more hours.
- One or more major transportation arteries or facilities are closed or shut down for one hour or more.
- Fire, breakage, spillage, or suspected radioactive contamination occurs.
- Fire, breakage, spillage, or suspected contamination occurs involving shipment of etiologic agents (bacteria or toxins).
- A situation exists of such a nature (e.g., continuing danger to life exists at the scene of an incident) that, in the judgment of the carrier, should be reported.

 The phone number of the National Response Center is (800) 424-8802. It's available 24 hours a day, and is toll-free.

Those making the immediate telephone report should be ready to give:

- their names
- the name and address of the carrier they work for
- the phone number where they can be reached
- the date, time, and location of the incident
- the extent of injuries, if any
- the classification, name, and quantity of hazardous materials involved, if available
- the type of incident and nature of hazardous material involvement and whether a continuing danger to life exists at the scene

If a reportable quantity of hazardous substance was involved, the caller should give the name of the shipper. Also, the caller should give the quantity of the hazardous substance discharged.

Be prepared to give your employer the required information. Carriers must make detailed written reports within 30 days.

Chemtrec

The Chemical Transportation Emergency Center (CHEMTREC) in Washington also has a 24-hour toll-free line. CHEMTREC was created to provide emergency personnel with technical information about the physical properties of hazardous products. The National Response Center and CHEMTREC are in close communication. If you call either one, they will tell the other about the problem when appropriate.

 CHEMTREC's phone number is (800) 424-9300.

Special Rules for Transporting Explosives

Some locations require permits to transport Division 1.1, 1.2, and 1.3 explosives. States and counties may also require drivers to follow special routes.

The federal government may require permits for special hazardous materials cargo, like rocket fuel. Find out about permits and special routes for places you drive.

Even the most commonplace cargo can be dangerous if transported in a defective vehicle or by an unskilled driver. Cargo that isn't properly secured can spill out on the roadway. Or, the driver can allow an accident to happen, spilling the cargo. Property nearby can be damaged, and others on the roadway can be injured.

When the cargo itself is hazardous, the smallest mistake can lead to disaster. So if you haul "hazmat," you must be very well informed and very skilled.

PASS POST-TRIP

Instructions: For each true/false test item, read the statement. Decide whether the statement is true or false. If it is true, circle the letter A. If it is false, circle the letter B. For each multiple-choice test item, choose the answer choice—A, B, C, or D—that correctly completes the statement or answers the question. There is only one correct answer. Use the answer sheet provided on page 325.

1. The _____ must make sure a hazardous product is being transported in the proper packages.
   A. shipper
   B. carrier
   C. driver
   D. consignee

2. A written route plan is something you must apply for before making a trip with explosives.
   A. True
   B. False

3. The "Hazardous Materials Table" and the "List of Hazardous Substances and Reportable Quantities" are _____.
   A. different names for the same thing
   B. available only to police and fire departments
   C. published in a different form by each state
   D. the two main lists used by shippers, carriers, and drivers

4. Hazardous materials markings can be a label, tag, or sign.
   A. True
   B. False

5. Your load contains more than 1,000 pounds of mixed hazard classes from Placard Table 2. You have not loaded more than 5,000 pounds of any one class at any one place. You _____.
   A. must have a separate placard for each hazard class in your load
   B. must have a separate placard for each hazard class in your load that totals 1,000 pounds
   C. must have a separate placard for each hazard class in your load that totals more than 5,000 pounds no matter where you got it
   D. can use the "DANGEROUS" placard all by itself

6. Shipping papers for a hazardous materials shipment must_____.
   A. have a shipper's certification
   B. be kept in a door pocket or on the seat when the driver is not at the controls
   C. be marked differently from other cargo documents
   D. all of the above

7. When you haul radioactive materials, you must have your written plan with you.
   A. True
   B. False

8. Trailers used to haul Division 1.1, 1.2, or 1.3 explosives must _____.
   A. have padded walls and floors
   B. use a floor liner that does not contain iron or steel
   C. have a date of manufacture after January 1, 1983
   D. be equipped with an air ride suspension

9. The radioactive "transport index" refers to radiation that _____.
   A. is in the packages
   B. surrounds each package and passes through nearby packages
   C. can reach to the outside of the packages
   D. is harmless

10. In addition to a special license and training, you may need a special permit from the federal, state, or local government to haul hazardous materials.
    A. True
    B. False

CHAPTER 13 ANSWER SHEET

Test Item	Answer Choices				Self - Scoring Correct Incorrect	
1.	A	B	C	D	☐	☐
2.	A	B	C	D	☐	☐
3.	A	B	C	D	☐	☐
4.	A	B	C	D	☐	☐
5.	A	B	C	D	☐	☐
6.	A	B	C	D	☐	☐
7.	A	B	C	D	☐	☐
8.	A	B	C	D	☐	☐
9.	A	B	C	D	☐	☐
10.	A	B	C	D	☐	☐

PART THREE

Chapter 14

Review

In this chapter, you will learn about:

- how to review what you've read
- general knowledge needed to get a CDL with no endorsements and the air brake restriction
- air brakes
- vehicle combinations
- tank vehicles
- hazardous materials

To complete this chapter, you will need:

- a pencil or pen
- a book of notes

You're almost at the end of this book. Just three more chapters to go! They'll help you put the finishing touches on the job of preparing to take the CDL tests.

You've read through a lot of pages and covered a lot of ground. If you plan to haul hazardous materials in a cargo tank with air brakes, you've probably read every chapter! What follows are questions on both the general and the endorsement knowledge areas. Answering the questions will help you measure how much you remember.

In this chapter, you'll also find tips on how to review what you've read if you find that necessary.

You can use this chapter in the way you think will work best for you. Take the tests first. Then use your test results to guide your review. Or, you can review your reading first, then take the tests.

HOW TO REVIEW

Quick—what was Chapter 4 about? What was the subject of Chapter 10?

You may recall Chapter 10 quite well, especially if you finished it recently. On the other hand, you may hardly be able to remember the subject of Chapter 4. If that's the case, it's not really that

surprising. It may be some time since you read Chapter 4. You've worked to absorb a lot of information since then. Before you take your CDL Knowledge Test, though, the information from Chapter 4 should be as fresh in your mind as that from Chapter 10. You may need to review.

You could read each chapter again from the start. You probably don't have time for this, though. Anyway, it's not necessary. Why review what you know? All you need to review is what you don't know as well.

How do you identify what you need to review? Try the systematic approach. Just as having a system helped you get through the material the first time, a system will help you do a quick and thorough review. Follow these steps:

- retake the PASS Pre-trip
- reread the chapter objectives
- scan the chapter
- read your notes
- retake the PASS Post-trip
- retake the diagnostic test
- take the Sample CDL tests

Retake the PASS Pre-trip

Take another look at the three questions that began each chapter in Part Two. If you know the material well, you should be able to answer each question correctly. If you can't, you should review the information tested by any question you missed.

Reread the Chapter Objectives

The chapter objectives list the major areas of information in the subject covered by the chapter. How confident do you feel in your knowledge of that area? Use your feelings to guide you to the part of the chapter you need to review.

Scan the Chapter

Mark for review any chapter that covers information you're still in doubt about. Look over the chapter main headings and subheadings. Pause to take stock of how familiar the words seem. Can't quite remember what a topic was about? Then plan to go over that part of the chapter in detail.

Pay special attention to any areas you marked with your highlighter. Those were areas that were new or hard for you at first. Make sure you feel confident about them now.

Take the time to reread thoroughly the parts of chapters that answer any test questions you may have missed.

If you have quite a lot of time left before you take your CDL Knowledge Test, scan Chapters 4 through 10 all the way through one more time. Start with the chapter that's the least fresh in your mind.

Also review completely any chapters you need to prepare for an endorsement.

Read Your Notes

As you read, you made notes of words that were new or ideas you wanted to remember. You wrote yourself a brief summary of each chapter. Use these notes to refresh your memory.

Retake the PASS Post-trip

Look at your answer sheets from the PASS Post-trip questions at the end of each chapter in Part Two. If you missed any the first time, review the part of the chapter covered by those questions. Then take the Post-trip again. You should be able to answer all of them easily and correctly. Try for a perfect score on the PASS Post-trips this time.

Retake the Diagnostic Test

Chapter 1 had a diagnostic test. Take the test again. Compare your score with the first time you took the test. Note which questions you missed, if any. They may be the same, or they may be different. Either way, they point to any area of information you could be stronger in before you take the CDL Knowledge Test.

Take the Sample CDL Tests

You can use the two review knowledge tests in this chapter before or after you review the other chapters. The results will pinpoint any areas of information you're still weak in.

Take the review tests under "actual" test conditions. Turn off the radio. Don't smoke, eat, or drink while taking the test. Put your books and dictionary away. You won't be able to use them when you take the actual CDL Knowledge Test.

Follow the instructions given.

For answers, please refer to pages 398–400.

SAMPLE TEST 1

Test Item	Answer Choices				Self - Scoring Correct Incorrect	
1.	A	B	C	D	☐	☐
2.	A	B	C	D	☐	☐
3.	A	B	C	D	☐	☐
4.	A	B	C	D	☐	☐
5.	A	B	C	D	☐	☐
6.	A	B	C	D	☐	☐
7.	A	B	C	D	☐	☐
8.	A	B	C	D	☐	☐
9.	A	B	C	D	☐	☐
10.	A	B	C	D	☐	☐
11.	A	B	C	D	☐	☐
12.	A	B	C	D	☐	☐
13.	A	B	C	D	☐	☐
14.	A	B	C	D	☐	☐
15.	A	B	C	D	☐	☐
16.	A	B	C	D	☐	☐
17.	A	B	C	D	☐	☐
18.	A	B	C	D	☐	☐
19.	A	B	C	D	☐	☐
20.	A	B	C	D	☐	☐

Cut here

Test Item	Answer Choices				Self - Scoring
					Correct Incorrect
21.	A	B	C	D	☐ ☐
22.	A	B	C	D	☐ ☐
23.	A	B	C	D	☐ ☐
24.	A	B	C	D	☐ ☐
25.	A	B	C	D	☐ ☐
26.	A	B	C	D	☐ ☐
27.	A	B	C	D	☐ ☐
28.	A	B	C	D	☐ ☐
29.	A	B	C	D	☐ ☐
30.	A	B	C	D	☐ ☐
31.	A	B	C	D	☐ ☐
32.	A	B	C	D	☐ ☐
33.	A	B	C	D	☐ ☐
34.	A	B	C	D	☐ ☐
35.	A	B	C	D	☐ ☐
36.	A	B	C	D	☐ ☐
37.	A	B	C	D	☐ ☐
38.	A	B	C	D	☐ ☐
39.	A	B	C	D	☐ ☐
40.	A	B	C	D	☐ ☐

Cut here

Test Item	Answer Choices				Self - Scoring
					Correct Incorrect
41.	A	B	C	D	☐ ☐
42.	A	B	C	D	☐ ☐
43.	A	B	C	D	☐ ☐
44.	A	B	C	D	☐ ☐
45.	A	B	C	D	☐ ☐
46.	A	B	C	D	☐ ☐
47.	A	B	C	D	☐ ☐
48.	A	B	C	D	☐ ☐
49.	A	B	C	D	☐ ☐
50.	A	B	C	D	☐ ☐
51.	A	B	C	D	☐ ☐
52.	A	B	C	D	☐ ☐
53.	A	B	C	D	☐ ☐
54.	A	B	C	D	☐ ☐

Cut here

SAMPLE TEST 1

1. One purpose of Commercial Driver Licensing is to disqualify drivers who operate commercial motor vehicles in an unsafe manner.
   A. True
   B. False

2. All CDL skill tests must be taken in _____.
   A. a representative vehicle
   B. a company vehicle
   C. a vehicle with air brakes
   D. a rented vehicle

3. To meet the driver qualification requirements for a CDL, you must _____.
   A. have at least a year of CMV driving experience
   B. be at least 18 years old for intrastate driving or at least 21 years old for interstate driving
   C. take prescription medication
   D. have perfect eyesight

4. If you are convicted of a traffic violation in a state other than your home state, you must make notification _____.
   A. to your employer
   B. within 30 days of the date of conviction
   C. in writing
   D. all of the above

5. A driver who is disqualified _____.
   A. must always receive a jail sentence
   B. has forfeited bond
   C. may not drive a CMV
   D. may not drive a motor vehicle

6. When operating a CMV, which of the following first offenses will result in the loss of your CDL for one year?
   A. driving with an expired or suspended CDL
   B. excessive speeding, reckless driving, or any traffic offense that causes a fatality
   C. DUI, DWI, and driving while on drugs
   D. driving with a load of hazardous materials that are not properly secured

7. Once you get your CDL for a specific vehicle group, you may never change it to another group.
   A. True
   B. False

8. The only sure cure for fatigue is _____.
   A. narcotics
   B. amphetamines
   C. real sleep
   D. caffeine

9. Medical certificates must be renewed every _____.
   A. year
   B. six months
   C. three years
   D. two years or when specified by a physician

10. Prescription drugs are allowed if a doctor says the drugs will not affect safe driving ability.
    A. True
    B. False

11. You are required to stop at a railroad grade crossing when_____.
    A. the crossing is located in a city or town with frequent train traffic
    B. when there are no warning signals at the crossing
    C. the cargo being carried makes a stop mandatory under state or federal regulations
    D. when a flagman tells you that it's safe to proceed

12. The law requires CMVs to have _____.
    A. service brakes
    B. emergency brakes
    C. parking brakes
    D. all of the above

13. You may not use tires that _____ on your vehicle.
    A. are belted
    B. are flat or have leaks
    C. have a tread depth of more than 2/32 of an inch
    D. are treaded

14. To drive your vehicle in a way that would cause it to break down or cause an accident is not only unsafe, it's illegal.
    A. True
    B. False

15. Which of the following is a hazardous materials class?
    A. "Requires Placards"
    B. "Other Regulated Materials"
    C. "Dangerous"
    D. none of the above

16. The color of the turn signals facing forward must be _____.
    A. amber only
    B. white
    C. white or amber
    D. whatever the manufacturer selected

17. When the engine starts, the ammeter jumps to the charge side and flutters. This is a sign _____.
    A. that the ammeter is faulty
    B. that the generator needs repair
    C. of normal operation
    D. that the engine is warmed up

18. When you first start your vehicle, the warning lights should come on.
    A. True
    B. False

19. Your vehicle's battery box must have _____.
    A. at least two batteries
    B. enough fluid to work properly
    C. at least one loose ground wire
    D. a secure cover

20. Which of the following creates the braking force in a braking system?
    A. air pressure
    B. hydraulic pressure
    C. vacuum pressure
    D. friction

21. Rust around wheel nuts often means that _____.
    A. the nuts are loose
    B. the nuts are broken
    C. the nuts are about to break
    D. the vehicle needs painting

22. The engine speed that you use for shifting should be based on _____.
    A. information in your owner's manual
    B. the vehicle's GVWR
    C. the vehicle's mpg
    D. what feels right for the situation

23. When roads are wet, icy, or covered with snow, you should _____.
    A. use your retarder for braking as much as possible
    B. turn the retarder off
    C. use the maximum setting if the retarder has power adjustment settings
    D. be ready to turn the retarder on the minute you start to skid

24. Lane changes, turns, merges, and tight maneuvers require _____.
    A. lots of luck to perform without accidents
    B. frequent checking and rechecking, using your mirrors
    C. maintaining a constant speed
    D. power steering

25. Total stopping distance is _____ plus reaction distance plus braking distance.
    A. visual distance
    B. perception distance
    C. vehicle length
    D. trip distance

26. Dirty headlights give about _____ as much light as clean ones.
    A. 100 percent
    B. 90 percent
    C. 75 percent
    D. 50 percent

27. To prepare for winter driving, check that your antifreeze will do the job _____.
    A. by inspecting the color
    B. by checking the level in the reservoir
    C. using a special coolant tester
    D. by draining the system and replacing the antifreeze

28. In hot weather, tire inflation pressures can be higher than normal. You should _____.
    A. inspect the tires less often
    B. let air out of your tires when the pressure exceeds 105 psi
    C. not let air out of the tires when they are hot
    D. spin the tires to cool them off

29. If you try to downshift while coming down a mountain, you might _____.
    A. damage the clutch
    B. damage the engine
    C. get stuck in neutral
    D. lose traction

30. A vehicle marked at the rear with a red triangle having an orange center _____.
    A. is hauling hazardous materials
    B. is moving slowly
    C. is a farm vehicle
    D. makes frequent stops

31. When steering to avoid a crash _____.
    A. keep one hand on the steering wheel and the other hand free for shifting
    B. turn and apply the brake at the same time for more control
    C. use both hands on the steering wheel and don't brake while turning
    D. none of the above

32. The most common skid is _____.
    A. rear wheels losing traction due to excessive braking or acceleration
    B. steering tires sliding due to front-brake lock-up
    C. trailer wheels sliding out on curves
    D. caused by a front tire blow-out

33. The first step in correcting a drive-wheel braking skid is to let off the brake.
    A. True
    B. False

34. Poorly distributed cargo can _____.
    A. cause the vehicle to pull to one side
    B. make the vehicle feel like it's going to tip over
    C. make the vehicle harder to put into motion and stop
    D. all of the above

35. Bridge laws _____.
    A. are the same as the maximum legal axle weight
    B. control traffic on a bridge
    C. apply only to drawbridges
    D. can lower the maximum axle weight limit

36. Loading a device beyond its rating is _____.
    A. illegal and unsafe
    B. impossible
    C. the smart way to increase a payload
    D. a good way to test your equipment

37. If your vehicle is overloaded to the rear, it is _____.
    A. very stable
    B. likely to tip over
    C. likely to go into a jackknife
    D. likely to go into a front-wheel skid

38. The legal size and weight distribution limits _____.
    A. should be your guide under all conditions
    B. are not changed by adverse conditions
    C. may not ensure safe operations in bad weather
    D. are often changed by states from season to season

39. Blocking used to prevent cargo movement _____.
    A. is secured to the cargo compartment floor
    B. is secured to the cargo itself
    C. is secured to the cargo and the walls
    D. must be placed every 2 1/2 feet

40. You must inspect cargo within _____ miles after starting a trip.
    A. 10
    B. 25
    C. 50
    D. 100

41. The lighter your load, _____.
    A. the less traction your vehicle has
    B. the longer your stopping distance
    C. the longer your stopping time
    D. all of the above

42. You inspect your vehicle because _____.
    A. it's important for safety
    B. it's required by federal regulations
    C. it's required by state law
    D. all of the above

43. You should do a post-trip inspection _____.
    A. at the end of each run for each vehicle you operate
    B. on the last vehicle you operate each day
    C. on whichever vehicle the dispatcher selects
    D. on the same vehicle every day

44. Drive tires must have at least _____ of tread, and no less.
    A. 1/4 inch
    B. 2/32 inch
    C. 1/2 inch
    D. 4/32 inch

45. A serious hazard of exhaust system leaks is _____.
    A. excess smoke can enter the cab
    B. exhaust smoke can damage the cargo
    C. poisonous fumes can enter the cab
    D. excess smoke can damage the vehicle

46. An air suspension _____.
    A. should not fill evenly all the way around
    B. should fill before the air brake system reaches normal pressure
    C. should allow the vehicle to tilt with the load
    D. should not leak more than three psi in five minutes at normal pressure

47. Mud flaps _____.
    A. should touch the ground
    B. should have advertising on them
    C. must be made of high-grade rubber
    D. may be required by state law

48. During the pre-trip inspection, approach the vehicle and _____.
    A. note the vehicle's general condition
    B. check for body damage and major leaks
    C. see if the vehicle leans to one side
    D. all of the above

49. Normal clutch travel is_____.
    A. less than one or two inches
    B. about one or two inches
    C. more than two inches
    D. not something the driver can measure

50. During the walk-around part of the pre-trip inspection, you should _____.
    A. leave the vehicle key in the switch so you won't lose it
    B. pull the key out of the switch and put it on the dash so you'll know where it is
    C. leave the vehicle key in the switch so it will be handy for the engine test
    D. put the key in your pocket so no one can move the vehicle while you are under it

And Now a Few Extras

Instructions: Match the letter for the vehicle system condition in Column B with the gauge reading in Column A.

Column A Gauge Reading	Column B System Condition
51. 180 to 250 degrees Fahrenheit	A. normal cooling system temperature
52. 165 to 185 degrees Fahrenheit	B. normal transmission oil temperature
53. 30 to 75 psi	C. normal operating oil pressure
54. 5 to 15 psi	D. normal idle oil pressure

SAMPLE TEST 2

Test Item	Answer Choices				Self - Scoring
					Correct Incorrect
1.	A	B	C	D	□ □
2.	A	B	C	D	□ □
3.	A	B	C	D	□ □
4.	A	B	C	D	□ □
5.	A	B	C	D	□ □
6.	A	B	C	D	□ □
7.	A	B	C	D	□ □
8.	A	B	C	D	□ □
9.	A	B	C	D	□ □
10.	A	B	C	D	□ □
11.	A	B	C	D	□ □
12.	A	B	C	D	□ □
13.	A	B	C	D	□ □
14.	A	B	C	D	□ □
15.	A	B	C	D	□ □
16.	A	B	C	D	□ □
17.	A	B	C	D	□ □
18.	A	B	C	D	□ □
19.	A	B	C	D	□ □
20.	A	B	C	D	□ □

Cut here

Test Item	Answer Choices				Self - Scoring
					Correct Incorrect
21.	A	B	C	D	☐ ☐
22.	A	B	C	D	☐ ☐
23.	A	B	C	D	☐ ☐
24.	A	B	C	D	☐ ☐
25.	A	B	C	D	☐ ☐
26.	A	B	C	D	☐ ☐
27.	A	B	C	D	☐ ☐
28.	A	B	C	D	☐ ☐
29.	A	B	C	D	☐ ☐
30.	A	B	C	D	☐ ☐
31.	A	B	C	D	☐ ☐
32.	A	B	C	D	☐ ☐
33.	A	B	C	D	☐ ☐
34.	A	B	C	D	☐ ☐
35.	A	B	C	D	☐ ☐
36.	A	B	C	D	☐ ☐
37.	A	B	C	D	☐ ☐
38.	A	B	C	D	☐ ☐
39.	A	B	C	D	☐ ☐
40.	A	B	C	D	☐ ☐

Cut here

Test Item	Answer Choices				Self - Scoring Correct Incorrect	
41.	A	B	C	D	☐	☐
42.	A	B	C	D	☐	☐
43.	A	B	C	D	☐	☐
44.	A	B	C	D	☐	☐
45.	A	B	C	D	☐	☐
46.	A	B	C	D	☐	☐
47.	A	B	C	D	☐	☐
48.	A	B	C	D	☐	☐
49.	A	B	C	D	☐	☐
50.	A	B	C	D	☐	☐
51.	A	B	C	D	☐	☐
52.	A	B	C	D	☐	☐
53.	A	B	C	D	☐	☐
54.	A	B	C	D	☐	☐

Cut here

SAMPLE TEST 2

1. All drivers who need a CDL must take the
   _____.
   A. air brakes test
   B. combination vehicles test
   C. chauffeur's license test
   D. general knowledge test

2. A driver who meets the requirements of the
   CDL laws does not have to meet the qualifica-
   tions set in FMCSR Part 391.
   A. True
   B. False

3. At least once a year, a driver must fill out
   a form listing all motor vehicle violations
   (other than parking) that occurred during the
   previous 12 months _____.
   A. even if there were no violations
   B. only if there was a conviction
   C. only if the bond was forfeited
   D. only if the carrier requires it

4. Your application for a CMV driving job must
   list the names and addresses of all employers
   who ever hired you.
   A. True
   B. False

5. Which of the following is a serious CMV
   driving violation?
   A. driving a representative vehicle
   B. reckless driving
   C. countersteering
   D. driving with a load of hazardous materials

6. Which of the following first offenses in a
   CMV will result in the loss of your CDL for
   life?
   A. leaving the scene of an accident involving
      a CMV you were driving
   B. using a CMV to commit a felony involving
      controlled substances
   C. driving any vehicle under the influence of
      alcohol or an illegal drug
   D. driving a CMV under the influence of
      alcohol or an illegal drug

7. You are pulled over for weaving between lanes.
   If you refuse to take a test for alcohol, you may
   be disqualified just as if you were DUI. This is
   because of the _____.
   A. higher standard of care law
   B. reasonable cause law
   C. implied consent law
   D. none of the above

8. If your employer gives you a road test, and
   you pass it, you don't have to take the CDL
   Performance Test.
   A. True
   B. False

9. Which of these statements about night driving
   is true?
   A. Most people are more alert at night than
      during the day because they drink more
      coffee.
   B. Most heavy vehicle accidents occur
      between midnight and 6 a.m.
   C. Most hazards are easier to see at night than
      during the day due to artificial lighting.
   D. If you become sleepy, it's best to push on
      and finish the long trip.

10. Which of these statements about alcohol is
    true?
    A. Some people aren't affected by drinking.
    B. A few beers have the same effects on driv-
       ing ability as a few shots of whiskey.
    C. Coffee and fresh air can sober up a person.
    D. Exercise can help you burn off alcohol
       faster.

11. When making an emergency stop on the high-
    way, you must put on your four-way flashers
    and _____.
    A. keep them on until you are underway
       again
    B. keep them on until you get your warning
       devices out
    C. hang a red flag from the rear of your vehicle
    D. blow your horn

12. Locked-up brakes are more often the result of panic stopping than faulty equipment.
    A. True
    B. False

13. Fatigued drivers should _____.
    A. drink coffee to combat sleepiness
    B. take a rest break until they are fully alert
    C. take medication
    D. do exercises to get energized

14. If your vehicle doesn't pass a roadside inspection _____.
    A. it can be declared "out of service"
    B. you cannot drive the vehicle, even to a repair station
    C. you may repair it on the spot, then resume your trip
    D. all of the above

15. Federal law requires _____.
    A. two white headlights, one at the left front and one at the right front of the tractor
    B. fog lamps for bad weather or dark roads
    C. stop lamps on projecting loads
    D. one red backup lamp

16. Trucks must carry a five-pound B:C fire extinguisher, unless they are placarded for hazardous materials.
    A. True
    B. False

17. Normal oil pressure while idling is _____.
    A. 165 to 185 degrees Fahrenheit
    B. 20 to 24 psi
    C. 30 to 75 psi
    D. 5 to 15 psi

18. Overcharging in a vehicle battery _____.
    A. means there isn't enough power to crank the engine
    B. leads to thickened battery fluid
    C. shortens battery life
    D. all of the above

19. Once a circuit breaker has opened, it must be replaced.
    A. True
    B. False

20. Tire inflation pressure should be checked _____.
    A. after the tire has warmed up
    B. when the tire is cold
    C. after the first 25 miles of a run
    D. every two hours or 100 miles of travel

21. Progressive shifting means _____.
    A. downshifting at lower rpm as you reach the lower gears
    B. downshifting at higher rpm as you reach the lower gears
    C. upshifting at lower rpm as you reach the higher gears
    D. upshifting at higher rpm as you reach the higher gears

22. You should downshift _____.
    A. when the tachometer or speedometer indicates it's necessary
    B. before starting down a steep hill
    C. before entering a sharp curve
    D. all of the above

23. Maintain good visual alertness by _____.
    A. always looking as far ahead as you can see
    B. fixing your eyes on the road right in front of you
    C. keeping a close watch on the road behind you at all times
    D. shifting your attention between the mirrors and the road ahead

24. Signaling other drivers when it is safe to pass is _____.
    A. a great aid to highway safety
    B. a courtesy professional drivers should extend to others
    C. an unsafe practice
    D. required

25. Traveling in the lane alongside other vehicles _____.
    A. is a good idea since they can always see you that way
    B. can cause you to be trapped when you need to change lanes
    C. will make traffic flow more smoothly
    D. will keep people from cutting in front of you

26. If another driver approaches you at night with high beams on, _____.
    A. get them to turn them off by flashing yours
    B. watching the approaching lights closely will show you where the vehicle is
    C. look slightly right in the right lane or at the right edge marking if there is one
    D. keep your high beams on until the other vehicle passes.

27. Ice on your radiator shutters or winterfront _____.
    A. will melt off after the engine warms up
    B. can cause the engine to overheat
    C. will help insulate the engine compartment
    D. is a minor winter inconvenience

28. In hot weather, bleeding tar can _____.
    A. damage your tires
    B. damage the road
    C. give your vehicle more traction
    D. make parts of the road very slippery

29. When going down a long grade, the gear selected by drivers of the latest, fuel efficient trucks is affected by _____.
    A. their streamlined shapes that reduce air drag
    B. their low friction parts
    C. their more powerful engines that allow you to climb hills in higher gears
    D. all of the above

30. Impaired drivers often _____.
    A. drive too fast, too slow, or change speed for no reason
    B. drive especially well because they are trying so hard
    C. are safer because they tend to drive slowly
    D. none of the above

31. You have to leave the road to avoid another vehicle. What should you not do?
    A. keep one set of wheels on the pavement
    B. stay on the shoulder until you can come to a stop
    C. turn widely to be sure of avoiding the other vehicle
    D. stay off the brake

32. The best way to stop a front-wheel skid is to _____.
    A. let the vehicle slow down
    B. brake hard
    C. turn sharply
    D. shift into neutral

33. Cargo that isn't properly secured can shift. This can _____.
    A. result in damaged cargo
    B. overturn the whole vehicle
    C. cause the cargo to spill out, resulting in a major highway hazard
    D. all of the above

34. State laws can regulate _____.
    A. the weight of your vehicle, but not the cargo
    B. the weight of your cargo, but not your vehicle
    C. both your vehicle and cargo weight
    D. neither vehicle nor cargo weight. Only the federal government can regulate these

35. Tire load is _____.
    A. the most weight a tire can carry safely
    B. the same as inflation pressure
    C. a measure of whether a tire is underinflated
    D. how much weight a tire puts on the road

36. An empty vehicle is _____.
    A. very stable
    B. likely to tip over
    C. likely to go into a jackknife
    D. likely to go into a rear-wheel skid

37. A vehicle with a high center of gravity is
_____.
    A. very stable
    B. likely to tip over
    C. likely to go into a jackknife
    D. likely to go into a front-wheel skid

38. When securing cargo, you should use _____.
    A. no fewer than three tiedowns, even for the smallest load
    B. one tiedown for every ten feet of cargo
    C. as few tiedowns as possible, since they only increase your overall weight
    D. none of the above

39. You may need to tarp a load both to protect the cargo and _____.
    A. yourself
    B. others on the road
    C. the vehicle
    D. the shipper

40. If your load is sealed, _____.
    A. you are not responsible for its weight
    B. break the seal, inspect the load, and reseal it every three hours or 150 miles
    C. break the seal and inspect the load when you are within 25 miles of your destination
    D. you are still responsible for exceeding gross weight or axle limits

41. Dry bulk tanks _____.
    A. are designed to control the shifting of the load
    B. are stable in curves and turns
    C. tend to have a high center of gravity
    D. present the fewest driving problems of all vehicles

42. If a state official conducts a roadside inspection and finds your vehicle to be unsafe, _____.
    A. the official will offer to repair it for you
    B. your vehicle will be put "out of service"
    C. your vehicle will be taken away from you
    D. your license to drive will be taken away from you

43. When you stop during a trip, you should check _____.
    A. the engine oil and coolant
    B. the post-trip inspection report made by the vehicle's last driver
    C. your cargo securement devices
    D. your disc brakes

44. Steering axle tires must have at least _____ of tread, and no less.
    A. 1/4 inch
    B. 2/32 inch
    C. 1/2 inch
    D. 4/32 inch

45. In many states, your vehicle will be placed "out of service" if there are _____ broken or missing leaves in your leaf spring suspension.
    A. more than one tenth
    B. more than one fifth
    C. more than one fourth
    D. any

46. A bent _____ is a steering system defect.
    A. torque rod
    B. tie rod
    C. spring hanger
    D. shock absorber

47. Snow chains _____.
    A. are required by federal regulations
    B. may be required by states during the winter
    C. are standard equipment on heavy vehicles
    D. are so sturdy they never break

48. When you start your vehicle's engine, the _____ should come up to normal with a few seconds.
    A. oil pressure
    B. fuel pressure
    C. coolant temperature
    D. all of the above

49. During the pre-trip inspection, check the brake (stop) lights by _____.
    A. applying the trailer hand brake if your vehicle has one, or getting someone to apply the treadle valve
    B. bleeding the air out of the system so the tractor protection valve will act
    C. fanning off air pressure so that the brakes will apply
    D. pulling the red knob

50. Regardless of the vehicle you have, the seven-step vehicle inspection is all you need to do.
    A. True
    B. False

And Now a Few Extras

Instructions: Match the letter for the description in Column B with the number of the term in Column A that fits the description.

Column A Weight Term	Column B Definition
51. GVW	A. a rating given to the vehicle by its manufacturer, which is the maximum weight of a combination vehicle plus cargo
52. GCW	B. a rating given to the vehicle by its manufacturer. It is the maximum weight for a single vehicle plus its load
53. GVWR	C. the total weight of a single vehicle, plus its load
54. GCWR	D. the total weight of the power unit or tractor, plus any trailers, plus the cargo

ENDORSEMENT TEST REVIEWS

The following sections will give you a brush-up on the questions specifically geared toward the endorsement tests we discussed earlier. The four categories covered are: Air Brakes, Combination Vehicles, Tank Vehicles, and Hazardous Materials. Use the Answer Sheet starting on page 361 to record your answers. The correct answers can be found starting on page 399.

Air Brakes Questions

The following questions should serve as a good review for you as you prepare for the Air Brakes endorsement test. Answer sheets are provided starting on page 361. For answers, refer to page 399.

1. Fanning air brakes _____.
   A. cools them off
   B. increases the air pressure
   C. increases the braking power
   D. decreases the air pressure

2. When some brakes in the system are doing more work than others, _____.
   A. those brakes will develop more heat
   B. vehicle handling will be affected
   C. those brakes will lose stopping power first
   D. all of the above

3. If your air compressor stops working, _____.
   A. you will lose your brakes immediately
   B. the safety relief valve will close
   C. you'll have some air pressure left stored in the air tanks
   D. your brakes won't be affected at all

4. An air brake system safety relief valve opens at about _____.
   A. 20 to 45 psi
   B. 60 psi
   C. 120 psi
   D. 150 psi

5. Your air brake safety relief valve has opened several times. This means _____.
   A. the system is working normally
   B. your air pressure is probably low
   C. the air compressor has failed
   D. you should have the system repaired

6. If your vehicle has a front brake limiting valve control, it should be in the _____.
   A. "slippery" position on wet roads
   B. "normal" position only on dry roads
   C. "normal" position under all road conditions
   D. "slippery" position under all road conditions

7. The service brake system _____.
   A. is an inspection done by the company maintenance staff
   B. applies and releases the brakes when you use the brake pedal during normal driving
   C. is the pump and check valves that keep the air tank pressure serviced
   D. is only on vehicles with hydraulic brakes

8. Spring brakes are _____.
   A. applied by air pressure
   B. held in the released position by air pressure
   C. not affected by air pressure
   D. have nothing to do with the emergency brake system

9. Most large vehicles with air brakes have spring brakes _____.
   A. that are parking brakes
   B. that are emergency brakes
   C. that are part of the parking and emergency brake systems
   D. that will stop the vehicle in a shorter distance than the service brakes

10. You should avoid setting the parking brakes _____.
    A. on a steep grade
    B. if the air pressure is low
    C. if the brakes are hot
    D. in hot weather if the brakes are wet

11. Spring brakes should come on automatically when you pump air pressure down to _____ psi.
    A. zero
    B. 20 to 45
    C. 60
    D. 90

12. If your brakes are out of adjustment, you won't have good _____ braking power.
    A. service
    B. emergency
    C. parking
    D. all of the above

13. On newer vehicles with air brakes, the parking brake control is _____.
    A. a lever
    B. a square, red, push-pull control knob
    C. a diamond-shaped, yellow, push-pull control knob
    D. a round, blue, push-pull control knob

14. If a low air pressure warning device comes on, _____
    A. pull off the road as soon as it's safe to do so
    B. you can safely continue until you get to a service station
    C. you may continue, but remember to make note of it later on your post-trip inspection report
    D. turn it off so it won't distract you while driving

15. The tractor protection valve _____.
    A. works automatically or can be operated manually
    B. protects the tractor air tanks in case of air pressure loss
    C. separates the tractor air supply from the trailer air supply
    D. all of the above

16. The tractor protection valve _____.
    A. cannot be operated manually
    B. is the same thing as the trailer brake control
    C. is also called the breakaway valve
    D. all of the above

17. The trailer hand brake _____.
    A. lets you control the amount of air to the trailer brakes
    B. may be used as a parking brake
    C. exhausts the air supply from the trailer brakes
    D. exhausts the air supply from the tractor brakes

18. Which of the following statements about glad hands is true?
    A. The service brake glad hands are color-coded red.
    B. The service brake glad hands are color-coded blue.
    C. The spring brake glad hands are color-coded blue.
    D. The spring brake glad hands are color-coded yellow.

19. If the service air line breaks, _____ (unless you have a dual air system).
    A. the air pressure will drop slowly
    B. you should apply the spring brakes
    C. the spring brakes will come on
    D. the check valve will prevent the dry tank from losing its air supply

20. If a spring brake line ruptures, _____ (unless you have a dual air system).
    A. the air pressure will drop slowly
    B. you should apply the spring brakes
    C. the spring brakes will come on
    D. the check valve will prevent the dry tank from losing its air supply

21. If the line from the compressor to the main supply tank ruptures, _____.
    A. the air pressure will drop slowly
    B. you should apply the spring brakes
    C. the spring brakes will come on when the service pressure drops below 45 psi
    D. the check valve will prevent the dry tank from losing its air supply

22. Brake drums or discs _____.
    A. must not have cracks
    B. must have linings that fit loosely on the shoes
    C. must not have cracks longer than half the width of the friction area
    D. should be well-greased between the drum or disc and the lining

23. Slack adjusters _____.
    A. never need adjustment themselves
    B. should only be adjusted by someone with an S endorsement
    C. should travel at least two inches from where the push rod is attached
    D. can be adjusted manually or automatically

24. Air tanks should be drained_____.
    A. at the end of each day or shift
    B. to keep sludge from clogging brake system valves
    C. manually when automatic devices fail
    D. all of the above

25. To determine if slack adjusters need adjustment, _____.
    A. apply the service brakes and release the parking brakes
    B. apply both the service and parking brakes
    C. pull out the automatic slack adjustment control knob
    D. release both the service and parking brakes and pull hard on the slack adjuster. It should not move more than one inch

26. To test the brakes on a single air system, run the engine at a fast idle to charge the air system. Your gauge should show you _____.
    A. pressure building from 50 to 90 psi within three minutes
    B. pressure building from 85 to 100 psi within 45 seconds
    C. the compressor cutting out below 50 psi or above 70 psi
    D. the governor stopping below 100 psi or above 125 psi

27. To test the brakes on a dual air system, run the engine at a fast idle to charge the air system. Your gauge should show you _____.
    A. pressure building from 50 to 90 psi within three minutes
    B. pressure building from 85 to 100 psi within 45 seconds
    C. the compressor cutting out below 50 psi or above 70 psi
    D. the governor stopping below 100 psi or above 125 psi

28. Your vehicle's single brake system needs adjustment if _____.
    A. pressure builds from 50 to 90 psi within three minutes
    B. pressure builds from 85 to 100 psi within 45 seconds
    C. the compressor cuts out between 70 psi and 90 psi
    D. the governor stops between 100 and 125 psi

29. In a single vehicle with a fully charged air system, air pressure loss (after an initial drop) should be less than _____ per minute.
    A. 2 psi
    B. 3 psi
    C. 4 psi
    D. 5 psi

30. When checking a single vehicle for air leaks with the brakes on, air pressure loss (after an initial drop) should be less than _____ per minute.
    A. 2 psi
    B. 3 psi
    C. 4 psi
    D. 5 psi

Combination Vehicles/Doubles/ Triples Questions

The following questions should serve as a good review for you as you prepare for this endorsement test. Answer sheets are provided starting on page 363. For answers, see page 399.

1. Before you begin coupling, _____.
   A. pre-position the fifth wheel
   B. check your path for hazards
   C. check the condition of the tractor frame
   D. put the spring brakes on

2. You can damage the landing gear by _____.
   A. aligning the tractor and trailer
   B. backing under the trailer at an angle
   C. positioning the trailer kingpin in the center of the fifth wheel V-slot
   D. backing under the trailer in a straight line

3. The trailer should be lowered so _____.
   A. the tractor strikes the nose of the trailer
   B. the trailer is well above the fifth wheel
   C. you can use the landing gear to make major adjustments
   D. it is raised slightly when the tractor is backed under it

4. Which of the following coupling steps comes first?
   A. apply the trailer brakes
   B. raise the landing gear
   C. put the transmission in reverse
   D. connect the air supply lines

5. When rolling up the landing gear to complete the coupling process, _____.
   A. begin in high gear to make the job go faster
   B. use low gear until the tractor is supporting the trailer
   C. leave the landing gear half-way down to speed the uncoupling process later
   D. use plenty of grease to make the job easier

6. If one of the glad hands on your blue air line is missing a seal, _____.
   A. it's a minor problem and you can proceed with the coupling
   B. you might end up with a service line air leak
   C. you might end up with an emergency line air leak
   D. you can take one off the red line and use that as a replacement

7. When uncoupling, if you park the trailer at an angle, _____.
   A. you'll save space in the yard
   B. you won't have to walk so far to get around the vehicle
   C. your job will be easier
   D. you could damage the landing gear

8. When uncoupling, it's a good practice to _____.
   A. couple the glad hands together
   B. couple the glad hands to dummy couplers
   C. hang the electrical cable with the plug end down
   D. all of the above

9. When you inspect the coupling, check to make sure that _____.
   A. there's a little slack in the air lines
   B. the landing gear handle is hanging free
   C. there's no slack in the air lines
   D. the electrical cable is unplugged

10. Inspect a converter dolly as if it were _____.
    A. cargo
    B. a trailer
    C. an axle with a fifth wheel
    D. an engine

11. A converter dolly may have its own air tank.
    A. True
    B. False

12. If you crossed your air lines on a new trailer with spring brakes, _____.
    A. you won't be able to release the trailer brakes
    B. you won't be able to release the tractor brakes
    C. you won't have any brakes at all
    D. you will have no way of knowing there's a problem

13. If you crossed the air lines on an old trailer, _____.
    A. you won't be able to release the trailer spring brakes
    B. you won't be able to release the tractor brakes
    C. you won't have any brakes at all
    D. you won't have any trailer brakes

14. To test the tractor protection valve, reduce the air pressure to _____. The valve should close automatically.
    A. zero
    B. 20 to 45 psi
    C. 60 psi
    D. 100 psi

15. To test the trailer emergency brake system, charge the trailer brakes. Then _____.
    A. press the treadle valve
    B. push in the blue, round knob
    C. pull the diamond-shaped, yellow knob
    D. pull the red, eight-sided knob

16. To test the trailer service brakes, _____.
    A. press the treadle valve
    B. use the trailer brake hand valve
    C. push in the blue round knob
    D. pull the red, eight-sided knob

17. To test for crossed air lines, _____.
    A. pull the red, eight-sided knob, then push it in and listen for brake movement air release
    B. pull the yellow knob out and push it in while listening for air flow
    C. turn the engine off, apply and release the brake pedal, and look for an air pressure drop
    D. turn the engine off, apply and release the trailer brakes with the hand valve, and listen for brake movement and air release

18. When you turn a corner, your trailer wheels follow a different path than your tractor wheels. This is _____.
    A. an alignment problem
    B. a steering problem
    C. a sign of a poorly coupled tractor-trailer
    D. normal

19. Trucks with double or triple trailers _____.
    A. have a dangerous "crack-the-whip" effect
    B. present a rearward amplification hazard
    C. can turn over in response to abrupt steering movements
    D. all of the above

20. If your vehicle starts to skid and you think it may jackknife, _____.
    A. put the tractor brakes on hard
    B. release the tractor brakes
    C. put on the trailer brakes
    D. turn the steering wheel sharply to the left, then back to the right

21. When coupling doubles, if the second trailer does not have spring brakes, _____.
    A. couple the second trailer to the first trailer before putting the tractor on
    B. drive the tractor close to the second trailer, connect the emergency line, charge the trailer air tank, and disconnect the emergency line
    C. you need a second tractor that can be left near the rear trailer
    D. put the rear trailer against a dock

22. When coupling doubles, start by _____.
    A. coupling the tractor to the second trailer
    B. backing the converter dolly under the second trailer
    C. coupling the converter tongue to the pintle hook on the first trailer
    D. putting the second trailer against a dock

23. On trailers used as doubles and triples you'll find shut-off valves (cut-off cocks) in the _____.
    A. service air lines
    B. emergency air lines
    C. service and emergency air lines
    D. parking brake system only

24. Should you unhook the pintle hook with the converter dolly still under a trailer?
    A. Yes. This is the standard procedure.
    B. Yes. This keeps the trailer from falling.
    C. No. This could damage the pintle hook.
    D. No. You could be injured if you do this.

25. Vehicles with double and triple trailers _____.
    A. have more parts that should be inspected
    B. need about the same amount of space and traffic gaps as other CMVs
    C. respond to steering corrections just like straight trucks
    D. are as stable as any other CMV

26. The dolly support _____.
    A. supports the dolly while it is being backed under a trailer
    B. supports the dolly air lines
    C. supports the spare tire carrier
    D. supports the tongue when the dolly isn't connected to anything

27. There is no way to check if the entire brake system in a triple is charged.
    A. True
    B. False

28. To make a right turn with a long vehicle combination, _____.
    A. swing to the left as you begin the turn
    B. use all the lanes you need before and during the turn
    C. guard against other vehicles trying to pass you on the left
    D. if you must use another lane to avoid running over the curb, swing wide as you complete the turn

29. Which has the most rearward amplification?
    A. a five-axle tractor-semitrailer
    B. turnpike doubles
    C. B-train doubles
    D. triples

30. You can prevent rollovers by keeping your load _____.
    A. low and centered between the trailer sides
    B. low and toward the right or curb side
    C. over the tractor drive wheels
    D. low and toward the left or road side

Tank Vehicles Questions

The following questions should serve as a good review for you as you prepare for the Tank Vehicles endorsement test. Answer sheets are provided starting on page 364. For answers, refer to page 400.

1. The best way to prevent rolling over when pulling a tanker through a curve is _____.
    A. travel at speeds below the posted limits
    B. travel faster than the posted speed limit
    C. get a running start going into the curve, then brake through the curve
    D. go into the curve at a slow speed, then speed up halfway through the curve

2. You will feel the effects of liquid surge less if you _____.
    A. turn slowly and carefully
    B. brake to a stop gradually
    C. haul thick liquids rather than thin ones
    D. all of the above

3. A smooth bore tanker is one that _____.
    A. is a long, hollow tube with no sharp corners
    B. is divided into compartments by bulkheads
    C. has baffles to control the surge factor
    D. can carry several different products at the same time

4. Dividers inside tankers that have openings at the top and bottom are called _____.
    A. bulkheads
    B. baffles
    C. barriers
    D. none of the above

5. Baffles in a tanker
    A. make this type of tanker easiest to clean
    B. control forward and back liquid surge
    C. eliminate side-to-side liquid surge
    D. allow you to haul several different products at the same time

6. Which is the most stable liquid tanker shape?
    A. van
    B. double conical
    C. cylindrical
    D. elliptical

7. The cladding in a tanker _____.
    A. cuts down on liquid surge
    B. cools down or heats up the cargo
    C. protects the tanker from corrosive cargo
    D. protects cargo from temperature extremes

8. What makes a bulk liquid tanker hard to handle?
    A. the cargo's high density
    B. the cargo's low center of gravity
    C. the cargo's high center of gravity
    D. friction

9. The amount of liquid to load into a tank depends on _____.
    A. the amount the liquid will expand in transit
    B. the weight of the liquid
    C. legal weight limits
    D. all of the above

10. Outage is _____.
    A. allowing for liquids to expand in transit
    B. the same as innage
    C. another name for a liquid level sensing device
    D. a dangerous practice when hauling liquid loads

11. When you have a liquid load, fanning the brakes will _____.
    A. cause the brakes to heat up and possibly fail
    B. increase the surge factor
    C. cause the vehicle to rock
    D. all of the above

12. Stop valves in a cargo tank _____.
    A. break off in an emergency
    B. close in an emergency
    C. can only be operated manually
    D. protect the tank and piping from rear-end collisions

13. A tanker that is "authorized" _____.
    A. has a DOT specification number
    B. may carry hazardous materials
    C. must be retested according to a specific schedule
    D. all of the above

14. Retest markings _____.
    A. must be stamped on the tank itself
    B. give the day, month, and year of the last retest
    C. show what type of test or inspection was performed
    D. are made by the driver

15. A retest marking reading "10-09, P, V, L" would tell you _____.
    A. that in October 2009, the cargo tank received and passed a pressure retest, external visual inspection and test, and a lining inspection
    B. that this is a DOT Specification 1009 tank carrying poisonous viscous liquid cargo
    C. that this tank passed a test on October 2009 and that it can carry various liquid loads
    D. nothing. This is not an official retest marking.

Hazardous Materials Questions

The following questions should serve as a good review for you as you prepare for the HazMat endorsement test. Answer sheets are provided staring on page 365. For answers, refer to page 400.

1. Requirements for the right kind of hazardous materials packages and the right way to load, transport, and unload bulk tanks are examples of _____.
   A. marking rules
   B. containment rules
   C. rules for communicating risk
   D. all of the above

2. Requirements to use the right shipping papers, package labels, and placards are examples of hazardous materials_____.
   A. marking rules
   B. containment rules
   C. rules for communicating risk
   D. all of the above

3. To assure that only safe drivers transport hazardous materials, drivers who transport hazmat must _____.
   A. have a CDL
   B. know the hazardous materials rules and pass a written test for the Hazardous Materials Endorsement
   C. complete special training for hauling certain materials
   D. all of the above

4. You are picking up a hazardous materials shipment and several packages are leaking. You should _____.
   A. wrap them in plastic
   B. be sure to wash out your truck when you finish unloading this shipment
   C. refuse this shipment
   D. note that the packages are leaking on your pre-trip inspection report

5. The person attending a vehicle placarded for hazardous materials _____.
   A. can be anyone you, as the driver, select
   B. must be the driver and no one else
   C. must have a perfect driving record
   D. must be qualified

6. A vehicle placarded for Division 1.1, 1.2, or 1.3 explosives _____.
   A. may never be left unattended under any condition
   B. may be left unattended in a safe haven
   C. may not be parked on the consignee's property
   D. may never be parked on private property

7. Which of these rules apply when hauling hazardous materials?
   A. Smoking is prohibited within 25 feet of a vehicle with hazardous materials.
   B. You may not park a vehicle with hazardous materials within 300 miles of a fire.
   C. You may only fuel a vehicle carrying hazardous materials at special fuel islands.
   D. When driving a vehicle with hazardous materials past a fire, you must stop and check the area before proceeding.

8. If you are hauling hazardous materials and have _____ tires on your vehicle, you must stop and check them every time you park.
   A. dual
   B. radial
   C. bias
   D. treaded

9. Hazardous waste may not be hauled in a vehicle that isn't marked with _____.
   A. the name or trade name of the private carrier operating the vehicle
   B. the motor carrier identification number
   C. the name of the person operating the vehicle, if that's not the carrier
   D. all of the above

10. If an X or an RQ is in the HM column of a shipping paper entry, the _____.
    A. material listed on that line is the largest part of the shipment
    B. entry refers to the materials that must be top loaded
    C. material listed on that line should be discarded
    D. shipment is regulated by hazardous materials regulations

11. Which of the following statements about hazardous materials is true?
    A. Contact with any hazardous material will kill you.
    B. Hazardous materials pose a risk to health, safety, and property during transportation.
    C. You must have a Hazardous Materials Endorsement on your CDL to drive a vehicle hauling any amount of hazardous material.
    D. A vehicle with any hazardous material on it must have placards.

12. On the Hazardous Materials Table, column 1 shows _____.
    A. how to ship an item
    B. to what shipping mode the information on that line applies
    C. how much of the material can be put in a vehicle without placarding
    D. what materials can be loaded together

13. On the Hazardous Materials Table, proper shipping names are shown _____.
    A. in plain type and alphabetical order
    B. in italic type and loading order
    C. so you know you must not transport that shipment
    D. so you know you can transport that shipment without placards

14. Which of these statements about shipping papers is true?
    A. Shipping papers may include hazardous and non-hazardous items.
    B. Hazardous items must be listed before non-hazardous items on the shipping paper.
    C. Reportable quantities will be identified differently from hazardous materials.
    D. all of the above

15. Hazardous waste shipments are identified by _____.
    A. the letters "HW" on the vehicle placards
    B. the word "waste" before the name of the material on the shipping papers
    C. the shipping name
    D. the name of the carrier

16. The Uniform Hazardous Waste Manifest must have _____.
    A. the quantity listed in pounds only
    B. an attached copy of the loading plan
    C. the signatures of everyone who released, transported, and received the shipment, with the dates of the transfer actions
    D. a record of the route taken

17. Tankers used to transport hazardous materials on vehicles must be marked with _____.
    A. the UN ID number of the product
    B. the date of manufacture
    C. the owner's PUCO or ICC number
    D. the CHEMTREC phone number

18. Which of the following statements about "Radioactive" labels is true?
    A. Yellow III indicates the highest level of radioactivity.
    B. Yellow II indicates the highest level of radioactivity.
    C. White I indicates the highest level of radioactivity.
    D. Black III indicates the highest level of radioactivity.

19. You are scheduled to transport 1,000 pounds each of non-flammable gas and pressurized liquid oxygen. Which of the following statements is true?
    A. You must refuse this load.
    B. You'll need two different types of placards.
    C. You'll need a liquid tanker with double-wall bulkheads.
    D. You'll need a "DANGEROUS" placard.

20. When a vehicle must be placarded, the placards must be _____.
    A. on the front, back, and both sides
    B. on both doors of the cab
    C. on the front and back, just above the license plate
    D. on each package

21. Tankers used to haul hazardous materials must _____.
    A. meet DOT specifications
    B. meet inspection, retest, and marking requirements
    C. have the month and year of the most recent test stamped into the metal of each tank or on a certification plate
    D. all of the above

22. Of the explosives, the least dangerous is _____.
    A. Division 1.1
    B. Division 1.2
    C. Division 1.3
    D. Division 1.6

23. Which of the following statements about flammable solids and fire is true?
    A. Friction can cause flammable solids to ignite.
    B. Flammable solids might retain heat from manufacturing or processing, and this heat can start a fire.
    C. Flammable solids may burn when combined with water.
    D. all of the above

24. Of the following hazardous material classes, which is the most dangerous?
    A. Division 6.1
    B. Division 6.2
    C. Division 6.3
    D. Division 6.4

25. ORM is regulated because _____.
    A. it's dangerous to transport because of the way it's packaged
    B. it is shipped only in large quantities
    C. it is an unknown material
    D. it is not properly labeled

26. Shipping papers _____.
    A. must have the shipper's certification
    B. must be marked differently from shipping papers for regular cargo
    C. must be carried in the vehicle so they are easy to get to in case of an accident, or for an inspection
    D. all of the above

27. Which of these statements about loading and unloading cargo tanks is false?
    A. The person attending the tanker must have a clear view of it.
    B. The person in attendance must be within 50 feet of the tanker.
    C. The person in attendance must be aware of the danger.
    D. The person in attendance must be authorized and able to move the vehicle.

28. Some hazardous materials may not be loaded together with other hazardous materials. The prohibited combinations are listed in the _____.
    A. Hazardous Materials Table
    B. List of Hazardous Materials and Reportable Quantities
    C. Segregation and Separation Chart
    D. Hazardous Waste Manifest

29. Do not load _____ with the engine running.
    A. explosives
    B. flammable liquids (unless they're needed to pump the product)
    C. compressed gases (unless they're needed to pump the product)
    D. all of the above

30. Which of the following statements about transporting hazardous materials is true?
    A. Trailers used to haul Division 1.1, 1.2, or 1.3 explosives must have a floor liner that doesn't contain iron or steel.
    B. You must never enter a tunnel when carrying cylinders of hydrogen or cryogenic liquids on your vehicle.
    C. You must stop before crossing a railroad track when hauling any amount of chlorine.
    D. all of the above

31. Which of the following statements about transporting chlorine is true?
    A. You must have a gas mask when you're hauling chlorine in a cargo tank.
    B. Before you couple or uncouple your tank, you must detach any loading and unloading connections.
    C. You must never leave the tank uncoupled from the tractor without chocking it first.
    D. all of the above

32. Which of the following statements about hauling hazardous materials with a cargo tank is true?
    A. The only time you should have liquid discharge valves open is during loading and unloading.
    B. For each shipment of flammable cryogenic liquid, you must make a written record of the cargo tank pressure and the outside temperature.
    C. You must complete your trip from start to finish within the one-way travel time.
    D. all of the above

33. You must control how far packages labeled "Radioactive II" or "Radioactive III" are located from people and cargo space walls by referring to _____.
    A. the transport index and the Separation Distances Table
    B. the Table of Hazardous Materials
    C. the List of Hazardous Materials and Reportable Quantities
    D. the Segregation and Separation Chart

34. Who is responsible for checking that the shipper has correctly named, labeled, and marked a hazardous materials shipment?
   A. the D.O.T.
   B. the carrier
   C. the shipper
   D. the manufacturer

35. Which of these statements about repairing vehicles with hazardous cargo is true?
   A. Devices that produce sparks may not be used to repair or maintain the cargo area or fuel system of your vehicle when you have a placarded load.
   B. While the work is being done, there must be someone able to move the vehicle immediately if that becomes necessary.
   C. The vehicle must be removed from the building as soon as the work is done.
   D. all of the above

36. When handling packages of explosives, you must _____.
   A. not use hooks or other metal tools
   B. keep bystanders 100 feet away
   C. roll the packages carefully with no sharp or jarring actions
   D. all of the above

37. Which of these statements about hazardous materials accidents is true?
   A. Open smoking packages of flammable solids if you can get to them.
   B. Remove broken and unbroken packages of flammable solids from the vehicle if it is safe to do so.
   C. Use a dry type of cleaner if a corrosive material leaks in your vehicle.
   D. all of the above

38. If hazardous material is leaking from your vehicle, _____.
   A. drive to a phone, truck stop, or service station as quickly as you can
   B. drive at as high a speed as is safe to spread the material thinly
   C. park the vehicle, secure the area, and send someone else for help
   D. get someone to watch the vehicle and go for help yourself since you know best what's needed

39. The markings on cargo tanks tell you about _____.
   A. the capacity
   B. the original test date
   C. the retest date
   D. all of the above

40. As the driver, your job at the scene of an accident is to _____.
   A. keep people away and upwind
   B. limit the spread of hazardous material, regardless of the risk to your safety
   C. make sure the shipping papers stay in the truck
   D. direct traffic

41. If someone is killed, injured and sent to the hospital, or total property damage exceeded $50,000 as a direct result of a hazardous materials incident, you or your employer must phone _____.
   A. your insurance agent
   B. the National Response Center
   C. the DOT
   D. CHEMTREC

42. A resource for local police and firefighters handling a hazardous materials incident is _____.
   A. the IMO
   B. the NRC
   C. the DOT
   D. the ICAO

43. If you are involved in a hazardous materials spill, you should call_____.
    A. either the National Response Center or CHEMTREC, but you may not call both
    B. either the National Response Center or CHEMTREC
    C. the National Response Center, instead of local police or firefighters
    D. the DOT

44. When you haul explosives, _____.
    A. some locations may require you to have special permits
    B. states may require you to follow special routes
    C. counties may require you to follow special routes
    D. all of the above

45. A vehicle involved in a leak of Division 2.3 or Division 6.1 must be _____.
    A. sent to a decontamination station
    B. checked for stray poison before being used again
    C. washed down by CHEMTREC
    D. never used again to haul food for humans

By now you should feel well-prepared for the knowledge part of your CDL test. If you've tackled every question in this book, you've had a lot of practice answering test questions. You can think of the CDL Knowledge Test as just another set of questions about material you're familiar with. And you can feel proud of the job you've done in this self-guided training course.

You know that you must take a Skills Test as well as a Knowledge Test to get your CDL. The next chapter will help you practice so you'll be ready for a typical CDL Skills Test.

ENDORSEMENT TESTS ANSWER SHEETS

Test Item	Answer Choices				Self - Scoring	
Air Brakes					Correct	Incorrect
1.	A	B	C	D	☐	☐
2.	A	B	C	D	☐	☐
3.	A	B	C	D	☐	☐
4.	A	B	C	D	☐	☐
5.	A	B	C	D	☐	☐
6.	A	B	C	D	☐	☐
7.	A	B	C	D	☐	☐
8.	A	B	C	D	☐	☐
9.	A	B	C	D	☐	☐
10.	A	B	C	D	☐	☐

Cut Here

Test Item	Answer Choices				Self - Scoring Correct Incorrect	
11.	A	B	C	D	☐	☐
12.	A	B	C	D	☐	☐
13.	A	B	C	D	☐	☐
14.	A	B	C	D	☐	☐
15.	A	B	C	D	☐	☐
16.	A	B	C	D	☐	☐
17.	A	B	C	D	☐	☐
18.	A	B	C	D	☐	☐
19.	A	B	C	D	☐	☐
20.	A	B	C	D	☐	☐
21.	A	B	C	D	☐	☐
22.	A	B	C	D	☐	☐
23.	A	B	C	D	☐	☐
24.	A	B	C	D	☐	☐
25.	A	B	C	D	☐	☐
26.	A	B	C	D	☐	☐
27.	A	B	C	D	☐	☐
28.	A	B	C	D	☐	☐
29.	A	B	C	D	☐	☐
30.	A	B	C	D	☐	☐

Cut Here

Test Item

Answer Choices

Combination Vehicles/
Doubles/Triples

1.	A	B	C	D
2.	A	B	C	D
3.	A	B	C	D
4.	A	B	C	D
5.	A	B	C	D
6.	A	B	C	D
7.	A	B	C	D
8.	A	B	C	D
9.	A	B	C	D
10.	A	B	C	D
11.	A	B	C	D
12.	A	B	C	D
13.	A	B	C	D
14.	A	B	C	D
15.	A	B	C	D
16.	A	B	C	D
17.	A	B	C	D
18.	A	B	C	D
19.	A	B	C	D
20.	A	B	C	D

Cut Here

364 Review

Test Item	Answer Choices				Self - Scoring Correct Incorrect	
21.	A	B	C	D	☐	☐
22.	A	B	C	D	☐	☐
23.	A	B	C	D	☐	☐
24.	A	B	C	D	☐	☐
25.	A	B	C	D	☐	☐
26.	A	B	C	D	☐	☐
27.	A	B	C	D	☐	☐
28.	A	B	C	D	☐	☐
29.	A	B	C	D	☐	☐
30.	A	B	C	D	☐	☐

Tank Vehicles

	Answer Choices				Correct	Incorrect
1.	A	B	C	D	☐	☐
2.	A	B	C	D	☐	☐
3.	A	B	C	D	☐	☐
4.	A	B	C	D	☐	☐
5.	A	B	C	D	☐	☐
6.	A	B	C	D	☐	☐
7.	A	B	C	D	☐	☐
8.	A	B	C	D	☐	☐
9.	A	B	C	D	☐	☐
10.	A	B	C	D	☐	☐

Cut Here

Test Item	Answer Choices				Self - Scoring Correct	Incorrect
11.	A	B	C	D	☐	☐
12.	A	B	C	D	☐	☐
13.	A	B	C	D	☐	☐
14.	A	B	C	D	☐	☐
15.	A	B	C	D	☐	☐
Hazardous Materials						
1.	A	B	C	D	☐	☐
2.	A	B	C	D	☐	☐
3.	A	B	C	D	☐	☐
4.	A	B	C	D	☐	☐
5.	A	B	C	D	☐	☐
6.	A	B	C	D	☐	☐
7.	A	B	C	D	☐	☐
8.	A	B	C	D	☐	☐
9.	A	B	C	D	☐	☐
10.	A	B	C	D	☐	☐

Cut Here

Test Item	Answer Choices				Self - Scoring Correct Incorrect	
11.	A	B	C	D	☐	☐
12.	A	B	C	D	☐	☐
13.	A	B	C	D	☐	☐
14.	A	B	C	D	☐	☐
15.	A	B	C	D	☐	☐
16.	A	B	C	D	☐	☐
17.	A	B	C	D	☐	☐
18.	A	B	C	D	☐	☐
19.	A	B	C	D	☐	☐
20.	A	B	C	D	☐	☐
21.	A	B	C	D	☐	☐
22.	A	B	C	D	☐	☐
23.	A	B	C	D	☐	☐
24.	A	B	C	D	☐	☐
25.	A	B	C	D	☐	☐

Cut Here

Cut Here

Test Item	Answer Choices				Self - Scoring Correct Incorrect	
26.	A	B	C	D	☐	☐
27.	A	B	C	D	☐	☐
28.	A	B	C	D	☐	☐
29.	A	B	C	D	☐	☐
30.	A	B	C	D	☐	☐
31.	A	B	C	D	☐	☐
32.	A	B	C	D	☐	☐
33.	A	B	C	D	☐	☐
34.	A	B	C	D	☐	☐
35.	A	B	C	D	☐	☐
36.	A	B	C	D	☐	☐
37.	A	B	C	D	☐	☐
38.	A	B	C	D	☐	☐
39.	A	B	C	D	☐	☐
40.	A	B	C	D	☐	☐
41.	A	B	C	D	☐	☐
42.	A	B	C	D	☐	☐
43.	A	B	C	D	☐	☐
44.	A	B	C	D	☐	☐
45.	A	B	C	D	☐	☐

Chapter 15

CDL Skills Tests

In this chapter you will learn about:

- what the CDL Skills Tests cover
- how the CDL Skills Tests test your ability to inspect your vehicle
- how the CDL Skills Tests test your basic ability to control your vehicle
- how the CDL Skills Tests test your safe driving ability

To complete this chapter, you will need:

- the owner's manual for your vehicle
- the Federal Motor Carrier Safety Regulations pocketbook (or access to U.S. Department of Transportation regulations, Parts 383, 393, and 396 of Subchapter B, Chapter 3, Title 49, Code of Federal Regulations)
- a CDL preparation manual from your state Department of Motor Vehicles, if one is offered
- the driver's manual from your state Department of Motor Vehicles

By now you should feel well prepared for the CDL Knowledge Test. You've seen many sample, pre-trip, post-trip, and review test questions. Did you answer every one of them? Then you should feel less anxious about this type of test-taking.

As you know, that's not all there is to CDL testing. You'll have to take a Skills Test as well. The main skill areas tested are:

- pre-trip inspection
- basic vehicle control
- safe driving
- air brakes (to avoid the Air Brake Restriction)

At least some of the skills must be tested in "on-street" conditions. Some of them may be tested off the street, or with a truck simulator.

You must take your CDL tests in a vehicle that is "representative" of the one you plan to drive.

This means that your test vehicle must belong to the same group, A, B, or C, as your work vehicle. It doesn't mean that the two vehicles must be the same make or model. They simply must belong to the same group.

The representative vehicle may have to be equipped with air brakes. If you wish to drive a CMV with an air brake system, you must take your Skills Tests in a vehicle with air brakes. If you take the Skills Tests in a vehicle without air brakes, an air brake restriction is put on your CDL. This would also be the case if you don't pass the air brake part of the Skills Tests. This means you are not allowed to drive a CMV with an air brake system. This includes braking systems that rely in whole or in part on air brakes.

Refer to the table below to see what tests you must take for the different vehicle groups.

Required CDL Skills Tests

Vehicle Group	Skills Tests Required
Group A	Pre-trip Inspection Basic Control Skills Road Test
Group B	Pre-trip Inspection Basic Control Skills Road Test
Group C	Road Test

"Passing" on the Skills Tests depends on what's being tested. In all cases, anyone who breaks a traffic law automatically fails the test. So does anyone who causes an accident during the test.

Your state may excuse military drivers from having to take the Skills Tests. You must meet certain conditions, though. You must have a current, valid license, and have a good driving record. A "good driving record" means that, in the past two years, you have not had your license suspended, revoked, or canceled. You must not have been disqualified from driving in the past two years. Your driving record for the past two years must be free of traffic violations connected with an accident (other than parking violations).

Other restrictions may apply.

Let's assume, though, that you will be taking the Skills Tests. In this chapter, we'll give you an idea of what the tests will be like. You'll learn what the examiners will be looking for. And, we'll give you some tips on how to "practice" and prepare for the Skills Tests.

PRE-TRIP INSPECTION

Part of the Skills Test will be on your ability to inspect your vehicle. When you take the Knowledge Test, you'll answer questions about vehicle inspection. When you take the Skills Tests, you will actually do one.

Having read Chapter 9, you know what a "basic" inspection involves. Keep this in mind as well. You must take your Skills Tests in, and therefore inspect, a representative vehicle. If you don't want the Air Brake Restriction, your vehicle must have air brakes. You'll have to show you know how to inspect the air brake system. Then, if you want one or more of the endorsements, your vehicle inspection will include extra steps. These extra steps are covered in the chapters that deal with the endorsements. Be sure to read those chapters thoroughly.

Most states will have you do an inspection as part of the Skills Tests. The purpose is to see if you know whether the vehicle is safe to drive. You may actually only do certain parts of a complete inspection. You will have to describe anything you would do if you were inspecting your vehicle completely.

During the Inspection Test, you may also be asked to describe in some detail the different parts and systems on your vehicle. Or, the examiner may have you stop your inspection from time to time and ask you questions about your equipment.

As you examine your vehicle, tell the examiner what you are inspecting. Describe what you find. You're not likely to take a defective vehicle to the test. However, the examiner will want to know you would recognize a defect if you saw one. So as you inspect your vehicle, mention the defects likely to be found at the different sites. Explain how those defects impair safety.

The examiner may ask you for more details. For example, you might say, "The hoses are not cracked or rubbing." The examiner may tell you to point out just which hoses you are talking about. You may be asked to state the function of the hoses.

Or, you might point to the battery and state that it's in good shape. The examiner might ask you to name the part and ask how you know it's in good shape. You'll have to respond like this: "This is the battery. It's securely mounted, and it's not cracked. There's no corrosion. The cables are securely attached to the correct posts," and so on.

The examiner will not prompt you or give you hints. If you forget a step, the examiner will just assume you don't know how to do a complete inspection. For this reason, you may want to have an Inspection Aid with you. Usually, you may have a checklist with you when you take the Inspection Test. Check with your state to see if for some reason this is not allowed. Otherwise, feel free to use the checklist. You'll be less likely to overlook something if you check off items as you go.

You'll usually find just such Inspection Aids in the CDL manual your state provides. There will likely be one for straight trucks, and another for tractor-trailers. You'll also find Inspection Aids at the end of this section. Your state may allow you to use the aids it provides, but not the ones in this book. You could ask about this when you arrange to take your Skills Tests. Or, bring both with you just in case.

Inspection Test Site

You'll usually take the Inspection Test in a flat parking area or open lot. Examiners will avoid using a parking space on a street, or any place where traffic passes close by. If you do have to take the test in a busy area, don't get so involved taking the test that you forget to check for traffic and other hazards.

Safety Tips

Do keep your own safety in mind while you take the test. Never get under, in front of, or behind a vehicle when there's any chance at all that the vehicle might move. Don't brace your foot on top of the bumper when you pull the engine hood open.

Use care getting in and out of the vehicle. Know where the cab footholds are on your vehicle. Make sure they're free of dirt and grease. Then use them. Use the three-point stance.

Appendix C

Motor Transport Associations

Alabama
Alabama Trucking Association
P.O. Box 242337
Montgomery, AL 36124-2337
(877) 277-TRUK
www.alabamatrucking.org

Alaska
Alaska Trucking Association
3443 Minnesota Dr.
Anchorage, AK 99503
(907) 276-1149
www.aktrucks.org

Arizona
Arizona Trucking Association
7500 West Madison St.
Tolleson, AZ 85353
(602) 850-6000
www.arizonatrucking.com

Arkansas
Arkansas Trucking Association
P.O. Box 3476
Little Rock, AR 72203

1401 West Capitol Ave.
Little Rock, AR 72201
(501) 372-3462
www.arkansastrucking.com

California
California Trucking Association
4148 E. Commerce Way
Sacramento, CA 95834
(916) 373-3500
www.caltrux.org

Colorado
Colorado Motor Carriers Association
4060 Elati St.
Denver, CO 80216
(303) 433-3375
www.cmca.com

Connecticut
Motor Transport Association of Connecticut
60 Forest St.
Hartford, CT 06105
(860) 520-4455
www.mtac.us/

Delaware
Delaware Motor Transport Association
445 Pear St.
Dover, DE 19904
(302) 734-9400
http://www.dscc.com/Trucking/Delaware-Motor-Transport-Association-1314

Florida
Florida Trucking Association
350 E. College Ave.
Tallahassee, FL 32301
(850) 222-9900
www.fltrucking.org

Georgia
Georgia Motor Trucking Association
2060 Franklin Way, Suite 200
Marietta, GA 30067
(770) 444-9771
www.gmta.org

Hawaii
Hawaii Transportation Association
P.O. Box 30166
Honolulu, HI 96820
(808) 833-6628
www.htahawaii.org

Idaho
Idaho Trucking Association
3405 East Overland Rd., Suite 175
Meridian, ID 83642
(208) 342-3521
www.idtrucking.org

Illinois
Illinois Trucking Associations
7000 Adams Suite 130
Willow Brook, IL 60527
(630) 654-0884
www.iltrucking.org

Indiana
Indiana Motor Truck Association
1 North Capitol Ave., Suite 460
Indianapolis, IN 46204
(317) 630-4682
http://www.intrucking.org/

Iowa
Iowa Motor Truck Association
717 East Court Ave.
Des Moines, IA 50309
(515) 244-5193
www.iowamotortruck.com

Kansas
Kansas Motor Carriers Association
2900 S.W. Topeka Blvd.
P.O. Box 1673
Topeka, KS 66601
(785) 267-1641
www.kmca.org

Kentucky
Kentucky Motor Transport Association
617 Shelby St.
Frankfort, KY 40601
(502) 227-0848
http://kmta.net/

Louisiana
Louisiana Motor Transport Association, Inc.
4838 Bennington Ave.
P.O. Box 80278
Baton Rouge, LA 70898
(225) 928-5682
http://www.louisianatrucking.com/

Maine
Maine Motor Transport Association
P.O. Box 857
142 Whitten Rd.
Augusta, ME 04332
(207) 623-4128
www.mmta.com

Maryland
Maryland Motor Truck Association, Inc.
3000 Washington Blvd.
Baltimore, MD 21230
(410) 644-4600
www.mmtanet.com

Massachusetts
Massachusetts Motor Transportation Association
12 Post Office Square
6th Floor
Boston, MA 02109
(617) 695-3512
www.mass-trucking.org

Michigan
Michigan Trucking Association
1131 Centennial Way
Lansing, MI 48917
(517) 321-1951
www.mitrucking.org

Minnesota
Minnesota Trucking Association
2277 Highway 36 West, Suite 302
Roseville, MN 55113
(651) 646-7351
www.mntruck.org

Mississippi
Mississippi Trucking Association
825 North President St.
Jackson, MS 39202
601-354-0616
www.mstrucking.org

Missouri
Missouri Trucking Association
102 East High St.
Jefferson City, MO 65101
(573) 634-3388
www.motrucking.org

Montana
Motor Carriers of Montana
501 N. Sanders #201
Helena, MT 59601
(406) 442-6600
www.mttrucking.org

Nebraska
Nebraska Trucking Association
1701 K St.
P.O. Box 81010
Lincoln, NE 68501
402-476-8504
www.nebtrucking.com

Nevada
Nevada Motor Transport Association
8745 Technology Way, Suite E
Reno, NV 89521
(775) 673-6111
http://nevadatrucking.com/

New Hampshire
New Hampshire Motor Transport Association
19 Henniker St.
Concord, NH 03302
(603) 224-7337
http://www.nhmta.org/

New Jersey
New Jersey Motor Truck Association
160 Tices Lane
East Brunswick, NJ 08816
(732) 254-5000
www.njmta.org

New Mexico
New Mexico Trucking Association
4700 Lincoln NE
Albuquerque, NM 87109
(505) 884-5575
www.nmtrucking.org

New York
New York State Motor Truck Association
7 Corporate Drive
Clifton Park, NY 12065
(518) 458-9696
www.nytrucks.org

North Carolina
North Carolina Trucking Association
4000 Westchase Blvd., Suite 210
Raleigh, NC 27607
(919) 281-2742
http://nctrucking.wildapricot.org/

North Dakota
North Dakota Motor Carriers Association, Inc.
1937 East Capitol Ave.
Bismarck, ND 58501

P.O. Box 874
Bismarck, ND 58501
(701) 223-2700
www.ndmca.org

Ohio
Ohio Trucking Association
21 E. State St., Suite 900
Columbus, OH 43215
(614) 221-5375
http://ohiotrucking.org/

Oklahoma
Oklahoma Trucking Association
3909 N. Lindsay Ave.
Oklahoma City, OK 73105
(405) 525-9488
http://oktrucking.org/

Oregon
Oregon Trucking Associations
4005 SE Naef Rd.
Portland, OR 97267
(503) 513-0005
www.ortrucking.org

Pennsylvania
Pennsylvania Motor Truck Association
910 Linda Lane
Camp Hill, PA 17011
717-761-7122
www.pmta.org

Rhode Island
Rhode Island Trucking Association
660 Roosevelt Ave.
Pawtucket, RI 02860
(401) 729-6600
www.ritrucking.org

South Carolina
South Carolina Trucking Association
P.O. Box 50166
Columbia, SC 29250

2425 Devine St.
Columbia, SC 29205
(803) 799-4306
www.sctrucking.org

South Dakota
South Dakota Trucking Association
P.O. Box 89008
Sioux Falls, SD 57109
(605) 334-8871
www.southdakotatrucking.com

Tennessee
Tennessee Trucking Association
4531 Trousdale Dr.
Nashville, TN 37204
(615) 777-2882
www.tntrucking.org

Texas
Texas Trucking Association
700 East 11th St.
Austin, TX 78701
(800) 727-7135
www.tmta.com

Utah
Utah Trucking Association
4181 West 2100 South
Salt Lake City, UT 84104
(801) 973-9370
www.utahtrucking.com

Vermont
Vermont Truck & Bus Association, Inc.
P.O. Box 3898
Concord, NH 03302
(802) 479-1778
www.vtba.org

Virginia
Virginia Trucking Association
1707 Summit Avenue, Suite 110
Richmond, VA 23230
(804) 355-5371
www.vatrucking.org

Washington
Washington Trucking Associations and WTA
Services, Inc.
2102 Carriage Dr. SW, Bldg. F
Olympia, WA 98502
(800) 732-9019, (253) 838-1650
www.wtatrucking.com

West Virginia
West Virginia Trucking Association
2006 Kanawha Blvd. E
Charleston, WV 25311
(304) 345-2800
http://www.wvtrucking.com/

Wisconsin
Wisconsin Motor Carriers Association
P.O. Box 44849
Madison, WI 53744
(608) 833-8200
www.witruck.org

Wyoming
Wyoming Trucking Association
555 N. Poplar St.
Casper, WY 82601

P.O. Box 1175
Casper, WY 82602
(307) 234-1579
www.wytruck.org

National
American Trucking Associations (ATA)
950 North Glebe Rd., Suite 210
Arlington, VA 22203
(703) 838-1700
www.trucking.org

Canadian Trucking Alliance
555 Dixon Rd.
Toronto, ON M9W 1H8
(416) 249-7401
www.cantruck.ca

Appendix D

Transportation Agencies

Federal Motor Carrier Safety Administration

http://www.fmcsa.dot.gov

Motor Carrier Safety Service Centers

Eastern Service Center
802 Cromwell Park Drive, Suite N
Glen Burnie, MD 21061
Phone: (443) 703-2240
Fax: (443) 703-2253
Connecticut, DC, Delaware, Massachusetts,
Maryland, Maine, New Hampshire, New Jersey,
New York, Pennsylvania, Puerto Rico, Rhode
Island, Virginia, Vermont, West Virginia,
Virgin Islands

Midwestern Service Center
4749 Lincoln Mall Dr., Suite 300A
Matteson, IL 60443
Phone: (708) 283-3577
Fax: (708) 283-3579
Iowa, Illinois, Indiana, Kansas, Michigan,
Minnesota, Missouri, Nebraska, Ohio, Wisconsin

Southern Service Center
1800 Century Blvd., Suite 1700
Atlanta, GA 30345
Phone: (404) 327-7400
Fax: (404) 327-7349
Alabama, Arkansas, Florida, Georgia, Kentucky,
Louisiana, Mississippi, North Carolina,
Oklahoma, South Carolina, Tennessee

Western Service Center
Golden Hills Office Centre
12600 West Colfax Ave., Suite B-300
Lakewood, CO 80215
Phone: (303) 407-2350
Fax: (303) 407-2339
Alaska, American Samoa, Arizona, California,
Colorado, Guam, Hawaii, Idaho, Northern
Mariana Islands, Montana, New Mexico, North
Dakota, Nevada, Oregon, South Dakota, Texas,
Utah, Washington, Wyoming

Appendix E

FMCSR Part 395

Federal Motor Carrier Saftey Regulations (FMCSR) Part 395 covers the Hours of Service of Drivers. It requires drivers to keep a Record of Duty Status. The subjects covered by this Part include the following:

- maximum driving and on-duty time
- travel time
- driver's record of duty status
- adverse driving conditions
- emergency conditions
- relief from regulations
- drivers declared "out of service"

Driving is different from almost every other profession. You usually don't work a set schedule. You don't stop driving just because the clock says it's 5:00 P.M. You don't stop driving just because Friday is about to turn into Saturday. You don't park the truck just because you've been on-duty for eight hours.

Instead, you work the number of hours your schedule or run requires, within the limits set in FMCSR Part 395. These limits are called the "hours of service regulations." The regulations state that you can work just so many hours at a time. Your legal day is the number of hours the regulations permit you to work before you must stop to rest. The number of hours you can work and the kind of work you can do on any day depends on the hours you worked the day before, up to eight days in the past.

You record the hours you worked and the kind of work you did in a log book. This log is called your "record of duty status." It helps you stay within the hours of service limits.

The first section in FMCSR Part 395 defines terms used throughout the rest of the Part. They are as follows:

On-duty time. From the moment you begin your work day until the time you are relieved of your duties, you are on-duty. If you are required to be ready for work, then you are on-duty. Even if you are just sitting at the terminal waiting for your truck to be loaded, you are on-duty. All of the time you spend working but not driving is called on-duty (not driving) or (ON) time. Here are some examples of on-duty not driving time:

- waiting to be dispatched
- inspecting or servicing your vehicle
- time spent as a co-driver (unless you are in the sleeper berth)
- loading and unloading, including supervising and taking care of paper work
- repairing, getting help for, or waiting with a disabled vehicle
- complying with the requirements of alcohol- and drug-testing programs
- providing a service for the carrier
- any other work that you are paid for by the trucking company or another job

You are on-duty (driving) or (D) when you are at the vehicle's controls. This is also referred to as "driving time" or simply "driving."

The on-duty and off-duty times add up to 24, the number of hours in an ordinary day.

Seven consecutive days. This is seven days, one right after the other. It can be any seven days in succession. (A "day" is any 24-hour period. A "24-hour period" is also defined in this section.)

Eight consecutive days. This is eight days, one right after the other.

Twenty-four-hour period. This is a period of 24 hours, one right after the other. You start counting based on what time it was at the terminal from which you are normally dispatched. That is, you don't add or subtract hours as you cross time zones.

Sleeper berth. When this term is used, it means that area of the truck meeting the specifications in

FMCSR Part 393. You'll see later that time spent in the sleeper is logged separately from ON or D (driving). You'll also see you can't log time as spent in the sleeper if you're napping on the seat. You must be "officially in" the "official sleeper."

Driver-salesman. Some drivers who work for private carriers are called "driver-salesmen." They sell products as well as transport them. Driver-salesmen drive within 100 miles of the terminal where they report for work. They do not spend more than 50 percent of their ON time driving.

Multiple stops. All stops made in any one village, town, or city may be counted as one stop.

Automatic on-board recording device. Your vehicle may have a device that completes your log for you. You may hear this called an ELD—an electronic logging device. It must record at least engine use, road speed, miles driven, the date, and time of day.

Figure E-1. An electronic logging device or on-board computer.

MAXIMUM DRIVING AND ON-DUTY TIME

FMCSR Part 395 sets the limits for how long you may drive. These rules limit the amount of total work that you may do and the total number of hours that you may spend driving. After 10 straight hours of off-duty time, you may drive for no more than 11 hours. After 10 straight hours of off-duty time, you may be on-duty for no more than 14 hours. Of the 14 hours, 11 may be spent driving.

As you might expect, there are exceptions. Drivers may extend the 14-hour-on-duty period to 16 hours on-duty under the following conditions:

- they are released from duty at the location to which they normally report for work for the five previous duty tours and

- they return to that normal work-reporting location and are released from duty within 16 hours and
- they haven't used this exception in the previous seven days except following a 34-hour restarting of a 7/8 day period.

This "restart" period allows drivers to begin a new weekly cycle if they take 34 consecutive (one right after the other) hours off.

In no case may the total number of hours that you spend driving exceed 11 hours.

These are rules for drivers of cargo-carrying vehicles. There are different rules for drivers who carry passengers.

You must get at least 10 hours of rest off-duty. You may split this into two very specific rest periods. In other words, you can combine one period of at least eight consecutive hours of rest in the sleeper berth with another rest period of at least two consecutive hours. You may take this second rest period in the sleeper berth, or you may be off-duty, or it may be a combination of these two. Note that for the sleeper berth time, you must be in the sleeper berth. You cannot be in the passenger seat and log that as sleeper berth time. The driving time immediately before and after these rest periods must not exceed 11 hours. Also, the total on-duty time before and after these rest periods must not include any driving beyond the 14th hour.

You may not return to driving without taking

- at least 10 consecutive hours off-duty or
- at least 10 consecutive hours in the sleeper berth or
- a combination of at least eight consecutive hours of sleeper berth and at least two consecutive hours of off-duty time

Drivers at natural gas or oil wells may rest elsewhere other than the sleeper berth but must get the same amount of rest.

If your company does not work every day of the week, you must not drive after being on-duty for 60 hours in seven straight days. This is often called the 60 hours/7-day rule. If your company does work every day of the week, you must not drive after being on-duty for 70 hours in a period of eight straight days. You may hear this referred to as the 70 hours/8-day rule. Drivers in Alaska are sometimes exempt from these rules. They may not drive more than 15 hours after being off-duty for eight hours. They may not drive after being on-duty for 20 hours or more after an eight-hour off-duty period. They may not drive after being on-duty for 70 hours in seven consecutive days for a carrier that doesn't work every day. They may not drive after being on-duty for 80 hours in eight consecutive days for a carrier that does work every day.

Drivers in Alaska may encounter adverse driving conditions. These drivers may drive as long as they need to in order to complete the run. After that, these drivers must be off-duty for at least 10 consecutive hours before driving again.

Driver-salesmen are exempt from these rules if driving time doesn't go over 40 hours in seven consecutive days.

Drivers who only work to make deliveries from retail stores to consumers are exempt from December 10 through December 25. They are limited to driving within 100 miles of where they normally report for work.

For some drivers of oil-well servicing vehicles, on-duty (ON) time does not always include waiting time. They must carefully account for all their waiting time.

TRAVEL TIME

Sometimes you may have to travel for your motor carrier. You are not driving or doing any other kind of work. Perhaps you're just flying to another state to collect a broken-down tractor. This is still counted as on-duty time unless you take 10 straight hours off when you reach the destination. If you do take the off-duty time, then you'll be considered off-duty for the entire time. That's the travel time plus the 10 straight hours off.

LOG BOOKS

You must keep a "record of duty status." Most people in the industry call this a "log book" or "log." A log book shows how you spent your time for each 24-hour period. You can use a handwritten log. If you do, you must make two copies. You must record the information on a form that meets the requirement of FMCSR Part 395. This is referred to as a "grid." There are examples of dif-

ferent types of grids in the FMCSR. You may also use Forms MCS-59, MCS-139, and 193A. These are older forms that still meet the requirements of FMCSR Part 395.

You may also record your hours with an electronic logging device (ELD). If ELDs are used on the trucks you are to drive, your carrier will make sure you know how to use them. You should still know how to do a log by hand. ELDs can break down. You will have to do your log by hand until the ELD is repaired.

You will log four different types of duty status. They are:

- off-duty or OFF
- sleeper berth or SB (but only if the sleeper berth is used)
- driving or D
- on-duty (not driving) or ON

Note that you don't record sleeper berth time if your vehicle doesn't have a sleeper.

Every time you change from one duty status to the other, you log it. You log where you were when this change occurred. You can show this with the highway number, the nearest milepost, the name of the nearest town, city or village, and the state abbreviation. If you are at a truck stop or service station, you can put the name of the business in place of the milepost. If you are at an intersection of two highways, put the number of the two roads instead of the milepost.

The log calls for other information besides change of duty status and location. You must also record:

- the date
- the total miles you drove the day you fill out the log
- the truck or tractor and trailer number
- the name of your motor carrier
- the driver's signature or certification
- the starting time of this 24-hour period
- the motor carrier's main office address
- remarks (the information about where your change of duty status took place)
- the co-driver's name, if there's a co-driver
- total hours
- shipping document numbers, or the name of the shipper and the freight

If your work isn't properly logged, both you and your motor carrier may be prosecuted. Your log must meet the following requirements:

Entries to be current. At all times, your log must be current to your last change of duty status.

Entries made by driver only. The log reflects the driver's duty status. If you are the driver, your handwritten log must be in **your** handwriting. It must be readable.

Date. Put the month, day, and year for the start of each 24-hour period.

Total mileage driven. "Total mileage driven" is NOT the total of the miles the truck moved. Don't include miles driven by the co-driver. (The co-driver's mileage goes on the log the co-driver completes.) Record the total miles driven by the driver.

Vehicle identification. Look for tractor numbers on the front of the cab or on the door. You can find trailer numbers on the front panel or the rear doors. If you cannot find the vehicle identification numbers, use the license plate number.

Name of carrier. This is the name of the motor carrier you are doing this run for. It may be different from the motor carrier you usually work for. You may work for more than one carrier in a 24-hour period. In that case, show both names. Follow each name with the start and finish time worked for that carrier. Don't forget to include AM and PM with these start and finish times.

Signature/certification. When you, as the driver, sign the log, you are saying everything is true and correct. You must use your legal signature, not your nickname or initials.

Twenty-four-hour period. Use the time in effect at your home terminal. Don't try to account for changes in time as you cross time zones. Start the 24-hour period, seven and eight consecutive days with the time your motor carrier specifies for your home terminal.

Main office address. If your motor carrier has more than one terminal, the address of the main office is the one called for here.

Recording days off-duty. You may have two or more consecutive 24-hour periods off-duty. You may record all of them on one log.

Total hours. Total all the hours spent in each duty status. Record the total for each to the right of the grid. They should add up to 24. If they don't, you've made an error somewhere. Either you added wrong or you forgot to record something.

Shipping document numbers. If you do not have a shipping document number to put here, use the name of the shipper and what's being shipped.

GRID PREPARATION

You must fill out the grid as described in FMCSR Part 395. You can use the form horizontally or vertically. The following description assumes you're using the form horizontally.

The four rows in the grid are for the length of time spent in each duty status. The columns mark off time segments. Each block in each row is one hour. Each long line in the middle of each block is the half hour (30 minutes). The short lines are quarter hours (15 minutes). The first one is one-fourth (15 minutes after the hour) and the second is three-fourths (45 minutes after the hour). In other words, each hour is broken into fourths. Each line within each box is one-fourth hour. You record your duty status to the nearest quarter of an hour.

To record the length of time spent in each duty status, start at the vertical line that represents the start time, to the nearest quarter hour. Put your pencil on that vertical line in the row for the duty status you are about to begin. Draw an unbroken horizontal line. The line stops at the quarter hour marker that stands for the time when you next switch duty status. Draw an unbroken vertical line up or down along the line that represents the time you switch status. Stop when you get to the row for the next duty status. Then start a new unbroken horizontal line in the new duty status.

This is easier to do than to describe! Figure E-2 may clear up any confusion you may have at this point.

Whenever you change duty status, you must record the location where the change took place. This is done in the remarks section. You recall there are three ways to describe the locations where the duty status change took place.

FILLING OUT THE LOG

You will have to fill out an original and one copy of each log. You must send the original log to your carrier within 13 days after you complete the form. If you drive for more than one carrier, you must send each carrier a complete copy of your log.

You must keep the copies of your logs for the past seven straight days with you.

EXEMPTIONS

Most drivers have to keep logs just as we've described. Some drivers are exempt. To be exempt, they must meet all these conditions:

- they work within a 100 air-mile radius of where they normally report for work
- they return to where they normally report for work within 12 consecutive hours
- they have eight consecutive hours off-duty between each 12-hour on-duty shift
- they don't exceed 10 hours driving time after eight consecutive hours off-duty
- their motor carrier keeps a record of their time as described in FMCSR Part 395

Some drivers in Hawaii are also exempt from logging requirements. So are

- some drivers transporting agricultural commodities
- some drivers involved in ground water well-drilling operations
- some transporters of construction materials and equipment
- some utility service drivers

While you may use an electronic logging device, you do need to know how to complete a paper log should the device fail.

EMERGENCIES

You may exceed the maximum driving time allowed under certain conditions. You may drive for two extra hours if you find yourself driving under adverse conditions that prevent you from completing your run within the allowed 11 hours. Adverse driving conditions do not mean a route without a café! Instead, adverse conditions include:

- snow
- sleet
- fog
- highways covered with snow or ice

Also included are unusual road or traffic conditions if the dispatcher didn't know about them when you began your run. If you meet such conditions and can't safely complete your run in the maximum allowed driving time, you may drive longer. You may drive a CMV no more than two more hours to finish the run or reach a place of

Figure E-2. A sample of a completed log.

safety. Still, drivers of property-carrying CMVs may not drive

- for more than 14 hours total, following 10 consecutive hours off-duty
- after being on-duty after the end of the 14th hour after coming on-duty, following 10 consecutive hours off-duty

At least 10 consecutive hours off-duty must separate each 11 hours on-duty. Drivers of property-carrying CMVs must not exceed 11 hours maximum driving time, following 10 consecutive hours off-duty.

If you work in Alaska and you encounter adverse driving conditions, you may continue to drive for two more hours. Even still, you may not drive more than 13 hours altogether, following 10 consecutive hours off-duty. Nor may you drive after you have been on-duty after the end of the 14th hour after coming on-duty, following 10 consecutive hours off-duty.

If an emergency comes up that causes a delay in your run, you may complete your run. This is only if the run could have been finished within the usual time limit had there not been an emergency.

The hours of service rules are also set aside when a driver provides transportation to help in a natural disaster, like an earthquake or flood.

PENALTIES

If you don't keep track of your time properly or don't obey the rules about how much time you spend working, you can be declared "out of service." Any agent of the Federal Highway Administration (FHWA) may inspect your log book and declare you out of service. These agents include highway patrol officers, DOT inspectors, and weigh masters.

You may be put out of service for disobeying the hours of service regulations. This would be the case if you work more hours than FMCSR Part 395 allows. When that happens, you must go off-duty immediately. You may not go back on-duty until you have had all the off-duty or sleeper time you are supposed to have.

You can be put out of service for not having a current record of duty status. If your log is current for the past six days, but not for the present day, you are given a chance to bring it up to date.

Otherwise, you are put out of service. Then you must be off-duty for the number of consecutive hours that the regulations require. The hours may be spent as sleeper berth time. Your carrier cannot require or permit you to drive during this period. You must get a copy of the out-of-service form to your carrier within 24 hours.

ELECTRONIC LOGGING DEVICES (ELDs)

As you have seen, you may use ELDs to do your log. This device will show how much time you spent in each duty status. It will show your start time for that 24-hour period. Electronic logging devices must be able to produce a printed log (printout) for officials who want to check your hours. The driver must sign any such printouts. ELDs must store information for the past seven consecutive days. They must record the same information as the handwritten log. This includes not only the four duty-status types. It also includes the date, total mileage today, vehicle numbers, carrier name, main office address, and so on.

If handwritten entries are needed, they must be made by the driver, in the driver's own handwriting.

Should your ELD fail, you must make note of it. As the driver, you will have to recreate any lost or missing records for the past seven days. You will have to continue to do your log by hand until the ELD is repaired.

On your vehicle, you must have instructions telling you how to store information in the ELD. You must have instructions on how to get information out of the ELD. You must have enough blank log grids for the current run.

As the driver, you must still get each day's log to the carrier within 13 days. With an ELD, there may be a way to do this electronically. Before you send your log to your carrier, you must check that all the entries the ELD has made are correct. In sending the log to the carrier you certify that this is a true and correct record of your duty status.

Even though your vehicle has an ELD, the FHWA may require you or your motor carrier to return to handwritten logs. One reason for this is if the carrier's drivers set a pattern of exceeding the hours of service limits. It can also be required if the motor carrier or any of the drivers tamper with the electronic logging devices.

Glossary

The following section contains definitions and explanations of terms used in your text and in the industry.

A

AC Alcohol concentration.

Agent A person authorized to transact business for and in the name of another. For instance, a driver becomes an agent of the trucking company when signing for freight.

Air bag suspension Trailer suspension system using air bags for a greater cushion than conventional leaf spring.

Air brakes Brakes that use compressed air instead of fluid.

Air cleaner Cleans air that enters the engine, sometimes called air filter.

Air compressor Builds up and maintains required air pressure in the brake system reservoir.

Air filter restriction gauge Gauge on a truck dashboard that registers the flow of air through the air filter element and registers the condition of the filter.

Air line Carries compressed air from one part of the air brake system to another, and from tractor to trailer.

Air-over-hydraulic brakes Brakes on a vehicle that have a regular hydraulic system assisted by air pressure.

Air reservoir Storage tank for compressed air.

Air shutter Mounted on the front of the radiator to control air entering the radiator and thereby to control engine temperature.

Alcohol concentration (AC) A measure of how much alcohol is in a person's blood or breath. You may also see the term "blood alcohol concentration" (BAC) used.

Alcohol (or alcoholic beverage) Beer, wine, distilled spirits (liquor).

Alternator Produces electricity for the battery and electric power to operate the lights, radio, and other items when the engine is running.

Ammeter Measures the amount of current flowing in an electrical current.

Amphetamines "Bennies," "speed," or "pep pills." Stimulant drugs.

Application pressure air gauge Indicates pressure being applied by brakes during brake operation.

Approved Approval issued or recognized by the Department of Transportation.

Articulate Refers to the ability to move or bend, as a tractor-trailer articulates when it turns.

Atmospheric gases Argon, krypton, neon, nitrogen, oxygen, and xenon.

Axle The bar that connects opposite wheels.

Axle temperature gauge Indicates the temperature of lubricant in an axle.

Axle weight How much weight the axle (or set of axles) transmits to the ground.

B

Baffle Dividers in a tanker that keep the load from shifting.

Battery Converts chemical energy into electricity.

Bias A type of tire with diagonal body plies, and narrow plies under the tread going in the same direction.

Blocking Supports that keep cargo from shifting during transport.

Brake drum The rotating unit of the brake that is attached to the wheel.

Brake lining Material attached to the brake shoe that creates friction.

Brake shoe Non-rotating part of the brake that contacts the brake lining and supplies braking force.

Braking distance Perception time plus reaction time plus brake lag.

Bridge formula Determines how much weight is put on any point by any group of axles.

Bridge law Regulates how much weight can be put on a bridge at any one point.

Btu British thermal unit. It's a measurement of heat energy.

Bulk packaging A packaging, including a transport vehicle or freight container, with a capacity greater than 119 gallons (liquid), 882 pounds (solid), or 1,000 pounds water capacity (gas).

C

C or Celsius or Centigrade It's one scale used for measuring temperature.

Cab Part of the vehicle where the driver sits.

Cabover Vehicle with most of its engine under the cab.

Carbon monoxide A poisonous gas in exhaust fumes.

Carboy A glass, plastic, or metal bottle or container holding several gallons of liquid. Carboys are often cushioned in a wooden box.

Cargo Freight.

Cargo tank Any bulk liquid or compressed gas packaging. Cargo tanks can be portable or permanently attached to any motor vehicle. They can be loaded or unloaded without being removed from the motor vehicle. Packaging built to specifications for cylinders are not cargo tanks.

Carrier A person who transports passengers or property by land or water as a common, contract, or private carrier, or by civil aircraft.

CDL Commercial Driver's License.

Centrifugal force The natural force that pulls objects in motion outward from the center of rotation.

Check valve Seals off one part of the air brake system from another.

Chock A block placed in front of a tire to keep the vehicle from moving.

Circuit A closed electrical path.

Circuit breaker Breaks and opens an electrical circuit in an overload.

Clean bore A tanker without compartments or baffles.

Combination vehicle One that articulates. It has joined sections that can move independently of each other.

Combustible Able to ignite and burn.

Combustible liquid A liquid with a flash point at or above 140 degrees and below 200 degrees Fahrenheit.

Commerce Trade, traffic, or transportation in the United States (or any area controlled by the United States). The trade can be between a place in a state and a place outside the state, even outside the United States.

Commercial Driver's License CDL

Commercial vehicle Commercial vehicles are vehicles with gross vehicle weights of 26,001 pounds or more; trailers with gross vehicle weights of 10,001 pounds or more; vehicles that transport hazardous materials that require placards, and buses designed to carry 16 or more people (including the driver).

Compressed gas Compressed gases are held under pressure. When in the container, compressed gases have an absolute pressure of more than 40 psi (that is, 40 psia) at 70 degrees Fahrenheit. Or, if measured at 130 degrees Fahrenheit, they have a pressure of 104 psia. A liquid flammable material with a vapor pressure over 40 psia at 100 degrees Fahrenheit is also a compressed gas.

Conductor A material through which electricity flows.

Consignee A company or person who has agreed to purchase a specific load of freight and to whom a shipment is delivered.

Consignor The shipper.

Consumer commodity A material that is packaged and distributed for retail sale for use by individuals. The material is meant for personal care or household use. This term also includes drugs and medicines.

Controlled intersection An intersection with a traffic light or signs that control traffic.

Controlled substance A substance listed on Schedules I through V of the Code of Federal Regulations.

Converter gear or dolly A coupling device; one or two axles and a fifth wheel used to couple a tractor to a semitrailer.

Convex mirror "Spot mirror" that shows a wider area than a flat mirror of the same size.

Coolant The liquid that reduces engine heat.

Corrosive material A corrosive is a solid or liquid that harms human skin on contact.

Couple Connect two sections of a vehicle combination.

Cryogenic liquid A coolant gas. It will boil at minus 130 degrees Fahrenheit when it's at one atmosphere, absolute (1 psia).

Cylinder A pressure vessel designed for pressures higher than 40 psia. A portable tank or cargo tank is not considered a cylinder.

D

Deceleration To slow down, to come to a stop (the opposite of acceleration).

Department of Transportation (DOT) The federal department that establishes the nation's overall transportation policies.

Designated facility A hazardous waste treatment, storage, or disposal facility that has been named on the manifest by the generator (creator of the waste).

Differential A system of gears that permits each wheel to turn at different speeds on the same axle, as occurs when going around a curve.

Disc brakes Brakes that function by causing friction pads to press on either side of a disc rotating along with the wheel.

Disc wheel A single unit that combines a rim and a wheel. The most common type is the Budd wheel.

Disqualification Suspension or complete loss of driving privileges.

Dock A platform where trucks are loaded and unloaded.

DOD The U.S. Department of Defense.

Double-clutching Shifting the gears of a truck transmission without grinding them (that is, shifting from the present gear to neutral, then shifting from neutral to the desired gear).

Driveaway-towaway operation A hauling operation in which the cargo is one or more vehicles, with one or more sets of wheels on the roadway.

Drive axle An axle that transmits power to the wheels and actively pulls the load.

Driver's record of duty status Form submitted by driver to carrier for each 24-hour period of work.

Drive shaft A heavy-duty tube that connects the transmission to the rear end assembly of the tractor.

Drive train A series of connected mechanical parts for transmitting motion.

Drive wheel The wheel to which power is transmitted to drive the vehicle.

Duals A pair of wheels and tires mounted together on the same side of one axle.

DUI Driving a commercial motor vehicle while under the influence of alcohol.

Dummy coupler A fitting used to seal the opening in an air brake hose connection (glad hands) when the connection is not in use. Sometimes called a dust cap.

Dunnage The material used to protect or support freight in trucks.

E

Eighteen-wheeler A combination of tractor and trailer with five axles and dual wheel combinations totaling 18 rims and tires.

Electrical system Consists of the starter, wiring, battery, generator, alternator, and generator regulator that work together to crank the engine for starting.

Employee Anyone who operates a CMV either directly for or under lease to an employer.

Employer Anyone who owns or leases a CMV or assigns employees to operate one.

Endorsement A special allowance added to your CDL that permits you to drive certain vehicles or haul certain cargo.

Engine retarder An auxiliary device added to the engine to reduce its speed. Also referred to as an engine brake.

En route On the way.

EPA The U.S. Environmental Protection Agency.

Etiologic agents Microorganisms (germs). They cause disease.

Explosives Explosives are chemical compounds, mixtures, or devices that explode.

F

F or Fahrenheit It's another scale for measuring temperature.

Fan belt A belt attached to the engine block that drives the fan.

Federal Motor Carrier Safety Regulations (FMCSR) Govern the operation of trucks and buses operated in interstate or foreign commerce by common, contract, and private motor carriers.

Felony A crime that is punishable by death or a prison term of more than one year.

Fifth wheel Part of the locking device used to connect a semitrailer and a tractor.

Filling density Refers to how full tankers and cylinders should be loaded with bulk liquids and compressed gases.

First aid Immediate and temporary care given to the victim of an accident or sudden illness until the services of a medical professional can be obtained.

Fishyback Transporting motor truck trailers and containers by ship.

Flammable A substance that easily bursts into flames (also"inflammable").

Flammable compressed gas. Compressed gas is said to be flammable if a mixture of 13 percent or less will form a flammable mixture when combined with air or it passes the UN Manual of Tests and Criteria tests for flammability.

Flammable liquid A liquid with a flash point below 100 degrees Fahrenheit.

Flammable solids A flammable solid is a solid material, other than an explosive, that can cause fire.

Flash point The lowest temperature at which a substance gives off flammable vapors. These vapors will ignite if they come in contact with a spark or flame.

Flatbed A truck or trailer without sides or a top.

FMCSR Federal Motor Carrier Safety Regulations.

Foot brake valve Foot-operated valve that controls the amount of air pressure delivered to or released from the brake chambers.

Freight container A reusable container with a volume of 64 cubic feet or more. It's designed and built so it can be lifted with its contents intact. It's mainly used to hold packages (in unit form) during transport.

Friction Resistance between the surfaces of two objects.

Fuel pump In a vehicle, the pump that moves fuel from the fuel tank to the engine.

Fuel tank A tank other than a cargo tank used to transport flammable or combustible liquid. It's also a tank that holds compressed gas used to fuel the transport vehicle it's attached to, or equipment on that vehicle. This is different from a tank semitrailer that transports fuel as cargo.

G

GCWR Gross combination weight rating.

Generator In a vehicle, the device that changes mechanical energy into electrical energy to run the lights and battery.

Glad hands Air hose brake system connections between the tractor and trailer.

Governor (air) Device to automatically control the air pressure being maintained in the air reservoirs. Keeps the air pressure between 90 and 120 psi and prevents excessive air pressure from building up.

Groove On a tire, the space between adjacent tread ribs.

Gross combination weight (GCW) The total weight of the power unit or tractor, plus any trailers, plus the cargo. (This would also apply to a vehicle towing another vehicle as cargo.)

Gross combination weight rating (GCWR) Gross combination weight rating is defined as the maximum gross combination weight stated by the manufacturer for a specific combination of vehicles, plus the load.

Gross vehicle weight (GVW) The total weight of a single vehicle, plus its load.

Gross vehicle weight rating (GVWR) The maximum gross vehicle weight stated by the manufacturer for a single vehicle, plus its load.

Gross weight The weight of a packaging, plus the weight of its contents.

GVWR Gross vehicle weight rating.

H

Hand throttle A manually set throttle in a tractor that is used to maintain a certain engine speed.

Hazardous material A substance or material, including a hazardous substance, that the Secretary of Transportation judges to pose an unreasonable risk to health, safety, and property when transported in commerce.

Hazardous substance A material listed in the Appendix to Part 172.101.

Hazardous waste Any material that is subject to the Hazardous Waste Manifest Requirement of the U.S. Environmental Protection Agency.

Hazardous waste manifest A document (shipping paper) on which all hazardous waste is identified and that must accompany each shipment of waste from the point of pickup to its destination.

Highway A public roadway that carries through traffic.

Hydraulic brakes Brakes that depend on the transmission of hydraulic pressure from a master cylinder to the wheel cylinders.

I

ICAO International Civil Aviation Organization.

Ignition point The temperature at which a flammable substance will ignite or burn.

Ignition switch Allows current to flow from the battery to the starter motor.

Import To receive goods from a foreign country.

Inertia The tendency of an object to remain in the same condition (that is, to stay still or keep moving).

Injector In a diesel engine, the unit that sprays fuel into the combustion chamber.

Insulated tanker Truck or trailer designed to haul cargo at controlled temperatures, whether cooled or heated.

Intermodal container A freight container designed and built to be used in two or more modes of transport.

Intermodal portable tank or IM portable tanks A specific class of portable tanks designed mainly for international intermodal use.

Intersection The place where two roadways intersect.

Intrastate traffic Traffic within one state only.

Irritating material When exposed to air or flames, it gives off dangerous fumes.

J

Jacking Changing the direction of the trailer.

Jackknife When a trailer forms a "V" with the tractor instead of being pulled in a straight line, usually resulting from a skid.

Jake brake (slang) The Jacobs engine brake that is used as an auxiliary braking device on a tractor.

K

Kingpin Hardened steel pin on a semitrailer that locks into the fifth wheel for coupling.

L

Landing gear Supports the front end of a semitrailer when not attached to a tractor.

Leaf spring suspension Conventional type of suspension system.

Limited quantity The maximum amount of a hazardous material for which there is a specific labeling and packaging exception.

Load lock A pole-shaped piece of equipment used to hold cargo in place during transport by way of a tension spring.

Log book A book carried by truck drivers that contains daily records of hours, route, and so forth, which is required by the Department of Transportation.

Low air warning device A mechanical warning of brake failure by means of a buzzer, a flashing red light, or a small red flag that drops into the driver's line of vision.

M

Manifest A document describing a shipment or the contents of a vehicle or ship.

Marker lights Clearance or running lights.

Marking Putting the descriptive name, instructions, cautions, weight, or specification marks required by regulations on outer containers of hazardous materials.

Mixture A material composed of more than one chemical compound or element.

Mode Any of the following transportation methods: rail, highway, air, or water.

Motor carrier A business that transports passengers or goods by a motorized vehicle.

Motor vehicle A vehicle, machine, tractor, trailer, or semitrailer, or any combination of these. This term assumes the vehicle is driven or drawn by mechanical power, is on the highway, and is transporting passengers or property. It doesn't refer to vehicles used on rail. It also doesn't include a trolley bus running on a fixed overhead electric wire and carrying passengers.

Mph Miles per hour.

N

Name of contents The proper shipping name specified in Part 172.101 or 172.102.

Net weight A measure of weight referring only to the contents of a package and that does not include the weight of any packaging material.

Non-bulk packaging A package smaller than the capacities stated for bulk packaging.

Non-liquefied compressed gas A gas that is completely in the form of vapor at 70 degrees Fahrenheit.

N.O.S. "Not otherwise specified."

O

Oil pressure gauge Instrument that measures the pressure of engine lubricating oil.

Operator A person who controls the use of an aircraft, vessel, or vehicle.

Organic peroxide A chemical.

ORM Other Regulated Materials.

Oscillatory sway Side-to-side motion at the top of a vehicle.

Other Regulated Materials "Other Regulated Materials" are those that don't meet any of the other hazardous materials class definitions but that are dangerous when transported in commerce.

Outage The amount by which a packaging falls short of being full of liquid. Usually expressed as a percent of volume. Outage allows for liquids to expand as they warm.

Out-of-service driver Driver declared out of service by a government representative because of violations.

Out-of-service vehicle A vehicle that cannot pass the government safety inspection and is declared out of service until the problems are corrected.

Outside container The outermost enclosure used to transport a hazardous material. This is other than a freight container.

Overpack An enclosure that is used by a single consignor to provide protection or convenience in the handling of a package or to combine two or more packages. Does not include a freight container.

Oversized vehicle Any vehicle whose weight and/or dimensions exceed a state's regulations.

Oxidizer Oxidizers cause other materials to react with oxygen.

P

Packaging The assembly of one or more containers and any other part needed to comply with the minimum packaging requirements.

Piggyback Intermodal transportation system wherein trailers or containers are carried by rail.

Pigtail Cable used to transmit electrical power to the trailer.

Pintle hook Coupling device at the rear of the truck for the purpose of towing trailers.

Placards Signs placed on a tanker or trailer during shipment to identify hazardous material and that must be visible from all angles.

Ply ratings The number of ply cords in the sidewall and tread of a tire (from two for cars up to as many as 20 for large off-the-road trucks).

Point of origin The terminal at which a shipment is received by a transportation line from the shipper.

Poison A substance that is so harmful to humans that it is dangerous to transport. It can kill when swallowed or inhaled, or when absorbed by the skin.

Pole trailer Trailer composed of a single telescopic pole, a tandem rear wheel unit, and a coupling device used to join the trailer to a tractor.

Pollution The presence of toxic substances that have entered the air, water, or soil and that poison the natural environment.

Portable tank Any packaging (except a cylinder having a 100-pound or less water capacity) over 110 U.S. gallons capacity. This definition includes tanks designed to be loaded into or on or temporarily coupled to a transport vehicle or ship. These tanks are equipped with skids, mounting, or other parts that make mechanical handling possible.

Pot torches Safety equipment used on a highway to warn traffic of an obstruction or hazard.

Power Takeoff (PTO) A device mounted on the transmission or transfer case, used to transmit engine power to auxiliary equipment.

Preferred route (or preferred highway) A highway for shipment of highway route controlled quantities of radioactive materials. These routes are named by state routing agencies. When there is no other option, any interstate system highway can be named a preferred route.

Private carrier A company that maintains its own trucks to ship its own freight.

Progressive shifting Shifting technique whereby the vehicle is taken up to highway speed by using the least horsepower needed to get the job done, thereby saving fuel.

Proper shipping name The name of the hazardous material shown in Roman print (not italics) in Part 172.101.

psi (or p.s.i.) Pounds per square inch.

psia (or p.s.i.a.) Pounds per square inch absolute. Psia uses vacuum (or zero pressure) as a reference point.

psig (or p.s.i.g.) Pounds per square inch gauge. The difference between two pressures.

Pyrophoric liquid A liquid that will ignite by itself in dry or moist air at or below 130 degrees Fahrenheit.

R

Radial Tires constructed with the cords running directly across the top to better mold and flex their way around objects on the road, thereby offering less rolling resistance and increased mileage.

Radiator Part of the cooling system that removes engine heat from the coolant passing through it.

Radiator cap A cap that protects the radiator from impurities, allows pressure to build up, and releases excess pressure from the engine.

Radioactive material Material that gives off rays, usually harmful.

Reaction time The time that elapses between the point that a driver recognizes the need for action and the time the driver takes that action.

Rearward amplification The "crack-the-whip" effect found on tractors with trailers.

Recap Restore a tire by putting new tread on the carcass (body).

Reciprocity Mutual action; exchange of privileges such as between two states.

Reefer Commonly used industry term for refrigerated truck or trailer that hauls perishables.

Reflectors Light reflectors that, when placed along the road, warn motorists of an emergency.

Regrooved When new tread grooves have been cut into the crown of the tire after the original tread is worn down.

Regulation A law designed to control behavior. A governmental order with the force of law.

Relay emergency valve A combination valve in an air brake system that controls brake application and that also provides for automatic trailer brake application should the trailer become disconnected from the towing vehicle.

Reportable Quantity (RQ) The quantity of a material, fixed by the Environmental Protection Agency, that must be reported if spilled or released into the environment.

Representative vehicle One that stands for the type of motor vehicle that a CDL applicant plans to drive.

Restricted articles Commodities that can be handled only under certain specific conditions.

Rev To operate an engine at a high speed.

Right-of-way The right of one vehicle or pedestrian to proceed before or instead of another vehicle.

Road The traveled part of a roadway and any shoulder alongside it.

Roadside The part of a highway or street that is not used by vehicles and is not a sidewalk.

Roadway A general term that refers to any surface on which vehicles travel.

Rocky Mountain double Combination consisting of a tractor and two trailers.

RQ Reportable Quantity.

Runaway ramp A ramp on a steep downgrade that can be used by a truck driver to stop a runaway truck when brakes have failed. Sometimes called an escape ramp.

Rural The countryside.

S

Saddle tanks Barrel-type fuel tanks that hang from the sides of the tractor's frame.

SCF Standard Cubic Foot. One cubic foot of gas measured at 60°F and 14.7 psia.

Seal In the shipping industry, a security device to assure that truck doors have not been opened in transit.

Semitrailer Truck trailer equipped with one or more axles and constructed so that the front end rests upon a truck tractor.

Series parallel switch Used to connect two parallel batteries into a series circuit for a 24-volt starter motor.

Serious traffic violations These are going more than 15 miles over the posted speed limit; reckless driving; improper or erratic lane changes; following the vehicle ahead too closely; traffic violations that result in fatal accidents.

Shipper's certification A written statement signed by the shipper stating a shipment was prepared properly, according to law.

Shipping paper A shipping order, bill of lading, manifest, or other shipping document serving the same purpose. These documents must have the information required by Parts 172.202, 172.203, and 172.204.

Shoulder The part of a roadway that runs along next to it and can be used by stopped vehicles.

Sidewalk The part of a roadway that is to be used by people who are walking (pedestrians).

Sight glass or gauge Glass window for determining fluid levels, as in a radiator.

Sight-side The side of the tractor visible to the driver, opposite the blind side.

Sixty-hour/seven-day or seventy-hour/eight-day rule Department of Transportation regulation in which no driver is allowed to be on-duty for more than 60 hours in any seven-day period; or, if carriers are operating the vehicles every day of the week, they may permit drivers to be on-duty not more than 70 hours in any eight-day period.

Skid Failure of the tires to grip the road due to loss of traction.

Slack adjuster An adjustable device located on the brake chamber push rod that is used to compensate for brake shoe wear.

Sleeper Truck cab with a sleeping compartment.

Sleeper berth Area in a tractor where a driver can sleep.

Slider Nickname for a sliding fifth wheel.

Sliding tandem A semitrailer tandem suspension that can be adjusted forward and backward.

Sludge Thickened oil and sediment.

Smooth bore tanker A trailer shaped like a long hollow tube with no baffles and used for one liquid material at a time.

Snub braking A moderate brake-and-release technique to reduce speed by five or six miles per hour, using a brake application of about 20 to 30 psi.

Solution Any uniform liquid mixture of two or more chemical compounds or elements that won't separate while being transported under normal conditions.

Spontaneously combustible material (solid) A solid substance that may heat up or ignite by itself while being transported under normal conditions. This includes sludges and pastes. It also includes solids that will heat up and ignite when exposed to air.

Spotter mirror Small convex mirror mounted on the mirror frame that gives a different view.

Spring brake Conventional brake chamber and emergency or parking brake mechanism for use on vehicles equipped with air brakes.

Spring brake control Controls spring-loaded parking brakes.

Starter motor The motor that cranks the engine to get it started.

Starting system Made up of the starter battery, cables, switch, and controls.

State of domicile Your home state. This is the place you plan to return to when you are absent. It's where you have your main, permanent home.

Steering axle An axle that steers the vehicle. Can be powered or non-powered.

Stopping distance The distance the vehicle travels between the time the driver recognizes the need to stop and the time the vehicle comes to a complete stop.

Straight truck A truck with the body and engine mounted on the same chassis (rather than a combination unit, such as a tractor-semitrailer).

Street The entire width of a roadway that is maintained with public funds, including the shoulder, sidewalk, and roadway.

Suspension The system of springs and other supports that holds a vehicle on its axles.

T

Tailgating Following another vehicle too closely so that, if the need arose, there is not enough room to come to a safe stop.

Tandem Semitrailer or tractor with two rear axles.

Tandem axle An assembly of two axles, either of which may be powered.

Tank vehicle (or tanker) One that transports gas or liquids in bulk. Portable tanks that carry less than 1,000 gallons are not included in this definition.

Tarp Tarpaulin cover for an open-top trailer.

Technical name A recognized chemical name currently used in scientific and technical handbooks, journals, and text. Some generic descriptions are used as technical names.

Throttle Controls the engine speed.

Tire load The most weight a tire can carry safely.

TOFC Trailer-on-flat-car.

Traffic Anything using the roadway for the purpose of travel, including vehicles, pedestrians, herded animals, or streetcars.

Trailer Freight-hauling part of a rig, designed to be pulled by a tractor and that is generally divided into three groups: semitrailer, full trailer, and pole trailer.

Trailer brake Hand-operated remote control brake located on the steering column or dashboard for the trailer only.

Trailer spotting The job of moving a trailer from one place, or spot, to another in a terminal yard.

Transmission Mechanical device that uses gearing or torque conversion to change the ratio between engine RPM and driving RPM.

Transport vehicle A cargo-carrying vehicle, such as an automobile, van, tractor, truck, semitrailer, tank car, or rail car, used to transport cargo by any mode. Each cargo-carrying body is a separate transport vehicle.

Triple Combination rig consisting of tractor, semitrailer, and two full trailers coupled together. Also called triple headers or triple bottoms.

Trolley brake A hand valve used to operate the trailer brakes independently of tractor brakes. Also called trailer brake.

Trucking industry The business of carrying goods by truck, including carrier, drivers, warehouse and terminal employees, and all others involved in any phase of trucking.

U

Ullage The amount by which a packaging falls short of being full of liquid. It's usually stated in percent by volume.

Uncontrolled intersection An intersection without any form of traffic control, such as stop signs or stop signals.

Uncouple To disconnect sections of a trailer combination.

United States The fifty states, the District of Columbia, the Commonwealth of Puerto Rico, the Virgin Islands, American Samoa, and Guam.

Universal joint Joint or coupling that permits a swing of limited angle in any direction.

Unstable cargo Cattle, swinging meat, liquids, and the like that cannot be completely secured against movement.

Urban The city or referring to the city (the opposite of rural).

V

Vacuum brake system A brake system in which the brake mechanism is activated by a vacuum.

Valve A device that opens and closes openings in a pipe, tube, or cylinder.

Viscosity A measurement of a liquid's tendency to resist flowing. A liquid with a high viscosity doesn't flow as easily as one with a low viscosity.

Viscous liquid A liquid material that has a measured viscosity in excess of 2,500 centistokes at 25 degrees Centigrade (77 degrees Fahrenheit). Viscosity is determined using ASTM procedures.

Volatility How fast materials evaporate and become vapor.

Volt A unit of measurement of electrical potential.

Voltage regulator Part of the generator regulator used to control the voltage going from the generator to the battery.

W

Water pump Part of the cooling system that circulates coolant between the engine's water jackets and the radiator.

Water reactive material (solid) Any solid substance that will ignite when it comes in contact with water. Water reactive materials are also those that will give off flammable or toxic gases in dangerous amounts when they come in contact with water.

Wedge In a truck, a commonly used type of brake.

Wet tank Part of the air brake system with a tank that must be drained at least once a day.

Winterfront A protective device to shield the front of the vehicle from cold. Usually of canvas or other sturdy material, the two-piece construction can be fully open, fully closed, or cover just the bumper or the grille.

Wrecker Truck designed for hoisting and towing disabled vehicles.

Y

Yaw instability The side-to-side motion at the rear of a vehicle combination.

Yield Give way to a driver with the right-of-way.

Index